PASS TRAK 7

Questions & Answers

General
Securities
Representative

6th Edition/Revised

Dearborn
Financial Publishing, Inc.

The Series 7 Qualification Exam is copyrighted by the New York Stock Exchange. Each page of the examination contains the following notice:

"The contents of this examination are confidential. Neither the whole nor any part of this examination may be reproduced in any form or quoted or used in any way without the written consent of the New York Stock Exchange, Inc."

Dearborn Financial Publishing, Inc. and its employees and agents honor the copyrights of the New York Stock Exchange. We specifically urge each of our students to refrain from any attempts to remove a copy of the exam; or to copy or record any of the questions on the exam.

At press time, this 6th edition of PassTrak Series 7 contains the most complete and accurate information currently available for the NASD Series 7 license examination. Owing to the nature of securities license examinations, however, information may have been added recently to the actual test that does not appear in this edition.

While a great deal of care has been taken to provide accurate and current information, the ideas, suggestions, general principles and conclusions presented in this text are subject to local, state and federal laws and regulations, court cases and any revisions of same. The reader is thus urged to consult legal counsel regarding any points of law—this publication should not be used as a substitute for competent legal advice.

Executive Editor: Kimberly K. Walker-Daniels
Project Editor: Nicola Bell
Cover Design: Vito DePinto

91   92   93   10   9   8   7   6   5   4   3   2   1

Library of Congress Cataloging-in-Publication Data

PassTrak series 7, General securities representative. Questions &
    answers. —6th ed., revised
        p.   cm.
    ISBN 0-7931-0337-1
        1. Stockbrokers—United States—Examinations, questions, etc.
2. Securities—United States—Examinations, questions, etc.
I. Dearborn Financial Publishing.   II. Title: PassTrak series seven,
General securities representative.   III. Title: General securities
representative.
HG4928.5.P353 1991   90-26869
332.63'27'076—dc20   CIP

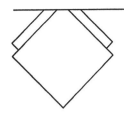

Contents

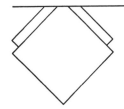

Introduction to PassTrak Series 7

Welcome to PassTrak Series 7. Because you probably have a lot of questions about the course and the exam, we have tried to anticipate some of them and provide you with answers to help you on your way.

The Course

How is the course structured?

PassTrak Series 7 is divided into three books: a textbook, a workbook and an exam book. The textbook, titled *Principles & Practices,* consists of 19 chapters, each devoted to a particular area of general securities sales and regulation that you will need to know in order to pass the General Securities Registered Representative Exam (Series 7). Each of these 19 chapters is subdivided into study sections devoted to more specific areas with which you need to become familiar.

The *Workbook* consists of 20 chapters. The first 19 chapters provide you with additional hands-on learning exercises that complement the 19 chapters of the *Principles & Practices*. Chapter 20 contains mnemonics and study aids designed to help you review important facts you need for the exam.

The exam book, titled *Questions & Answers,* contains 19 review exams that each cover a particular aspect of general securities sales and regulation. The book concludes with 2 final exams composed of questions similar to those you will encounter on the Series 7 exam.

What topics are covered in this course?

The information needed to pass the Series 7 exam is covered in PassTrak Series 7 through the following chapters:

Chapter 1: Equity Securities
Chapter 2: Corporate Debt Securites
Chapter 3: Corporate Special Securities
Chapter 4: U.S. Government Securities
Chapter 5: Money-market Securities and Interest Rates
Chapter 6: Issuing Securities
Chapter 7: Trading Securities
Chapter 8: Client Accounts
Chapter 9: Brokerage Office Procedures
Chapter 10: Margin Accounts
Chapter 11: Economics and Analysis
Chapter 12: Investment Recommendations and Taxation
Chapter 13: U.S. Government Rules and Regulations
Chapter 14: Self-regulatory Organizations Rules and Regulations
Chapter 15: Municipal Securities
Chapter 16: Option Contracts and Option Markets
Chapter 17: Investment Company Products
Chapter 18: Retirement Planning and Annuities
Chapter 19: Direct Participation Programs

How much time should I spend studying?

You should plan to spend approximately 90 to 120 hours reading the material and working through the questions. Your actual time, of course, may vary from this figure depending on your reading rate, comprehension, professional background and study environment.

Spread your study time over the six to eight weeks prior to the date on which you are scheduled to take the Series 7 exam. Select a time and place for studying that will allow you to concentrate your full attention on the material at hand. You have a lot of information to learn and a lot of ground to cover. Be sure to give yourself enough time to learn the material.

What is the best way to approach the exams?

Approach each review and final exam as if you were preparing to take the actual Series 7 test. Read each question carefully and write down your answer. Then check your answers against the key and read the accompanying rationale. Making yourself go through all of these steps (rather than simply reading each question and skipping directly to the rationale) will greatly increase your comprehension and retention of the information in the book.

Do I need to take the final exams?

The final exams test the same knowledge you will need in order to answer the questions on the Series 7 exam. By completing these exams and checking your answers against the rationale, you should be able to pinpoint any areas with which you are still having difficulty. Review any questions you miss, paying particular attention to the rationale for those questions. If any subjects still seem troublesome, go back and review those topics in *Principles & Practices*. At the end of each rationale, you will find a page reference that directs you to the page in *Principles and Practices* where the information is covered.

The Exam

Why do I need to pass the Series 7 exam?

Your employer is a member of the New York Stock Exchange (NYSE) or another self-regulatory organization (SRO) that requires its members and employees of its members to pass a qualifications exam in order to become registered. To be registered as a representative qualified to sell all types of securities (except commodities), you must pass the Series 7 exam.

What is the Series 7 exam like?

The Series 7 is a two-part, six-hour, 250-question exam administered by the NASD. The exam is given in two three-hour parts, each covering different areas of general securities sales and regulation. It is offered as a computer-based test at various testing sites around the country. A pencil-and-paper exam is available to those candidates who apply to and obtain permission from the NASD to take a written exam.

What topics will I see covered on the exam?

This course covers the wide range of topics the NYSE has outlined as being essential to the general securities registered representative. The NYSE exam is divided into six broad topic areas:

	No. of Questions	% of Exam
Advertising, Qualifying customers, Industry regulations	31	12%
Securities instruments	84	33%
Handling customer accounts, Taxation, Margins	34	14%
Securities markets, Order handling, Confirmations	34	14%
Economics, Securities analysis, Sources of financial information	29	12%
Portfolio analysis, Investment strategies, Retirement plans	38	15%
	250	100%

What score do I need to pass?

You must answer correctly at least 70% of the questions on the Series 7 exam in order to pass and become eligible for NYSE registration as a general securities registered representative.

How long does the exam take?

You will be allowed six hours in two three-hour sessions in which to finish the exam. If you are taking the computerized version of the exam, you will be given additional time before the test to become familiar with the PLATO® terminal.

Are there any prerequisites I have to meet before taking the exam?

There are no examinations you must take before sitting for the Series 7.

How do I enroll for the exam?

To obtain an admission ticket to the Series 7 exam, you must complete either a U-10 Form (if your firm is a non-NASD member) or a U-4 Form (if your firm is an NASD member) and file it with the NASD along with the appropriate processing fees. The NASD will then send you an entrance ticket that is valid for 90 days. To take the exam during this 90-day period, you must make an appointment with a Professional Development Center at least two weeks before the date on which you would like to sit for the test.

What should I take to the exam?

Take one form of personal identification that bears your signature and your photograph. You are not allowed to take reference materials or anything else into the testing area except a calculator. Your calculator must run silently and have an independent power source, no alphanumeric keys or programmable memory and no print device.

Scratch paper and pencils will be provided by the testing center, although you will not be permitted to take them with you when you leave.

What is PLATO®?

The Series 7 exam, like many professional licensing examinations, is administered on the PLATO® computerized testing system, which is an interactive computer network developed by Control Data as an educational and testing service.

Included with your notice of enrollment from the NASD, you will receive a directory of Professional Development Centers and a brochure describing how the exam is formatted and how to use the computer terminal to answer the questions.

When you have completed the exam, the PLATO® System promptly scores your answers and within minutes displays a grade for the exam on the terminal screen.

How well can I expect to do on the exam?

The examinations administered by the NASD are not easy. You will be required to display considerable understanding and knowledge of the topics presented in this course in order to pass the Series 7 exam and qualify for registration. If you study and complete all of the sections of this course, and consistently score at least 80% on the review and final exams, you should be well prepared to pass the Series 7 exam.

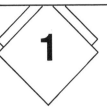

1 Equity Securities

1. At the annual meeting of Huron Corporation, five directors are to be elected. Under the cumulative voting system, an investor with 100 shares of Huron would have

   A. 100 votes that could be cast for each of five directors
   B. 100 total votes that could be cast in any way the investor chooses among five directors
   C. 500 votes that could be cast for each of five directors
   D. 500 total votes that could be cast in any way the investor chooses among five directors

2. Mountain Brewing would like to distribute treasury stock it currently holds to stockholders of record as a stock dividend. In order to do this, it must

   A. reregister the stock with the NASD
   B. reregister the stock with the NYSE
   C. apply to the SEC for permission to reissue the treasury shares
   D. take no special actions

3. Stockholders must approve

   A. the declaration of a stock dividend
   B. a 3-for-1 stock split
   C. the repurchase of 100,000 shares for the treasury
   D. the declaration of a 15% stock dividend

4. A client has 100 shares of XYZ. The stock undergoes a split. After the split, she will have

   A. a proportionately decreased interest in the company
   B. a proportionately increased interest in the company
   C. no effective change in position
   D. a greater exposure

5. A company may pay dividends in which of the following ways?

   I. Stock of another company
   II. Cash
   III. Stock
   IV. Product

   A. I only
   B. II and III only
   C. III only
   D. I, II, III and IV

6. Cumulative voting rights

   A. benefit the large investor
   B. aid the corporation's best customers
   C. give preferred stockholders an advantage over common stockholders
   D. benefit the small investor

7. XYZ declares a 3-for-2 stock split. How many additional shares will an investor who owns 200 shares be issued?

   A. 100
   B. 300
   C. 400
   D. 500

8. Acme Corp. common stock is currently selling for $75 per share with a quarterly dividend of $.75. The current yield for Acme common stock is

   A. 1.0%
   B. 4.0%
   C. 12.5%
   D. 25.0%

9. Inco, which has 7% $100 par cumulative preferred stock outstanding, has the following dividend record: last year, 5% was paid to preferred stockholders; the full preferred dividend was paid until last year. Now Inco wishes to declare a common dividend. Before Inco can pay dividends to the common stockholders, how much must it first pay on each preferred share outstanding?

   A. $3
   B. $7
   C. $9
   D. $15

10. ABC stock is $10.00 par value and is selling in the market for $60.00 per share. If the current quarterly dividend is $1.00, what is the current yield of ABC?

    A. 1.0%
    B. 1.7%
    C. 6.7%
    D. 10.0%

11. In a portfolio containing common stock, preferred stock, convertible preferred stock and guaranteed stock, changes in interest rates would be most likely to affect the market price of the

    A. common
    B. preferred
    C. convertible preferred
    D. guaranteed stock

◆ Answers & Rationale

1. **D.** With cumulative voting rights, this investor may cast 500 votes for the five directors in any way the investor chooses. (Page 5)

2. **D.** A company does not have to reregister treasury stock in order to distribute it to the stockholders. (Page 3)

3. **B.** Stockholder approval is required to change the stated value of stock as would occur with a stock split. Decisions regarding payment of dividends or repurchase of stock are made by the board of directors (management only) because these are considered to be operation decisions. (Page 10)

4. **C.** When a stock splits, the number of shares each stockholder has either increases or decreases. The customer experiences no effective change in position or proportionate interest. (Page 10)

5. **D.** A company may pay a dividend in any of the ways listed. (Page 9)

6. **D.** The cumulative method of voting gives an investor one vote per share owned, times the number of directorships to be voted on. For exam-ple, if an investor owns 100 shares of stock and there are five directorships to be voted on, the investor will have a total of 500 votes. The stockholder may cast all of his votes for one director, thereby giving the small investor more voting power. (Page 5)

7. **A.** Multiplying 3/2 by 200 shares gives 300, the total number of shares. To calculate how many additional shares are received, subtract 200 from the total of 300 for 100 additional shares. (Page 10)

8. **B.** $\dfrac{\$3.00\ \text{annual dividend}}{\$75\ \text{market price}} = 4.0\%$ (Page 9)

9. **C.** In order to pay this year's common dividend, the corporation must pay the preferred stockholders the 2% not paid last year and this year's 7% dividend; in total, 9%, or $9. (Page 12)

10. **C.** The quarterly dividend is $1.00; therefore, the annual dividend is $4.00. $4 divided by $60 (market price) equals 6.7% annual yield (current yield). (Page 9)

11. **B.** Preferred stock has the closest characteristics to bonds and would be most affected by a change in interest rates. (Page 11)

2 ◇ Corporate Debt Securities

1. Your customer holds 10 XYZ 6 bonds callable at 102 in 1995 and maturing in 2001. How much money will the customer receive in total at the debenture's maturity?

   A. $10,000
   B. $10,200
   C. $10,300
   D. $10,600

2. If you wanted to find out the price and yield to maturity of a particular bond at a given price, you would go to your basis book tables to convert

   I. decimals to dollars
   II. basis to dollars
   III. dollars to decimals
   IV. dollars to basis

   A. I and III
   B. I and IV
   C. II and III
   D. II and IV

3. If interest rates are changing, which of the following terms would best describe the relationship between prices and yields for corporate bonds?

   A. Reverse
   B. Inverse
   C. Coterminous
   D. Coaxial

4. Of the following bonds in your customer's portfolio, which would be most affected by the risk of changing interest rates?

   A. 8's of '98, yielding 7%
   B. 8.75's of '06, yielding 7.2%
   C. 8's of '13, yielding 7.3%
   D. 8.25's of '04, yielding 7.4%

5. Which of the following are considered to have an equity position in a corporation?

   I. Common stockholders
   II. Preferred stockholders
   III. Convertible bondholders
   IV. Mortgage bondholders

   A. I and II only
   B. I, II and III only
   C. II and III only
   D. I, II, III and IV

6. One of your clients owns two different 9% corporate bonds maturing in 15 years. The first bond is callable in five years, the second has 10 years of call protection, but is callable from then until it matures. If interest rates on bonds of this type begin to fall, which bond is likely to show a greater increase in price?

   A. Bond with the five-year call
   B. Bond with the ten-year call
   C. Both will increase by the same amount.
   D. Both will decrease by the same amount.

7. All of the following corporate bonds have a call option, and all have passed their call protection period. Which of these investments is least likely to be called away by the issuer?

A. 7 1/4% maturing in 2018, callable at 100
B. 7 1/4% maturing in 2017, callable at 101 1/2
C. 9 3/4% maturing in 2018, callable at 103
D. 9 3/4% maturing in 2024, callable at 100

8. In order to read about all of the limitations, promises and agreements about a new corporate bond issue, you would go to the

A. legal opinion
B. tombstone
C. agreement among underwriters
D. indenture

9. The board of Mountain Brewing has come to you for advice. They see a need to increase the company's working capital, but don't want to incur additional fixed charges. Unless there are no other alternatives, they would rather not increase the company's capitalization until the next fiscal year. Which of the following alternatives would you recommend they NOT take over the next six months?

A. Issue stock dividends in lieu of cash dividends for the next two quarters.
B. Issue additional shares of common stock to current stockholders through a preemptive rights offering.
C. Issue two-year notes with no call protection.
D. Sell a wholly owned foreign subsidiary.

10. Acme Sweatsocks, Inc. has created a sinking fund for the purpose of retiring bonds issued several years ago. The sinking fund is large enough to redeem the outstanding bonds at 102 1/2. If the bonds are trading in the market at 97, Acme's board of directors should

A. call in part of the issue
B. purchase bonds at market
C. wait until the bonds reach parity
D. convert Acme stock into bonds and arbitrage

11. All of the following are true about bonds registered as to principal only EXCEPT that

A. coupons are attached
B. the registered owner may sell the bonds prior to maturity
C. interest payments are sent directly to the owner twice a year
D. such bonds can be purchased today in the secondary market

Use the following information to answer questions 12 through 14.

Company	Sales	High	Low	Close	Change
Best 7 3/4's '95	5	92 1/2	91 1/4	92	− 1/2
Bre 7's '96	10	84 1/4	83 3/8	83 7/8	− 3/8
Bzdt 7 1/2's '99	30	95 3/8	95	95 7/8	+ 5/8

12. How many dollars worth of Bzdt bonds were sold on this day?

A. $30
B. $300
C. $3,000
D. $30,000

13. Best's bonds closed the day before at

A. 91 1/2
B. 92
C. 92 1/2
D. This cannot be determined from information given.

14. The current yield for Bre's 7% bonds is

A. 8.25%
B. 8.30%
C. 8.35%
D. 8.54%

15. With fluctuating interest rates, the price of which of the following will fluctuate most?

A. Common stock
B. Preferred stock
C. Short-term bonds
D. Long-term bonds

16. A corporation will call in its debt during a period of

A. rising interest rates
B. declining interest rates
C. volatile interest rates
D. stable interest rates

17. Funded debt is

A. flower bonds
B. municipal bonds
C. U.S. government bonds
D. corporate bonds

Use the following tombstone to answer questions 18 and 19.

```
┌─────────────────────────────────────────┐
│                                           │
│   Northern New Jersey Electric Company    │
│                                           │
│            Mortgage Bonds                 │
│             Senior Debt                   │
│               7 7/8%                       │
│                                           │
│            Price: 95.75                   │
│                                           │
└─────────────────────────────────────────┘
```

18. These bonds pay an annual interest per $1,000 of

A. $77.50
B. $78.75
C. $85.00
D. $95.75

19. What is used to secure the debt?

A. Power plant built with the proceeds of the issue
B. Full faith and credit of the company
C. Property owned by the company
D. Principal mortgages of property owned by the residents of northern New Jersey

20. JEDCO bonds, with a 1993 maturity, are callable as of 1987 as follows: 100 plus 1/2 for each year between call date and maturity with the call price not to exceed 103. The redemption price of the bond in 1990 is

A. 100 1/2
B. 101 1/2
C. 102
D. 103

21. How do you calculate the current yield on a bond?

A. Yield to maturity ÷ Par value
B. Yield to maturity ÷ Dollar market price
C. Annual interest payments ÷ Par value
D. Annual interest payments ÷ Dollar market price

22. The current yield on a bond priced at $950 with a coupon bearing interest at 6% is

    A. the same as the nominal yield
    B. the same as yield to maturity
    C. 6%
    D. 6.3%

23. The newspaper reports a Burlington Northern bond is priced at $1,012.50. This price is written as

    A. 100 1/8
    B. 101 1/4
    C. 101 1/2
    D. 101.25

24. The current yield on a bond with a coupon rate of 7 1/2% currently selling at 95 is approximately

    A. 7.0%
    B. 7.4%
    C. 7.9%
    D. 8.0%

25. Jim Michels purchases $50,000 of 10% corporate bonds at par. At the end of the day, the bonds close down 1/2 point. The investor has a loss of

    A. $25
    B. $250
    C. $2,500
    D. $5,000

26. Your customer has two $5,000 bonds. One has a coupon of 5.1%; the other has a coupon of 5.3%. What is the difference in annual interest payments between the bonds?

    A. $1
    B. $2
    C. $10
    D. $20

Use the following information from Moody's bond page to answer questions 27 and 28.

GMAC ZR '12 54 1/4
Ogden 5's '93 78 7/8

27. The annual interest on the GMAC bond is:

    A. nothing until the bond matures
    B. $ 12.00
    C. $ 24.00
    D. $ 54.25

28. The annual interest on 50 Ogden bonds is

    A. $93
    B. $500
    C. $930
    D. $2,500

29. Currently, a corporation issues 8 1/2% Aaa bonds in the primary market at par. Two years earlier, the corporation had issued 8% Aaa rated debentures at par. Which two statements are true regarding the outstanding 8% issue?

    I. The dollar price per bond will be higher than par.
    II. The dollar price per bond will be lower than par.
    III. The current yield on the issue will be higher.
    IV. The current yield on the issue will be lower.

    A. I and III
    B. I and IV
    C. II and III
    D. II and IV

30. Which of the following are characteristics of bearer bonds?

    A. They come in registered form.
    B. They have interest coupons attached to the bond.
    C. They have interest coupons detached from the bond.
    D. They pay interest quarterly.

31. A trust indenture spells out the covenants between

    A. trustee and underwriter
    B. issuer and underwriter
    C. issuer and trustee
    D. issuer and trustee for the benefit of a bondholder

32. Which statement would be true for an investor who purchased $50,000 face value of 5.10 bonds at par due in 2002 and held them to maturity?

    A. The investor would receive more than the $50,000 and would have a long-term taxable gain at maturity.
    B. The investor would receive less than $50,000 and would have a tax-deductible long-term capital loss at maturity.
    C. The investor would receive $50,000 and would have a taxable long-term capital gain at maturity.
    D. The investor would receive $50,000 and would have no taxable gain or loss at maturity.

33. Which bonds are issued all at once and mature over several years?

    A. Serial
    B. Term
    C. Balloon
    D. Series

34. A bond purchased at $900 with a 5% coupon and a five-year maturity has a current yield of

    A. 5.0%
    B. 5.6%
    C. 7.0%
    D. 7.7%

35. Serial bonds, in comparison to term bonds, have

    A. stable interest payments and stable principal
    B. increasing interest payments and increasing outstanding principal
    C. declining interest payments and declining outstanding principal
    D. declining interest rates and stable principal

36. A bond at par has a coupon rate

    A. less than current yield
    B. less than yield to maturity
    C. the same as current yield
    D. higher than current yield

37. What is the calculation for determining the current yield on a bond?

    A. Annual interest ÷ Par value
    B. Annual interest ÷ Current market price
    C. Yield to maturity ÷ Par value
    D. Yield to maturity ÷ Current market price

38. The difference between par and a lower market price on a bond is called the

    A. reallowance
    B. spread
    C. discount
    D. premium

39. Which of the following factors would be least important in rating a bond?

    A. Interest rates
    B. Amount and composition of existing debt
    C. Stability of issuer's cash flows
    D. Asset protection

40. A customer purchased a 5% corporate bond yielding 6%. A year before the bond matures, new corporate bonds are being issued at 4% and the customer sells the 5% bond. The customer

    I.   bought it at a discount
    II. bought it at a premium
    III. sold it at a premium
    IV. sold it at a discount

    A. I and III
    B. I and IV
    C. II and III
    D. II and IV

41. In case of bankruptcy, debentures rank on a par with

    A. first-mortgage bonds
    B. equipment trust certificates
    C. unsecured debts of private creditors
    D. collateral trust bonds

42. Bonds that are guaranteed are

    A. insured by AMBAC
    B. required to maintain a self-liquidating sinking fund
    C. guaranteed as to payment of principal and interest by another corporation
    D. guaranteed as to payment of principal and interest by the U.S. government

43. Which of the following statements are true regarding corporate zero-coupon bonds?

    I.   Interest is paid semiannually.
    II. Interest is not paid until maturity.
    III. The discount must be prorated and is taxed annually.
    IV. The discount must be prorated annually, with taxation deferred to maturity.

    A. I and III
    B. I and IV
    C. II and III
    D. II and IV

44. An indenture has a closed-end provision. This means that

    A. additional issues will have junior liens
    B. the bonds must be called before maturity
    C. a sinking fund must be established
    D. no additional bonds may be issued

45. Southern California Electric Company issued mortgage senior lien bonds at 8 7/8, price 96.353. These bonds pay annual interest, per $1,000 bond, of

    A. $85.00
    B. $85.51
    C. $88.75
    D. $96.35

46. In the liquidation of the assets of General Gizmo, Inc., in what order would the following list of organizations and individuals receive payment?

    I.   Internal Revenue Service
    II. Holders of debentures
    III. General creditors
    IV. Common stockholders

    A. I, II, III, IV
    B. I, III, II, IV
    C. III, I, II, IV
    D. IV, III, II, I

47. Consolidated Codfish has filed for bankruptcy. Interested parties will be paid off in which of the following orders?

    I.   Holders of secured debt
    II. Holders of subordinated debentures
    III. General creditors
    IV. Preferred stockholders

    A. I, II, III, IV
    B. I, III, II, IV
    C. III, I, II, IV
    D. IV, I, II, III

48. New issues of corporate bonds are MOST likely to be offered

    A. in bearer form
    B. registered as to interest only
    C. registered as to principal only
    D. fully registered as to both principal and interest

49. Which of the following represents a corporate bond quote?

    A. 8.20–8.00
    B. 8.5%
    C. 85.24–85.30
    D. 85 1/2

50. Max Leveridge wants to sell his 20 Datawaq bonds, but tells you that they are registered in book-entry form. What must occur in order for Max to sell his bonds?

    A. Your firm must send the signed Datawaq bond certificate to the transfer agent.
    B. Your firm will send the certificate to the transfer agent who will then destroy the old certificate and issue a new one.
    C. The transfer agent will input the necessary changes in the ownership records on a computer.
    D. The issuer will make the necessary changes in its customer bond record books.

51. Which two of the following statements are true about bearer bonds?

    I. Interest coupons are attached.
    II. Interest is sent directly to the bondholders on a semiannual basis.
    III. Proof of ownership is required at maturity.
    IV. The person who holds such bonds is presumed to be the owner.

    A. I and III
    B. I and IV
    C. II and III
    D. III and IV

52. Moody's A rated bonds can be accurately described as being

    I. of investment grade
    II. of high or upper-medium quality
    III. speculative

    A. I
    B. I and II
    C. II
    D. III

53. Which of the following bonds on a broker-dealer inventory sheet would MOST likely be quoted at a price based upon the probability of a call or refunding?

    A. Bond trading at 95, callable at par
    B. Bond trading at 95, callable at premium
    C. Bond trading at 105, callable at par
    D. Bond trading at 105, callable at premium

◆ Answers & Rationale

1.   **C.**   10 bonds (sometimes printed as 10M) equal $10,000 in principal amount to be received by the bondholder at maturity. Each bond pays 6% annual interest, or $60; thus, ten bonds pay a total of $600 per year in two semiannual payments of $300. At maturity, the bondholder will receive the $10,000 face amount plus the final semiannual payment ($10,000 + $300 = $10,300).   (Page 21)

2.   **D.**   The basis is defined to be the yield to maturity of a bond at a given price. The basis book contains tables that give the basis to dollar and dollar to basis conversions.   (Page 33)

3.   **B.**   As yields increase, the price of outstanding debt decreases and vice versa. Because the face and coupon on a debt instrument remain unchanged, the market value fluctuates to account for changes in yields.   (Page 28)

4.   **C.**   Interest rate risk is the danger that interest rates will change while a long-term debt is outstanding. The bond with the most years remaining to maturity and the lowest coupon will be exposed to the greatest risk.   (Page 29)

5.   **A.**   Owners have equity positions. Common and preferred stockholders are owners.   (Page 20)

6.   **B.**   The price of the bond that has the longer call protection will be more volatile, and the basis is therefore likely to increase more as general interest rates fall.   (Page 36)

7.   **B.**   The bond with an earlier maturity and a lower coupon is less likely to be called than one with a higher rate. A call price above par is more expensive for the issuer to pay. It is least likely that the 7 1/4% bond callable at 101 1/2 will be called.   (Page 36)

8.   **D.**   The indenture is the contract between an issuer and the trustee on behalf of its bondholders and contains information regarding all terms, conditions and repayment provisions of a corporate debt issue.   (Page 41)

9.   **C.**   The issuing of short-term debt securities would result in an increase in fixed charges, something the company wants to avoid. The call feature is a "red herring"; it doesn't affect the answer. The other options would increase working capital without increasing fixed charges, although answer B would also increase capitalization.   (Page 21)

10.   **B.**   If the company is prepared to pay $1,025 for each bond at redemption, it can save $55 per bond by purchasing the bonds back in the market at 97.   (Page 36)

11.   **C.**   A bond that is registered as to principal only will have a certificate registered in some person's name and have bearer coupons attached to the bond certificate. Only the person to whom the bond is registered may sell the securities. Interest will be paid on the bond only if the interest coupons are sent to the paying agent of the bond.   (Page 32)

12.   **D.**   Sales on bonds are quoted in $1,000 par value unit. 30 = 30 $1,000 bonds = $30,000 face amount.   (Page 43)

13.   **C.**   Today, Best closed at 92, down 1/2. Therefore, Best closed the day before at 92.50, or 92 1/2.   (Page 43)

14.   **C.** $$\frac{\text{Annual interest}}{\text{Bond price}} = \frac{\$70}{\$838.75}$$

$$= .0835 \times 100 = 8.35\%$$
(Page 26)

15.   **D.**   Long-term debt prices will fluctuate more than short-term debt prices as interest rates rise and fall. When one buys a note or a bond, one is really buying the interest payments and the final principal payment. Money has a time value: the farther out in time money is to be received, the less it is worth today. With a 10% five-year bond, an investor buying at market interest rates will pay $1,000 for one bond. If interest rates go to 15%, the

bond price will fall to approximately $800. As payments move out to later years, they are worth less and less, due to the interest rate compounding effect. This same compounding effect causes longer term bonds to increase or decrease more in value (as interest rates change) than short-term bonds. (Page 29)

16. **B.** A corporation will generally call in its debt when interest rates are declining. It can then replace old, high interest rate debt with a new, lower interest rate issue. (Page 36)

17. **D.** *Funded debt* is the term used to describe long-term corporate debt. (Page 20)

18. **B.** The annual interest can be determined by looking at the coupon. The annual interest is 7 7/8% of $1,000 face value, or $78.75. (Page 21)

19. **C.** Senior debt (also known as senior lien) bonds are backed by property owned by the company. They are backed by a first mortgage. (Page 38)

20. **B.** Using the data given, the call schedule for the bond is:

Year	Price
1987	103
1988	102 1/2
1989	102
1990	101 1/2
1991	101
1992	100 1/2
1993	100

(Page 36)

21. **D.** The current yield of a bond equals the annual interest payment divided by the current market price. (Page 26)

22. **D.** The current yield is:

$$\frac{\$ \text{Coupon}}{\text{Bond market price}} = \frac{\$60}{\$950} = 6.3\%$$

(Page 26)

23. **B.** Corporate bond prices are expressed as percentages of the principal amount of a bond, or

$1,000. Each bond point is equal to $10, with the minimum variation for bond quotes at 1/8 of a point. Therefore, a quote of 101 1/4 is equal to $1,012.50 (101.25 × $10). A quote expressed as 101:25 or 101-25 is used for government securities quotations and is equal to 101 25/32. (Page 25)

24. **C.** Each $1,000 7 1/2% bond pays $75 of interest annually.

$$\text{Current yield} = \frac{\text{Annual interest}}{\text{Bond market price}}$$
$$= \frac{\$75}{\$950} = 7.89\%$$

7.89% is approximately 7.9%. (Page 26)

25. **B.** The investor holds 50 $1,000 bonds. If each bond decreases by 1/2 point, the loss is $5 per bond multiplied by 50 bonds equals $250. (Page 25)

26. **C.** To determine the dollar difference between the bonds, calculate the two interest payments and find the difference between them ($5,000 × 5.1% = $255; $5,000 × 5.3% = $265; $265 − $255 = $10). (Page 21)

27. **A.** The GMAC bond is a zero-coupon bond (ZR), meaning that no interest payments are made. These bonds sell at a deep discount and the tax law requires annual accretion of the discount. (Page 40)

28. **D.** "Ogden 5's" means 5% bonds. 5% of $1,000 par equals $50 interest per bond annually. For 50 bonds, the annual interest is $2,500. (Page 21)

29. **C.** Because interest rates in general have risen since the issuance of the 8% bond, the bond's price will now be discounted to give a higher current yield on the bond, making it competitive with the new issues now being sold at 8 1/2%. (Page 28)

30. **B.** Bearer bonds, also called *unregistered bonds*, must have the interest coupons attached to the bond. (Page 32)

31. **D.** The trust indenture is a contract between the issuer and trustee for the benefit of a bondholder. It spells out the covenants to be honored by the issuer and gives the trustee the power to monitor compliance with the covenants and the ability to take action on behalf of the bondholder(s) if a default of the covenants is found.   (Page 41)

32. **D.** Because the 2002 bonds were purchased at par ($1,000 per bond) and will be redeemed at par ($1,000 per bond), there will be no capital gain upon redemption.   (Page 25)

33. **A.** Serial bonds, by definition, have maturity dates scheduled at regular intervals until the issue is retired. Other bonds may also mature serially, but they don't have to.   (Page 22)

34. **B.** The current yield is the annual interest payment divided by the current market price. Therefore, $50 divided by $900 equals 5.6% current yield.   (Page 21)

35. **C.** Serial bonds are bonds that mature over a series of years. From the issuer's standpoint, as bonds mature, interest payments and the outstanding principal amount will decline.   (Page 21)

36. **C.** When a bond is selling at par, its coupon rate, nominal rate and current yield are the same.   (Page 26)

37. **B.** Dividing the annual interest received by the current market price of the bond will give the current yield.   (Page 26)

38. **C.** The difference between the par (or face) value of a bond and a market price lower than par is known as the bond's discount from par.   (Page 25)

39. **A.** The interest rate that a bond pays is not a factor in rating a bond, although the rating that a bond could receive may significantly impact the interest rate the issuers must set.   (Page 30)

40. **A.** If the current yield of a bond is higher than its coupon rate, the bond is selling at a discount from par. If interest rates of newly issued bonds are lower than the rate of a secondary market bond, it is likely that the older bond could be sold at a premium.   (Page 28)

41. **C.** Debentures represent unsecured loans to an issuer. All of the other bonds are backed by one form or another of collateral.   (Page 39)

42. **C.** A guaranteed bond has additional backing supplied by a corporation other than the issuer (typically a parent corporation guaranteeing the bonds of a subsidiary).   (Page 39)

43. **C.** The investor in a corporate zero-coupon bond receives his return in the form of growth of the principal amount during the bond's life. The bond is purchased at a steep discount and the discount is accrued by the investor and taxed by the government annually.   (Page 40)

44. **A.** A closed-end provision in a bond indenture assures investors in the bonds that no other bonds will be issued with a higher claim against company assets.   (Page 42)

45. **C.** A coupon of 8 7/8 represents an annual interest payment of 8 7/8% of $1,000, or $88.75.   (Page 21)

46. **A.** The order in a liquidation is as follows: the IRS (and other government agencies), secured debt holders, unsecured debt holders, general creditors, holders of subordinated debt, preferred stockholders and finally common stockholders.   (Page 41)

47. **B.** The order in a liquidation is as follows: the IRS (and other government agencies), secured debt holders, unsecured debt holders, general creditors, holders of subordinated debt, preferred stockholders and finally common stockholders.   (Page 41)

48. **D.** Most corporate bonds are currently being issued in fully registered form.   (Page 32)

49. **D.** Corporate bond quotes, like dollar bond quotes, are based upon a percentage of face

amount. Corporate bonds have a par value of $1,000. Therefore, a quote of 85 1/2 is 85 1/2% of $1,000, or $855. (Page 43)

50. **C.** Bonds that are registered in book-entry form are not evidenced by a paper certificate. All records of ownership are retained in computerized form. The transfer agent will make any necessary changes in the computer's records. (Page 33)

51. **B.** A bearer bond must have all unpaid coupons attached to the bond. Interest payments are mailed only to owners of registered bonds; demonstration of ownership is not necessary to redeem a bearer bond; it is payable to the bearer, who is presumed to own the bond. (Page 32)

52. **B.** Moody's rating service defines its rating categories as follows: "Aaa" is the best quality, and along with "Aa" is known as high grade. "A" is upper-medium grade. "Baa" is medium grade. Bonds rated in these top four categories are considered to be investment grade. Anything below these ratings is considered speculative. (Page 31)

53. **C.** Bonds must be quoted based on the most conservative yield an investor may receive. Any discount bond callable at par or above will have a yield to call that is greater than its yield to maturity. The higher the call price and the sooner the bond is called, the greater the yield to call for a discount bond. A premium bond callable at par or below always has a yield to call that is less than its yield to maturity. The lower the call price and the sooner the bond is called, the lower the yield to call for any premium bond. Recall the rule of thumb method that illustrates these principles:

1. Add the prorated discount to, *or* subtract the prorated premium from, the coupon rate.
2. Divide the result by the average price, which is the price paid for the bond plus the price received upon maturity, divided by 2.

(Page 32)

3 Corporate Special Securities

1. Mrs. Swensen owns shares of ABC convertible preferred stock. ABC convertible preferred is currently trading at 9 1/2 per share. ABC has just announced that it is offering to redeem shares of ABC convertible preferred at $10 per share. Each share is convertible into one half of a share of the common, currently trading at 18 1/4. What should you advise Mrs. Swensen to do with her 1,000 shares of ABC convertible preferred?

   A. Sell them in the open market
   B. Convert them immediately into the common
   C. Tender the shares to the corporation
   D. Hold the shares

2. Mrs. Swensen owns shares of ABC convertible preferred stock. ABC convertible preferred is currently trading at 9 1/2 per share. ABC has just announced that it is offering to redeem shares of ABC convertible preferred at $10 per share. Each share is convertible into one half of a share of the common, currently trading at 18 1/4. Assuming that the market price of the ABC common remains stable, what will happen to the market price of the convertible preferred as the expiration date of the tender offer approaches?

   A. It will slowly decline below the current 9 1/2.
   B. It will slowly rise to just under 10.
   C. It will slowly rise to just under 18 1/4.
   D. It will stabilize at 9 1/8.

3. Acme Motors has issued both common stock and convertible preferred stock. The convertible preferred has a par value of $100 per share. It is convertible into the common at $25 per share. Acme convertible is trading at 110. What is the parity price of the common?

   A. 25
   B. 27 1/2
   C. 35
   D. 37 1/2

4. Acme Motors has issued both common stock and convertible preferred stock. The convertible preferred has a par value of $100 per share. It is convertible into the common at $25 per share. Due to a change in interest rates, the market price of the Acme preferred declines to $90 per share. Assume that the common is trading at 20% below parity. What is the market price of the Acme common?

   A. 15 3/4
   B. 18
   C. 22 1/2
   D. 25

5. A corporation has $20,000,000 of 8% convertible debentures outstanding. The bonds have a conversion price of $25 per share. The trust indenture has a provision that prevents dilution of the debenture holder's potential ownership in the corporation. The corporation declares a 10% stock dividend. How will the corporation comply with the dilution covenant of the indenture?

   A. Adjust the conversion price to $16 per share
   B. Adjust the conversion price to $16.67 per share
   C. Adjust the conversion price to $22.73 per share
   D. Offer bondholders the choice of receiving 10 shares of stock or $40 cash

6. The XYZ Corporation has a $20 million convertible debenture issue outstanding. Each bond converts into 20 shares of XYZ common stock. The bond indenture contains antidilutive covenants. XYZ Corporation declares a 10% stock dividend. What would be the new conversion price of the bonds?

   A. $32
   B. $33.33
   C. $36.66
   D. $45.45

7. A $1,000 Central Development Corp. bond can be converted at $50 per share into CDC common stock. The bond is currently selling at 110% of parity while the current market value of the stock is $55 per share. What is the bond selling for in the market?

   A. $1,000
   B. $1,100
   C. $1,210
   D. $1,350

8. An investor who wants to subscribe to a rights offering will mail those rights to the

   A. corporation's underwriting department
   B. rights agent
   C. bursar
   D. subscription agent

9. ABC Corporation has a rights offering. Before the rights offering, ABC had 10,000,000 shares of common stock authorized, with 4,000,000 issued and 1,000,000 shares of treasury stock. In a standby rights offering, there are 1,000,000 additional shares offered to the current stockholders. Assume that the existing stockholders subscribe to 600,000 of these shares. After the completion of the rights offering, how many shares of common are outstanding?

   A. 3,000,000
   B. 3,600,000
   C. 4,000,000
   D. 5,000,000

Use the following tombstone to answer questions 10 and 11.

Seven Seas Sailboat Corporation

600,000 Units – $5.00 Per Unit

Each unit represents 4 shares of Preferred, plus 1 perpetual Warrant. Warrants may be exercised for 1/2 share of common stock at a value of $50 per share.

Churnim, Burnum & Spurnem Inc.

10. A customer of yours who owns SSS Corp. common saw the tombstone in the local business daily, and has called you with some questions. If SSS's offering is successful, she wants to know, how much money will it be raising?

   A. $2,400,000
   B. $3,000,000
   C. $12,000,000
   D. Cannot be determined from the information given

11. On completion of the offering of SSS Corp., and if all of the warrants were exercised, how many shares would be outstanding?

    I.   2,400,000 preferred shares
   II. 600,000 preferred shares
  III. 600,000 common shares
  IV. 300,000 common shares

    A. I and III
    B. I and IV
    C. II and III
    D. II and IV

12. Which of the following statement(s) is(are) true concerning ADRs?

    I.   They are issued by large commercial U.S. banks.
   II. They encourage foreign trading in U.S. markets.
  III. They facilitate U.S. trading in foreign securities.
  IV. They are registered on the books of the bank that issued the ADR.

    A. I and III
    B. I, III and IV
    C. II
    D. II and IV

13. What would be the benefits to a corporation of attaching warrants to a new issue of debt securities?

    A. Dilution of shareholder's equity
    B. Reduction of the interest rate of debt securities
    C. Reduction of the number of shares outstanding
    D. Increase in earnings per share

14. Which of the following statements are true of convertible and callable bonds?

    I.   If called, the owners have the option of retaining the bonds and they will continue to receive interest.
   II. After the call date, interest will cease.
  III. Upon conversion, there will be dilution.
  IV. The coupon rate would be less than the rate for a nonconvertible bond.

    A. I and III
    B. I, III and IV
    C. II, III and IV
    D. II and IV

15. Twin City Barge is attempting to sell new shares through a rights offering. John Quick, who chooses to exercise his rights, sends his check to the

    A. company
    B. underwriter
    C. customer's broker
    D. rights/transfer agent

16. Which of the following is NOT true concerning convertible bonds?

    A. Coupon rates are usually higher than nonconvertible bond rates of the same issuer.
    B. Convertible bondholders are creditors of the corporation.
    C. Coupon rates are usually lower than nonconvertible bond rates of the same issuer.
    D. If the underlying common stock were to decline to the point where there is no advantage to convert the bonds into common stock, the bonds would sell at a price based on their inherent value as bonds, disregarding the convertible feature.

17. All of the following will remain relatively stable in value in a period of stable interest rates EXCEPT

   A. convertible preferred stock
   B. senior preferred
   C. participating preferred
   D. cumulative preferred

18. A corporate offering of 200,000 additional shares to existing stockholders is a

   A. tender offer
   B. secondary offering
   C. preemptive offer
   D. rights offering

Use the following tombstone to answer questions 19 and 20.

This announcement appears as a matter of record only.

New Issue   May 5, 1995

$42,000,000

Acme Sweatsocks, Inc.

10 5/8 Convertible Debentures Due 5/31/2025

Price $1,000

Each bond is convertible into Acme Sweatsocks, Inc. common at $10.50 per share through May 31st, 2005.

Dewey, Cheatham & Howe, Inc.   Capital Bankers, Inc.

---

19. If an investor wishes to convert, approximately how many whole shares of common stock can she expect per bond?

   A. 90
   B. 95
   C. 100
   D. 105

20. On December 4, 1996, the bonds were trading at 102. Calculation of the parity price of common stock on that date shows it to be approximately

   A. 1 7/8
   B. 9 1/8
   C. 9 3/4
   D. 10 3/4

21. Which of the following do NOT pay a dividend?

   A. Warrants
   B. Mutual funds
   C. ADRs
   D. Unit investment trusts

22. Inco is offering 600,000 units to the public at $5 per unit. Each unit consists of two shares of Inco preferred stock and one perpetual warrant for 1/3 share of common stock, exercisable at $5. Through the sale of this issue, Inco raised

   A. $1,500,000
   B. $1,750,000
   C. $3,000,000
   D. $6,000,000

23. Inco is offering 600,000 units to the public at $5 per unit. Each unit consists of two shares of Inco preferred stock and one perpetual warrant for 1/3 share of common stock, exercisable at $5. Upon the exercise of all warrants, Inco will be capitalized with

   A. 600,000 preferred shares and 200,000 common shares
   B. 600,000 preferred shares and 600,000 common shares
   C. 1,200,000 preferred shares and 200,000 common shares
   D. 1,200,000 preferred shares and 600,000 common shares

24. XYZ common stock is currently trading at 56 1/2. Your client owns one XYZ 6% convertible debenture that closed at 115 1/2 on Friday. Before the open of the market Monday, it was announced that the debenture would be called at 102 1/4. The debenture is convertible into common stock at $59.25 per share. What should he do?

   A. Sell the debenture at 115 1/2
   B. Convert the debenture and immediately sell the converted shares in the market
   C. Sell the common stock short against the box
   D. Allow the debenture to be called

25. A corporation issues new stock with a subscription price of $28. The stock is currently selling at $32. Under the terms of the offering, four rights are needed to subscribe to one new share. Using the ex-rights formula, what is the value of a right?

    A. $.80
    B. $1.00
    C. $4.00
    D. Cannot be determined from the information given

26. Acme Co. decides to sell additional shares to its existing stockholders through a rights offering. The current market price of Acme is $32 and the subscription price has been set at $18. Twenty rights will be necessary to purchase one new share. What, approximately, will be the price of the right before the ex-date?

    A. $.67
    B. $.70
    C. $1.00
    D. $1.12

27. What is the conversion ratio of a convertible bond purchased at face value and convertible at $50?

    A. 2:1
    B. 3:1
    C. 20:1
    D. 30:1

28. An investor purchases two newly issued $1,000 par, 5% convertible corporate bonds at parity. The bonds are convertible into common stock at $50 per share. During the period in which the investor holds the bonds, the market price of the common stock increases 25% over her purchase price. The parity price of the bond, after the increase in the common stock price, is

    A. $750
    B. $1,000
    C. $1,025
    D. $1,250

29. An investor purchases two newly issued $1,000 par, 5% convertible corporate bonds at parity. The bonds are convertible into common stock at $50 per share. During the period in which the investor holds the bonds, the market price of the common stock increases 25% over her purchase price. Each bond is equivalent to how many converted shares?

    A. 2
    B. 3
    C. 20
    D. 30

30. Acme convertible bonds are convertible at $50. If the bonds are selling in the market for 90 and the common stock is selling for $45, which two of the following statements are true?

    I. The bond can be converted into 20 shares of common stock.
    II. There would be a profitable arbitrage situation.
    III. The bonds are trading below parity.
    IV. The stock is selling on conversion parity.

    A. I and II
    B. I and III
    C. I and IV
    D. II and III

31. A new bond issue will include warrants to

    A. increase the spread to the underwriter
    B. compensate the underwriter for handling the issue
    C. increase the price of the issue to the public
    D. increase the attractiveness of the issue to the public

32. John Evans purchases a 9% convertible bond maturing in 20 years. The bond is convertible into common stock at $50 per share. If the price of the common stock is at parity (57 1/2), how much does John Evans pay for the bond?

    A. $850.00
    B. $942.50
    C. $1,057.50
    D. $1,150.00

33. Ms. Smith owns some $100 par 5 1/2% callable convertible preferred stock that is convertible into common stock at $25. What should she be advised to do should the board of directors call all the preferred at 106 when the common stock is trading at $25.50?

    A. Convert her preferred stock into common stock because the common stock is selling above parity.
    B. Present the preferred stock for the call in order to realize a $6-per-share premium.
    C. Place irrevocable instructions to convert the preferred stock into common stock and sell short the common stock immediately.
    D. Hold the preferred stock in order to continue the 5 1/2% yield.

34. ADRs facilitate which of the following?

    I.   Foreign trading of domestic securities
    II. Foreign trading of U.S. government securities
    III. Domestic trading of U.S. government securities
    IV. Domestic trading of foreign securities

    A. I and II
    B. III
    C. III and IV
    D. IV

35. Jacklyn Smith owns a convertible bond for ABC Corp. She is, therefore,

    A. an owner
    B. a creditor
    C. both owner and creditor
    D. neither owner nor creditor

36. All of the following pay dividends EXCEPT

    A. common stock
    B. preferred stock
    C. convertible preferred stock
    D. warrants

◆ Answers & Rationale

1. **C.** Mrs. Swensen should do whatever will result in the greatest value. She currently holds 1,000 shares of the preferred with a CMV totaling $9,500 (1,000 × $9.50). She can sell each share in the open market for $9.50. If she converts her preferred, she will get two shares of common for each share of preferred, a conversion value per share of $18.25, and a total market value of $9,125 (500 × 18 1/4). If she tenders the stock, she will receive $10 per share, or $10,000. She can hold the stock, but its retirement by the company means it will no longer earn dividends. She would just be postponing the time at which she receives the $10 per share from the corporation.   (Page 52)

2. **B.** If the corporation is redeeming the entire issue of preferred stock at $10 per share, that fixes the value of those shares as of the call date. As the call date nears, the stock should trade at a slight discount to $10, the call price. This reflects the present value of the funds to be received for tendering the shares to the corporation.
(Page 52)

3. **B.** Acme preferred may be converted into four shares of common (100 ÷ $25 = 4). With the convertible preferred trading at 110, the common stock must be trading at 27 1/2 for four shares of common stock to be of equivalent value with one share of preferred. To calculate the parity price of the common stock, divide the current market price of the preferred stock by the number of shares of common stock that would be received for converting to the preferred ($110 ÷ 4 = 27 1/2).
(Page 51)

4. **B.** The parity price of the common would be 22 1/2 (90 ÷ 4 = 22 1/2). Because the common is trading at 20% below parity, you know that its market price is 80% of 22 1/2 (.80 × 22 1/2 = 18).
(Page 51)

5. **C.** To comply with the dilution covenant, the corporation must adjust the conversion price of the debentures downward to compensate for the 10% stock dividend being received by common stockholders. The new conversion price is calculated as follows: $1,000 par value divided by $25 conversion price equals 40 shares. Forty shares multiplied by 10% stock dividend equals four shares plus 40 shares equals 44 shares. $1,000 par value divided by 44 shares equals $22.73, the new conversion price.   (Page 50)

6. **D.** Before the dividend, the conversion ratio was 20 and the conversion price was $50 ($1,000 ÷ 20 = $50). Each bondholder received 20 shares of stock per $1,000 face value or par value of bonds owned. After the dividend, the conversion ratio must be increased by 10% to maintain the bondholder's equivalent equity position upon conversion as specified by the antidilutive covenants. The following calculations illustrate the mechanics: 20 (old conversion ratio) multiplied by 110% equals 22 (new conversion ratio), and the new conversion price equals $1,000 divided by 22, or $45.45.   (Page 50)

7. **C.** This is a two-step problem: first, the parity price of the bond must be found. The parity price of a bond equals the market value of common stock times the conversion rate. $55 multiplied by 20 conversion rate (which is $1,000 divided by $50) equals parity price of $1,100 for the bond. If the price of the bond is 110% of parity, then parity times 1.1 equals the market price ($1,100 × 1.1 = $1,210).   (Page 51)

8. **B.** The issuing corporation will appoint a firm to serve as its rights agent. The rights agent will receive the subscription rights sent to it by those individuals who wish to exercise their rights to acquire the corporation's stock.   (Page 55)

9. **C.** Because there were 4,000,000 shares issued, and 1,000,000 shares of treasury stock, this means there were 3,000,000 shares outstanding. The existing stockholders subscribed to 600,000 new shares. However, because a standby (firm) underwriting was used, the additional 400,000 shares were also issued. Hence, a total of 4,000,000 shares will be outstanding.   (Page 55)

10.   **B.**   600,000 units are being offered for a price of $5 per unit. If the offering is successful and all of the units are sold, the company will raise $3,000,000.   (Page 56)

11.   **B.**   600,000 units each represents four shares of preferred stock for a total of 2,400,000 shares of preferred. Each unit also contains a warrant exchangeable into 1/2 of a share of common stock, for a total of 300,000 shares of common.
                                    (Page 56)

12.   **B.**   ADRs are issued by large commercial U.S. banks to facilitate American trading in foreign securities and are registered on the books of the banks that issued them.   (Page 58)

13.   **B.**   Usually the warrant is issued as a sweetener to make the debt instrument more marketable. This enhancement allows the issuer to pay a slightly lower rate of interest. A warrant may be issued together with bonds or preferred stock, entitling the owner to purchase a given number of common stock shares at a specific price, for a number of years.   (Page 57)

14.   **C.**   When a bond is called and the owner does not redeem, the interest payments cease. Conversion causes dilution and generally interest rates on convertible bonds are less than straight debt issues.   (Page 52)

15.   **D.**   The rights (or transfer) agent receives the checks for a rights offering. The agent can be the company's transfer agent or a special rights agent for the rights offering only.   (Page 55)

16.   **A.**   Coupon rates are not higher; they are lower because of the value of the conversion feature. The bondholders are creditors, and if the stock price falls, the conversion feature will not influence the bond's price.   (Page 48)

17.   **A.**   Because interest rate movements drive the prices of preferred stocks, in a period of stable interest rates, preferred stocks will not fluctuate in value. However, convertible preferred stocks will fluctuate with movements in the price of common stock into which the preferred can be converted.
                                    (Page 49)

18.   **D.**   The question defines a rights offering.
                                    (Page 54)

19.   **B.**   Because the debentures are convertible at $10.50, they are convertible into 95.23 shares (95 whole shares).

$$\frac{\$1{,}000 \text{ per bond}}{\$10.50} = 95.23 \text{ shares}$$

                                    (Page 49)

20.   **D.**

$$\frac{\text{Debenture principal } (\$1{,}000)}{\text{Conversion price } (\$10.50) \text{ common stock}} =$$

$$\frac{\text{Debenture market value } (\$1{,}020)}{\text{Parity price } (X)}$$

$$\frac{\$1{,}000}{\$10.50} = \frac{\$1{,}020}{(X)}$$

$$(X) = \frac{\$10.50 \times \$1{,}020}{\$1{,}000}$$

$$= \$10.71, \text{ rounded to } 10\ 3/4 \qquad \text{(Page 49)}$$

21.   **A.**   Warrants are long-term options to buy stock and do *not* pay dividends.   (Page 56)

22.   **C.**   600,000 units are being offered at $5 each; $3,000,000 will be raised.   (Page 56)

23.   **C.**   Each unit consists of two preferred shares and 1/3 of a common share if the warrant is exercised. 600,000 multiplied by 2 equals 1,200,000 preferred shares and 600,000 multiplied by 1/3 equals 200,000 common shares.
                                    (Page 56)

24. **A.** If the debenture is converted and sold, the sale amount is:

$$\frac{\$1,000}{\$59.25} = 16.877 \text{ shares}$$

$$16.877 \times \$56.50 = \$953.55$$

If the debenture is called, the proceeds would be $102 1/4 or $1,022.50. Therefore, the best option is to sell in the market at the open of trading on Monday. There is no guarantee that your client will receive 115 1/2 (the price at market close on Friday), but there is still a chance that he will be able to get a better price than if he waits for the call to take effect. (Page 53)

25. **B.** To determine the value of a right, use the ex-rights formula.

$$\frac{\text{Market price} - \text{Subscription price}}{N \text{ (number of rights)}}$$

= Value of right

$$\frac{\$32 - \$28}{4} = \$1 \text{ per right}$$

(Page 56)

26. **A.** Use the cum rights formula.

$$\frac{\text{Market price (\$32)} - \text{Sub. price (\$18)}}{N(20) + 1}$$

$$= \frac{14}{21} = .67$$

(Page 56)

27. **C.** $\frac{\$1,000 \text{ par value}}{\$50 \text{ conversion}} = 20$ shares per bond

(Page 49)

28. **D.** The bond is convertible into 20 shares ($1,000 ÷ 50 = 20 shares). The market price of the shares appreciates by 25% ($50 × 1.25 = $62.50). 20 multiplied by $62.50 (price of the stock) equals $1,250. (Page 56)

29. **C.** $1,000 divided by $50 equals 20 shares. (Page 51)

30. **C.** Parity for the bond is $1,000 bond price divided by $50 share price equals 20 shares per bond. If the bond is now selling for 900 and the stock for $45, the conversion rate is $900 divided by 45, which equals 20. The bond and the stock are at parity. (Page 51)

31. **D.** Warrants are used as a "sweetener" to increase the attractiveness of a new issue to the public. (Page 56)

32. **D.** Because the bond is convertible at $50 per share, each bond can be converted into 20 shares of stock ($1,000 ÷ $50 = 20). The price of the common stock is now 57 1/2. For the bond to be selling at parity, it must sell for 20 multiplied by $57.50 equals $1,150. (Page 52)

33. **B.** If the preferred is called, each share is worth $106. If the preferred is converted, and the equivalent common shares are sold in the market, the dollar value received will be $102 ($100 par at $25 equals four shares of common (4 × $25.50 = $102). Therefore, the stockholder will not retain the stock because dividends cease upon the call. (Page 53)

34. **D.** ADRs (American depositary receipts) are tradeable securities issued by banks, with the receipt's value based on the underlying foreign securities held by the bank. In this way, Americans can trade foreign securities in the United States. (Page 58)

35. **B.** A bondholder is a creditor (whether or not the bond is convertible). Only after the bond is converted to stock is she considered to be an owner. (Page 48)

36. **D.** Warrants do not pay dividends under any circumstances. The other instruments listed will pay dividends when declared by the board of directors. (Page 56)

 **4** # U.S. Government Securities

1. Treasury bills can be described as

   A. issued at par
   B. callable
   C. issued in bearer form
   D. registered

2. Which of the following statements are true of Freddie Mac?

   I. It issues pass-through securities.
   II. It purchases student loans.
   III. It purchases conventional residential mortgages from financial institutions insured by an agency of the U.S. government.
   IV. It issues securities directly backed by the full faith and credit of the U.S. government.

   A. I and III
   B. I and IV
   C. II and III
   D. II and IV

3. Securities offered by the Federal Intermediate Credit Bank are

   A. backed by the full faith and credit of the issuer
   B. issued either in the form of discounted notes or as long-term bonds
   C. neither A nor B
   D. both A and B

4. Which of the following debt instruments pays no interest?

   A. Treasury STRIPS
   B. Treasury note
   C. Treasury bond
   D. Treasury stock

5. Which of the terms below would NOT be used to describe the securities the Federal Intermediate Credit Bank issues?

   A. Stock and equities
   B. Mortgage-backed
   C. Supporting farmers and agricultural producers
   D. Bonds and debentures

6. A client could be assured of federal government backing for an investment in which of the following agencies?

   A. Federal National Mortgage Association
   B. Inter-American Development Bank
   C. Government National Mortgage Association
   D. Federal Intermediate Credit Bank

7. In describing GNMAs to a potential investor, you would tell him that

   A. the certificates have the full faith and credit guarantee of the U.S. government
   B. each bond is backed by a pool of insured mortgages
   C. interest payments received by the investor are exempt from both local and federal income taxes
   D. a GNMA can be purchased for as little as $10,000

27

8. The securities issued by the Federal Farm Credit System could be described as

   A. being issued only in the form of long-term bonds
   B. making federally tax-free interest payments
   C. having the same low risk as direct Treasury issues
   D. being backed by the full faith and credit of the issuer

9. An investor interested in monthly interest income should invest in

   A. GNMAs
   B. Treasury bonds
   C. stock of a utility company
   D. corporate bonds

10. Which of the following maturities is available to investors in Treasury bills?

    A. One week
    B. One month
    C. Six months
    D. Nine months

11. Agency-issued securities and direct federal government issues have which of the following characteristics in common?

    I.   Yields quoted in 1/32nds
    II. Interest-bearing securities quoted as a percentage of par
    III. Redeemable by the purchaser
    IV. Redeemable by the issuer

    A. I and III
    B. I and IV
    C. II and III
    D. II and IV

12. The Federal Intermediate Credit Bank issues all of the following types of securities EXCEPT

    I.   discount notes
    II. debentures
    III. pass-through securities
    IV. preferred stock

    A. I and II
    B. I and IV
    C. II and III
    D. III

13. Which of the following is true of a Treasury STRIP but not of a Treasury receipt?

    A. It may be stripped and issued by a securities broker-dealer.
    B. It is backed by the full faith and credit of the federal government.
    C. Its stripped-off interest coupons are sold separately.
    D. Investors may purchase them at a discount.

14. A customer who watches the T bill auctions noticed that the average return to investors in the latest T bill auction fell to 4.71%, down from 4.82% at the previous week's sale. When he asks you for your interpretation, you should tell him that

    A. the decline in yields indicates that the supply of short-term funds has decreased relative to demand
    B. investors who purchased bills at this auction paid more for them than purchasers last week
    C. investors who purchased T bills 12 weeks ago paid less than subsequent purchasers
    D. the federal funds rate and other short-term interest rate indicators are probably rising

15. One of your customers would like to invest in a fairly safe security, but is not interested in regular income. Which of the following securities is offered at a discount and would meet his needs?

    A. GNMA certificates
    B. FHLB securities
    C. FNMA certificates
    D. U.S. Treasury STRIPS

16. If interest rates in general are rising, the price of new T bills should

    A. fluctuate
    B. rise
    C. fall
    D. remain steady

17. Which of the following represents a Treasury note quote?

    A. 8.20–8.00
    B. 8.5%
    C. 85.24–85.30
    D. 85 1/2

18. Which of the following represents a Treasury bill quote?

    A. 8.20–8.00
    B. 8.5%
    C. 85.24–85.30
    D. 85 1/2

◆ Answers & Rationale

1. **D.** A registered security is any security for which ownership is recorded in files maintained for this purpose. Even though T bills are book-entry securities (no certificates are issued), ownership records are maintained, and therefore they are considered registered. (Page 62)

2. **A.** Freddie Mac stands for Federal Home Loan Mortgage Corporation. Like Ginnie Mae, it issues mortgage-backed pass-through securities. Unlike Ginnie Mae, however, it deals only in conventional residential mortgages. (Page 69)

3. **D.** Farm Credit System loans are made through Federal Land Banks, Federal Intermediate Credit Banks and Banks for Cooperatives. These banks are federally charted and supervised by the Farm Credit Administration, an independent agency of the federal government. Securities issued by these organizations are not direct obligations of or guaranteed by the U.S. government, but rather by the Farm Credit Agency. The securities are issued in the form of discount notes, six- and nine-month bonds and longer term bonds. Interest is exempt from state and local taxes but is subject to federal income taxes. (Page 69)

4. **A.** STRIPS (Separate Trading of Registered Interest and Principal of Securities) are T bonds with the coupons removed. STRIPS don't pay interest separately, they are sold at a deep discount and mature at face (par) value. Treasury stock is not a debt instrument and pays neither interest nor dividends. (Page 64)

5. **B.** The FICBs make loans to credit companies, agricultural institutions and commercial banks, which in turn lend that money to farmers. Some of these loans take the form of discounted purchases of agricultural "paper" from various financial institutions. FICBs are private corporations and, as such, issue both common and preferred stock in themselves. They raise the funds they lend

by issuing short-term debentures, but these bonds are not backed by mortgages on any underlying land, buildings or equipment. (Page 69)

6. **C.** Only the Government National Mortgage Association issues securities backed by the full faith and credit of the U.S. government. The remainder are considered government agencies and, although their securities are considered second only to U.S. government issues in safety, they do not have direct U.S. government backing. (Page 70)

7. **A.** The certificates issued by GNMA represent interests in government-insured mortgages pooled by mortgage brokers (who guarantee the monthly cash flow), but it is the U.S. government that actually "backs" GNMA pass-through certificates. GNMA pass-throughs are issued in minimum denominations of $25,000, and all interest earned is subject to federal income tax. (Page 70)

8. **D.** The Federal Farm Credit Consolidation System was set up in 1980 as a means of organizing and reducing the costs of issuing securities for the Federal Land Banks, the Federal Intermediate Credit Banks and the Federal Farm Credit Banks. Issues of the consolidated system are backed in various manners, although, as agencies, none has the full faith and credit backing of the U.S. government. Interest income from all government agency issues is subject to federal income taxes at the ordinary income tax rate. (Page 68)

9. **A.** The mortgages underlying GNMA modified pass-through certificates pay interest on a monthly basis. GNMA then passes this monthly income through to investors in GNMA pass-through certificates. (Page 70)

10. **C.** Investors can acquire Treasury bills at the weekly T bill auction in denominations of $10,000 and up with maturities of three months, six months and twelve months. The U.S. government can issue nine-month certificates, but doesn't currently. (Page 62)

11. **D.** Agency issue yields are typically quoted on a percentage of par basis. Investors who desire to liquidate their investment must either sell it on the secondary market or wait for the issue to mature. (Page 65)

12. **D.** The Federal Intermediate Credit Bank makes loans to other banks to back agriculture and related financing business. As a private corporation, it can issue stock in itself. (Page 69)

13. **B.** Treasury receipts are stripped treasuries and, as such, are issued in stripped form by an institution other than the federal government. Only direct issues of the U.S. government are backed by its full faith and credit. (Page 64)

14. **B.** As rates for T bills drop, T bill prices climb (T bill rates and prices have an inverse relationship). T bills are priced at their yield, so an investor who bids 4.71% is actually paying *more* for a T bill than one who bids 4.82%. (Page 66)

15. **D.** U.S. Treasury STRIPS (Separate Trading of Registered Interest and Principal of Securities) are direct obligations of the U.S. Treasury issued in the form of zero-coupon bonds. Zero-coupon bonds pay no interest. They are issued at a discount and appreciate in value each period until maturity. (Page 64)

16. **C.** Bill prices decrease as the interest rates go up. (Page 66)

17. **C.** All Treasury notes and bonds maturing in one year or more are quoted in 1/32nds. Thus a quote at 85.24 to 85.30 means 85 24/32 to 85 30/32. (Page 65)

18. **A.** Treasury bills are quoted on a yield basis, which is based on a discounted price to par. This results in a yield quote where the bid is greater than the offer. The greater the discount to par (the lower the actual dollar price) the greater the yield. (Page 65)

5 Money-market Securities and Interest Rates

1. You would advise an investor interested in low volatility of interest rates to invest in a security that has a return tied to the

   A. passbook rate
   B. prime rate
   C. federal funds rate
   D. broker call rate

2. Federal funds are used primarily by

   A. large commercial banks
   B. mutual insurance companies
   C. independent broker-dealers
   D. savings and loans

3. One of the most important functions of a banker's acceptance is its use as a means of

   A. facilitating trades in foreign goods
   B. facilitating trades of foreign securities in the United States
   C. assigning previously declared distributions by foreign corporations
   D. guaranteeing payment of an international bank's promissory note

4. The federal funds rate is charged to banks for

   A. short-term bank loans from the government
   B. loans offered by major New York City banks
   C. loans from other banks and can change daily
   D. loans from broker-dealers

5. Which of the following types of corporations typically do NOT issue commercial paper?

   A. Commercial banks and holding companies
   B. Investment and finance companies
   C. Industrial and service companies
   D. Brokerage and insurance firms

6. Corporations issue commercial paper with maturities ranging from as little as 1 day to as long as

   A. 7 days
   B. 90 days
   C. 270 days
   D. 365 days

7. The price an investor pays would include face value plus any accrued interest in which of the following securities?

   A. Bankers' acceptances
   B. Negotiable certificates of deposit
   C. Reverse repurchase agreements
   D. Treasury bills

8. A repurchase agreement is usually initiated by

   I. the U.S. Treasury
   II. a Federal Home Loan Bank
   III. a commercial bank
   IV. the Federal Reserve Board

   A. I and III
   B. I and IV
   C. II and IV
   D. III and IV

9. The rate at which Japanese yen could be converted into U.S. dollars, or British pounds could be converted into Swiss francs, would be set in the

   A. exchange rate market
   B. interbank market
   C. secondary market
   D. fourth market

10. If a client asked you to explain how the effective federal funds rate she saw quoted in the paper is determined, you would say that the rate reflects the

    A. opening rate for the day
    B. noon rate
    C. closing rate for the day
    D. average rate for the day

11. What organization or institution would insure a jumbo certificate of deposit issued by a savings and loan?

    A. SIPC
    B. FRB
    C. FDIC
    D. FSLIC

12. What organization or institution would insure a jumbo certificate of deposit issued by a bank?

    A. SIPC
    B. FRB
    C. FDIC
    D. FSLIC

13. Which of the following use federal funds as an investment?

    A. Individuals
    B. Commercial banks
    C. Industrial corporations
    D. Federal Reserve Banks

14. Federal funds are often loaned between which of the following institutions?

    I.   Small commercial banks
    II. Corporations
    III. Large commercial banks
    IV. National banks

    A. I and II
    B. I and III
    C. II and III
    D. II and IV

15. Which of the following would be considered a money-market instrument?

    A. Rights with 269 days remaining until expiration
    B. Warrants with seven months remaining to maturity
    C. New issue of T bills
    D. GMAC direct paper

16. Which of the following are characteristics of negotiable jumbo CDs?

    I.   Issued in amounts of $100,000 to $1,000,000
    II. Fully insured by the FDIC
    III. Mature in less than 270 days
    IV. Trade in the secondary market

    A. I, II and III
    B. I and IV
    C. II, III and IV
    D. III and IV

17. Which of the following would be considered Eurodollars?

    A. European currencies deposited in U.S. banks
    B. U.S. currency deposited in foreign banks
    C. European currencies deposited in Japanese banks
    D. Japanese currency deposited in European banks

18. Which of the following are characteristics of commercial paper?

   I. Backed by money-market deposits
   II. Negotiated maturities and yields
   III. Issued by commercial banks
   IV. Not registered as securities

   A. I and II
   B. I, II and III
   C. II and IV
   D. III and IV

19. Your company would like to import raw wool from New Zealand to make into yard goods for shipping next fall. Which of the following instruments could provide your firm with the best means of financing this purchase?

   A. Banker's acceptance
   B. Commercial paper
   C. Eurodollars
   D. Repurchase agreement

20. Because of the cyclical nature of the industry, your firm is experiencing a shortage of cash just at the time it needs to tool up to manufacture new inventory. Which of the following instruments could be used to improve your company's cash flow?

   A. Banker's acceptance
   B. Commercial paper
   C. Repurchase agreement
   D. Reverse repurchase agreement

21. One of your clients is involved in the importation of exotic nuts and oils for a commercial bakery. If the bakery wants to delay payments on purchases of nuts until it is able to sign contracts with a wholesaler, it would use

   A. bankers' acceptances
   B. commercial paper
   C. Eurodollars
   D. foreign currency exchanges

22. If the Treasury wants to improve the U.S. dollar's value in comparison to Japan's yen, it can engage in which of the following activities?

   I. Devaluation
   II. Revaluation
   III. Pegging
   IV. Stabilization

   A. I and II
   B. I, II and IV
   C. II and III
   D. II, III and IV

23. Which of the following entities can issue Eurobonds?

   I. Domestic corporations
   II. Foreign corporations
   III. Domestic governments
   IV. Foreign governments

   A. I, II and IV only
   B. I and III only
   C. II and IV only
   D. I, II, III and IV

24. Your firm has entered a number of spot trades for British pounds and Swiss francs in the interbank market. What are the settlement terms it will have to meet?

   A. Same business day
   B. One or two business days
   C. Five business days
   D. One to eighteen months

25. Because of the changes it anticipates in the exchange rates for various foreign currencies, your firm has entered several forward trades for Japanese yen and German deutsche marks. What are the settlement terms it will have to meet?

   A. Same business day
   B. One or two business days
   C. Five business days
   D. One to eighteen months

26. Transactions in foreign currencies typically use which of the following settlements?

   I.   Same day
   II. Spot
   III. Regular way
   IV. Forward

   A. I, II and III only
   B. I and III only
   C. II and IV only
   D. I, II, III and IV

27. A central bank can cause a strengthening in the value of its own country's currency in the interbank market by

   I.   buying its own country's currency
   II. selling its own country's currency
   III. buying foreign currency
   IV. selling foreign currency

   A. I and III
   B. I and IV
   C. II and III
   D. II and IV

28. A central bank can cause a weakening in the value of its own country's currency in the interbank market by

   I.   buying its own country's currency
   II. selling its own country's currency
   III. buying foreign currency
   IV. selling foreign currency

   A. I and III
   B. I and IV
   C. II and III
   D. II and IV

29. If the federal funds rate has been on the upswing over the past few months, which of the following is probably also occurring?

   A. Increase in the prime rate
   B. Decrease in the prime rate
   C. Increase in Federal Reserve member bank deposits
   D. Decrease in Federal Reserve member bank deposits

30. One of your corporate clients is interested in learning more about money-market instruments. You would provide him with more information on which of the following?

   I.   Commercial paper
   II. T bill offerings
   III. TANs
   IV. Repos

   A. I, II and III
   B. I, II and IV
   C. I, III and IV
   D. II, III and IV

31. An investor interested in the most stable rate of return would NOT want an investment tied to the

   A. prime rate
   B. long-term interest rate
   C. federal funds rate
   D. discount rate

32. All of the following are money-market instruments EXCEPT

   A. Treasury bills
   B. municipal notes
   C. commercial paper
   D. newly issued Treasury bonds

33. Which of the following is a money-market instrument?

   A. Short-term debt
   B. Long-term debt
   C. Short-term equity
   D. Long-term equity

34. Commercial paper has a maximum maturity of how many days?

   A. 90
   B. 180
   C. 270
   D. 360

35. Which of the following statements are true of negotiable certificates of deposit?

 I. The issuing bank guarantees the instrument.
 II. They are callable.
 III. The minimum denominations are $1,000.
 IV. They can be traded in the secondary market.

 A. I, II and III only
 B. I and IV only
 C. II and III only
 D. I, II, III and IV

36. Commercial paper is a

 A. secured note issued by a corporation
 B. guaranteed note issued by a corporation
 C. promissory note issued by a corporation
 D. promissory note issued by a broker-dealer

37. A banker's acceptance is a

 A. promissory note
 B. capital-market instrument
 C. time draft
 D. means to facilitate the trading of foreign securities

38. Which of the following trade with accrued interest?

 A. Zero-coupon Treasury obligations
 B. Treasury bills
 C. Certificates of deposit
 D. Bankers' acceptances

39. A U.S. government bond dealer sells bonds to another dealer with an agreement to buy back the securities in a specified period of time. This is a(n)

 A. repurchase agreement
 B. reverse repurchase agreement
 C. open market certificate
 D. open market note

40. The effective federal funds rate quoted in the business news represents the average rate for the previous

 A. hour
 B. day
 C. week
 D. two weeks

41. The federal funds rate is calculated by taking the

 A. daily average rate charged by the largest money center banks
 B. daily average rate charged by the national Federal Reserve member banks
 C. weekly average rate charged by the largest money center banks
 D. weekly average rate charged by the national Federal Reserve member banks

42. Of the following interest rates, which is considered the MOST volatile?

 A. Discount rate
 B. Federal funds rate
 C. Prime rate
 D. Passbook savings rate

43. Which of the following interest rates is considered the LEAST volatile?

 A. Discount rate
 B. Federal funds rate
 C. Prime rate
 D. Passbook savings rate

44. Which of the following statements would constitute a valid reason for investing in Eurobonds?

 A. Eurobonds can provide diversification to a portfolio.
 B. Eurobonds can be purchased more inexpensively than comparable U.S. bonds.
 C. Eurobonds are traded in an unregulated market, free from government intervention.
 D. Eurobonds can provide an exchange rate hedge against a fall in the U.S. dollar.

45. Interbank transactions in foreign currencies occur in which of the following markets?

   I. Spot
   II. Forward
   III. Pegged
   IV. Stabilized

   A. I and II only
   B. I and III only
   C. III and IV only
   D. I, II, III and IV

46. The interbank market was formed to trade which of the following?

   A. Foreign currencies
   B. American depositary receipts
   C. Commercial paper
   D. Foreign stocks

47. An international, unregulated, decentralized market for trading currencies, as well as debt obligations, where prices are affected by economic policies and conditions, is the

   A. Federal Reserve Board
   B. interbank system
   C. London Stock Exchange
   D. International Monetary Fund

48. Which of the following could be money-market instruments?

   I. Newly issued Treasury bonds
   II. Commercial paper
   III. Treasury bills
   IV. Municipal notes

   A. I and III only
   B. II, III and IV only
   C. II and IV only
   D. I, II, III and IV

49. A time draft is similar to which of the following money-market instruments?

   A. CDs
   B. Commercial paper
   C. Treasury bills
   D. Bankers' acceptances

50. When the Federal Reserve and a U.S. government securities dealer agree that the Fed will sell securities to the dealer subject to Fed repurchase in a specified time period, they make a(n)

   A. open market note
   B. open market certificate
   C. reverse repurchase agreement
   D. repurchase agreement

51. When the Fed makes an agreement with a U.S. government securities dealer specifying that it will buy the securities from the dealer subject to repurchase in a specified time period, it agrees to a(n)

   A. reverse repurchase agreement
   B. repurchase agreement
   C. open market certificate
   D. open market note

52. The maturity on commercial paper is set at 270 days or less in order to

   A. avoid the attachment of bearer coupons
   B. give the investor an option not offered by T bills
   C. reflect the normal production cycle of a corporation
   D. avoid the SEC registration requirement

53. Which of the following statements about Eurodollar bonds are true?

   I. Payment of principal and interest is always in U.S. dollars.
   II. Payment of principal and interest is always in the designated foreign currency of the issuer.
   III. The issuer of Eurodollar bonds may be either a U.S. corporation or a foreign corporation.
   IV. The bonds may be issued either in the U.S. or abroad.

   A. I and III
   B. I and IV
   C. II and III
   D. II and IV

54. Mountain Brewing, a subsidiary of a U.S. corporation, is looking for debt financing by offering a bond denominated in Japanese yen that will be sold in Canada. This bond is a(n)

A. ADR
B. Eurobond
C. Eurodollar bond
D. foreign exchange bond

55. Which of the following entities would NOT be permitted to issue debt securities in the Eurobond market?

A. U.S. domestic corporations
B. Foreign corporations
C. Foreign banks
D. None of the above

◆ Answers & Rationale

1. **A.** Using volatility (or likelihood of changing) as the benchmark, the passbook savings rate is the least volatile of those listed because it is usually fixed for long periods of time. All of the other rates fluctuate from occasionally to frequently.   (Page 82)

2. **A.** Federal funds are those funds deposited at Federal Reserve banks, typically funds in excess of bank reserve requirements. The rate at which large commercial banks are willing to lend those funds to other banks is called the federal funds rate.   (Page 81)

3. **A.** A banker's acceptance is a time draft typically used to facilitate overseas trading ventures. It is guaranteed by a bank on behalf of a corporation in payment for goods or services.   (Page 78)

4. **C.** The federal funds rate is the rate of interest at which member banks of the Federal Reserve System can borrow excess funds from other members, usually on an overnight basis. The rate is subject to change and often does change daily.   (Page 81)

5. **A.** Commercial paper is unsecured short-term debt issued by corporations as a means of financing short-term needs. It is issued at a discount from face value and generally matures within 270 days. Commercial banks issue CDs and BAs.   (Page 79)

6. **C.** Commercial paper is issued by corporations with a maximum maturity of 270 days, in part to avoid certain registration requirements under the act of 1933.   (Page 79)

7. **B.** Of the securities listed, only CDs are sold at face value, pay interest and trade with accrued interest. All of the other securities listed are sold at a discount from face value and are redeemed at face value.   (Page 80)

8. **D.** Repurchase agreements (or *repos*) are entered into by a government securities dealer (usually a bank) or by the Federal Reserve Board with an investor (usually a corporation).   (Page 77)

9. **B.** The foreign exchange rate for international currencies is determined by buying and selling interest in the interbank market.   (Page 86)

10. **D.** The federal funds rate is the rate charged by one bank to another on loans of excess reserves. The rate quoted in the paper is typically the average rate of interest charged by banks on the reporting day.   (Page 81)

11. **D.** The Federal Savings and Loan Insurance Corporation guarantees money on deposit in savings and loans that are members of the FSLIC system.   (Page 80)

12. **C.** The Federal Deposit Insurance Corporation guarantees money on deposit in banks that are members of the FDIC system.   (Page 80)

13. **B.** Federal funds are overnight loans among members of the Federal Reserve System (commercial banks). The Federal Reserve Banks themselves do not use federal funds. When member banks borrow from the Federal Reserve Bank, they borrow at the discount rate and are said to be *going to the discount window*. Individuals and industrial corporations do not borrow at the federal funds rate. Some corporations may borrow at the prime rate, which is the rate at which banks lend to their best *prime* corporate customers. The federal funds rate is the most volatile interest rate, and it reacts sooner to economic changes than other interest rates.   (Page 81)

14. **B.** Federal funds are usually loaned by small commercial banks, located away from the major money centers, to large commercial money-center banks to help them meet their reserve requirements.   (Page 81)

15. **D.** Only the GMAC direct commercial paper would be considered a money-market instrument. Even though the rights and the warrants have

less than 270 days remaining to maturity, they represent rights to equity ownership and do not serve the same purpose as the cash-equivalents normally found in the money market. T bills do not become part of the money market until they begin secondary trading.   (Page 77)

16. **B.** Negotiable jumbo CDs are issued for $100,000 to $1,000,000 and, as money-market instruments, are commonly traded in the secondary market. Most jumbos are issued with maturities of less than a year, but initial maturities of three to five years can be arranged. The FDIC insures nonnegotiable CDs up to $100,000 each.   (Page 80)

17. **B.** Because the question asks about *Eurodollars,* the only correct answer specifies that U.S. currency (U.S. dollars) is deposited in a foreign country. All of the other answers contain examples of *Eurocurrency.*   (Page 84)

18. **C.** Commercial paper represents the unsecured debt obligations of corporations in need of short-term financing. Both yield and maturity are open to negotiation. Because commercial paper is issued with maturities of less than 270 days, it is exempt from registration under the act of 1933.
                    (Page 79)

19. **A.** The import and export of goods is often made easier by the use of bankers' acceptances. BAs provide the seller with ready cash, and the buyer with an extended time frame in which to pay.   (Page 78)

20. **B.** The primary purpose of commercial paper is to provide corporations with short-term financing at reasonable rates. Bankers' acceptances are used to finance imports and exports. Repos and reverse repos are used by securities dealers and banks to finance securities inventories.   (Page 79)

21. **A.** Bankers' acceptances can be used to delay payment on imports and provide the seller with a bank's guarantee that an account will be paid.   (Page 78)

22. **D.** The Treasury can employ revaluation, pegging and stabilization as tools in its efforts to improve the value of the U.S. dollar. Devaluation occurs when the interbank market's perception of a currency's value falls markedly, and demand for that currency decreases.   (Page 86)

23. **D.** Any entity, public or private, domestic or foreign, can issue bonds in foreign markets that are denominated in U.S. dollars. Many companies and governments do issue Eurobonds to avoid the complexities of U.S. securities registration or to tap a larger market of potential investors.
                    (Page 84)

24. **B.** Spot trades in foreign currencies are settled in one or two business days. Forward trades settle in more than two business days, and are normally scheduled to settle between one and eighteen months.   (Page 85)

25. **D.** Forward trades settle in more than two business days, and are normally scheduled to settle between one and eighteen months. Spot trades in foreign currencies are settled in one or two business days.   (Page 85)

26. **C.** Foreign currency transactions use spot settlement (same or next day) or forward settlement (one to eighteen months).   (Page 85)

27. **B.** If a central bank wanted to strengthen the value of its own currency, it could decrease the currency's supply (and therefore increase its price) by buying it in the interbank market. It could also increase the supply of foreign currencies (and therefore decrease their price) by selling them in the interbank market.   (Page 86)

28. **C.** If a central bank wanted to weaken the value of its own currency, it could increase the currency's supply (and therefore decrease its price) by selling it in the interbank market. It could also decrease the supply of foreign currencies (and therefore increase their price) by buying them in the interbank market.   (Page 86)

29. **D.** The federal funds rate is the interest rate charged by member banks with excess funds to

other member banks that need to borrow funds to meet their reserve requirements. A rising rate usually indicates that member banks are more reluctant to lend their funds, and therefore want a higher rate of interest in return. A higher rate is usually the result of a shortage of funds to lend, and probably indicates that deposits in general are shrinking. (Page 81)

30.   **C.**   T bills do not become part of the money market until they begin secondary trading. All of the others are money-market instruments. (Page 76)

31.   **C.**   The federal funds rate is the rate at which banks lend money *overnight* to each other to maintain reserve requirements. It is the most volatile rate and can fluctuate widely even during a business day. The effective federal funds rate is considered to be the average rate each day throughout the country. (Page 82)

32.   **D.**   Newly issued Treasury bonds have a minimum maturity of ten years. Money-market instruments have a maximum maturity of one year. (Page 76)

33.   **A.**   A money-market instrument is short-term debt with one year or less to maturity. (Page 76)

34.   **C.**   Commercial paper is normally issued for a maximum period of 270 days. (Page 79)

35.   **B.**   Negotiable certificates of deposit are primarily issued by banks and are backed (guaranteed) by the issuing bank. (Page 80)

36.   **C.**   Commercial paper is a short-term promissory note issued by a corporation. (Page 79)

37.   **C.**   A banker's acceptance is a time draft. It facilitates imports and exports, not the trading of foreign securities. (Page 78)

38.   **C.**   Only securities with a stated rate of interest will have accrued interest added to the transaction price. Zero-coupon securities, T bills and bankers' acceptances are all issued without a coupon, at a discount, and mature at face value. CDs are issued most often for their face amount (minimum of $100,000) with a stated coupon rate. (Page 80)

39.   **A.**   When the dealer sells the bonds with an agreement to repurchase, it is entering into a repurchase agreement. (Page 77)

40.   **B.**   The effective federal funds rate, as published, is a daily average calculated from the rates negotiated between the various banks. (Page 81)

41.   **B.**   The federal funds rate reflects the rate charged by member banks that lend funds to other member banks that need to borrow funds overnight to meet reserve requirements. (Page 81)

42.   **B.**   The federal funds rate is the interest rate that banks with excess reserves charge other banks that are associated with the Federal Reserve System and that need overnight loans to meet reserve requirements. Because the federal funds rate is set daily, it is the most sensitive indicator of interest rate direction. (Page 82)

43.   **D.**   Until recently, passbook savings rates were regulated by the Federal Reserve Board. The interest rate remained stable for long periods of time and was not indicative of fluctuations in other interest rates. The prime rate is periodically changed by banks and the discount rate is periodically changed by the Federal Reserve Board. (Page 82)

44.   **A.**   Eurobonds may provide a sophisticated investor with a means of adding diversification to her portfolio. All of the other answers are either untrue statements or represent disadvantages of investing in Eurobonds. (Page 87)

45.   **A.**   Foreign currency transactions occur in the spot market (same or next day settlement) or the forward market (one to eighteen months' settlement). (Page 85)

46. **A.** The interbank market is a decentralized, unregulated market formed for the sole purpose of trading foreign currencies.   (Page 85)

47. **B.** The interbank system is an international, unregulated, decentralized market involved in trading currencies and debt obligations. As with any market, changes in economic policies and conditions will influence prices.   (Page 85)

48. **B.** Newly issued Treasury bonds have a minimum maturity of 10 years. Money-market instruments have a maximum maturity of one year and are considered short-term debt instruments.   (Page 76)

49. **D.** Bankers' acceptances are time drafts.   (Page 78)

50. **D.** When the Fed sells, it is a repurchase agreement.   (Page 77)

51. **A.** When the Fed buys, it is a reverse repurchase agreement.   (Page 78)

52. **D.** Commercial paper is exempt from registration if the maturity is 270 days or less.   (Page 79)

53. **A.** Eurodollar bonds are issued outside the United States and are denominated in U.S. dollars by either a domestic or a foreign corporation. Payment of interest and principal on Eurodollar bonds can be made only in U.S. dollars.   (Page 84)

54. **B.** A Eurobond is a debt issue that is denominated and that pays principal and interest in the currency of a country other than that in which the issue is located. A Eurodollar bond is a Eurobond denominated in Eurodollars (U.S. dollars held in banks outside the continental United States).   (Page 84)

55. **D.** U.S. domestic corporations, state and municipal governments, foreign corporations and foreign banks would all be permitted to issue Eurobonds.   (Page 84)

6   Issuing Securities

1. In the underwriting of a new issue of securities, all of the following will occur before the public offering price is announced EXCEPT

   A. the formation of the syndicate and selling group
   B. due diligence meetings and investigation
   C. the preparation of the preliminary prospectus
   D. the preparation of legal feasibility documents

2. Why would a syndicate form a selling group?

   A. By forming a selling group, a syndicate cuts its losses if the price of the issue drops.
   B. By forming a selling group, smaller firms may take part in and assist with an underwriting they may not otherwise be able to handle.
   C. The Securities Act of 1933 requires a minimum of one active syndicate manager and three active, participatory selling group members for each new issue in order to provide the public with adequate due diligence.
   D. Permitting other firms into a selling group is a method of repaying those firms for any past favors.

3. For what period of time can the managing underwriter in a syndicate take action to stabilize an issue?

   A. Only during the offering period
   B. Through one day after the end of the offering period
   C. Through one week after the end of the offering period
   D. Through one month after the end of the offering period

4. What type of agreement would exist if the underwriter of an issue receives a guaranteed amount of money if the minimum amount of the issue is sold, but no more if the maximum is sold?

   A. Mini-max
   B. All or none
   C. Fill or kill
   D. Standby

5. All of the following factors are taken into consideration in determining the public offering price of a new issue of corporate stock EXCEPT

   A. past and projected earnings of the company
   B. dividend payment record of the company
   C. how the stock of other corporations in the same industry is priced
   D. selling group's opinion as to a marketable price level

6. Which of the following are terms for different types of underwritings?

    I. Best efforts
    II. All or none
    III. Firm commitment
    IV. Fail to receive

    A. I
    B. I, II and III
    C. I and III
    D. II, III and IV

7. Which of the following will NOT be found in a final prospectus?

    A. Underwriting agreements and the underwriters' compensation
    B. Stabilization plans
    C. Date and offering price
    D. Statement that the SEC neither approves nor disapproves of the issue

8. Which of the following statements about a red herring is FALSE?

    A. A red herring is used to obtain indications of interest from investors.
    B. The final offering price does not appear in a red herring.
    C. Additional information may be added to a red herring at a later date.
    D. A registered rep may send a copy of the company's research report with it.

Use the following information to answer questions 9 through 11.

Datawaq is raising money by issuing 1,000,000 new shares of common stock at $30 per share. Dewey, Cheatham & Howe, the managing underwriter, will receive $2.10 per share plus $.30 per share for expenses. The selling group will receive $1.80 per share.

9. The total spread is

    A. $.30
    B. $1.80
    C. $2.10
    D. $2.40

10. How much money will DCH receive from the underwriting to cover all of its advertising and other miscellaneous expenses?

    A. $300,000
    B. $1,800,000
    C. $2,100,000
    D. $2,400,000

11. How much money will Datawaq receive from the proceeds of the new issue after all sales and advertising expenses are deducted?

    A. $2,400,000
    B. $27,600,000
    C. $27,900,000
    D. $28,200,000

12. Which of the following is probably an example of a stabilizing bid for a new issue by a syndicate?

	Stabilizing Bid	Market Bid	Market Asked
A.	$18	$18	$18 1/4
B.	$21	$20 7/8	$21
C.	$25	$24 1/4	$24 1/2
D.	$35	$34	$34 7/8

13. Datawaq has filed a registration statement for its new issue of common stock with the SEC. As a registered rep you can do which of the following?

    I.   Send out your firm's most current research reports to your customers.
    II. Take indications of interest from your customers.
    III. Send a Datawaq preliminary prospectus to each of your customers.
    IV. Take orders for the stock from customers in cash accounts only.

    A. I only
    B. I, II and III only
    C. II and III only
    D. I, II, III and IV

14. Dewey, Cheatham & Howe is the managing underwriter for a new issue of 1,000,000 Microscam common. It has agreed to sell as much of the stock as possible in the market, and Microscam has agreed to take back the rest unsold. What is this type of offering known as?

    A. Standby
    B. Best efforts
    C. All-or-none
    D. Contingency

15. Dewey, Cheatham & Howe is the managing underwriter for a new issue of 1,000,000 Microscam common. It has agreed to sell all of the stock being offered, and has agreed to buy for its own account any stock that it cannot sell to the public. Microscam will receive the proceeds from the sale of 1,000,000 shares. What is this type of offering known as?

    A. Firm commitment
    B. Best efforts
    C. All-or-none
    D. Standby

16. Dewey, Cheatham & Howe is the managing underwriter for a new issue of 1,000,000 Microscam common. It has agreed to do its best to sell as much of the stock as possible in the market, but if it cannot sell it all, Microscam will cancel the offering. What is this type of offering known as?

    A. Standby
    B. Best efforts
    C. All-or-none
    D. Contingency

17. As a registered representative, you can use a preliminary prospectus to

    A. obtain indications of interest from investors
    B. solicit orders from investors for the purchase of a new issue
    C. solicit an approval of the offering from the SEC
    D. obtain the NASD's authorization to sell the issue

18. Which of the following statements about new issue underwriting is FALSE?

    A. Underwriting agreements can include a clause that relieves the underwriter of its obligation to sell an issue if certain restrictions are not met.
    B. The preliminary prospectus contains the date and price of the issue in order to assist brokers in obtaining indications of interest.
    C. If the underwriting syndicate discloses that it might engage in stabilization in the preliminary prospectus, it may do so under appropriate circumstances.
    D. If a selling group member sells securities back to the manager of the syndicate during the underwriting period, it may be penalized.

19. Microscam is engaged in a stock rights offering with the help of Dewey, Cheatham & Howe as managing underwriter. DCH has offered to purchase any of the stock Microscam is unable to sell to current stockholders. This arrangement is known as what type of underwriting?

    A. Special
    B. Best efforts
    C. Standby
    D. All-or-none

20. Consolidated Codfish would like to offer its new issue of 1,000,000 shares of common through Churnim, Burnum, Spernem to investors in the three states in which it has customers. What registration and sales restrictions will apply?

    I. The offering needs to be registered only in Consolidated Codfish's home state.
    II. COD shares can only be sold by registered reps licensed to sell securities in those states.
    III. CBS must arrange to have tombstones published in each of those states.
    IV. The offering must be blue-skyed in each of the three states in which the issue will be sold.

    A. I and III
    B. II, III and IV
    C. II and IV
    D. III and IV

21. Dewey, Cheatham & Howe is the managing underwriter for a new issue of 1,000,000 Microscam common on a firm commitment basis. If part of the Microscam issue remains unsold and results in a loss, the loss will be divided proportionately among the

    I. underwriting firms
    II. issuing corporation
    III. selling group firms

    A. I only
    B. I and III only
    C. II only
    D. I, II and III

22. All of the following will occur during the cooling-off period for a new issue EXCEPT

    I. due diligence meeting
    II. issuance of a preliminary prospectus
    III. stabilization of the issue
    IV. blue-skying the issue

    A. I
    B. I and II
    C. II
    D. III

23. This Can't Be Sushi (TCB) will be offering $2,000,000 of its common stock in its home state and in three other states. For the offering to be cleared for sale by the SEC, TCB must file a(n)

    A. offering circular
    B. standard registration statement
    C. letter of notification
    D. preliminary prospectus

24. I Can't Believe This Is Sushi (IBS) wants to offer $1,200,000 of its common stock in six states in the Midwest. For the offering to be cleared for sale by the SEC, IBS must file a(n)

   A. offering circular
   B. standard registration statement
   C. letter of notification
   D. preliminary prospectus

25. Churnim, Burnum, Spurnem is underwriting a new issue of Consolidated Codfish common. During the distribution period CBS starts buying COD stock in the open market. CBS is engaging in

   A. churning
   B. manipulation
   C. fixing
   D. stabilization

26. Which of the following is NOT required in a preliminary prospectus?

   A. Written statement in red that the prospectus may be subject to change and amendment and that a final prospectus will be issued
   B. Purpose for which the funds that are being raised will be used
   C. Final offering price
   D. Financial status and history of the company

27. Microscam is required to do all of the following if it intends to offer stock EXCEPT

   A. publish a tombstone
   B. issue a prospectus
   C. file a registration statement
   D. register the securities with the SEC

28. Datawaq plans to offer 300,000 shares of its 2,000,000-share new offering of common stock to its own employees. How many shares must it register as being publicly offered?

   A. 300,000
   B. 1,700,000
   C. 2,000,000
   D. 2,300,000

29. If the SEC has cleared an issue, which of the following statements is true?

   A. The SEC has guaranteed the issue.
   B. The underwriter has filed a standard registration statement.
   C. The SEC has endorsed the issue.
   D. The SEC has guaranteed the accuracy of the information in the prospectus.

30. Churnim, Burnum, Spurnem is the managing underwriter for a new stock offered at 18 1/2. CBS can stabilize the offering at which of the following prices?

   I.   17 3/4
   II.   18 1/4
   III. 19 1/4
   IV.   19 3/4

   A. I only
   B. I and II only
   C. I, II and III only
   D. I, II, III and IV

Use the following tombstone to answer questions 31 and 32.

```
  New Issue

       $20,000,000
  Tallawhosits City Waterworks
        Coupon 7%

      Price 100.65%

  Dewey, Cheatham & Howe
```

31. The Tallawhosits City Waterworks bonds are probably priced above par for what reason?

   A. The price reflects the fact that the coupon rate for the bonds at issuance is more than the rate of similar newly issued bonds available in the market.
   B. The amount in excess of par includes accrued interest.
   C. The amount in excess of par represents the underwriter's spread.
   D. The municipality has applied the standard municipal bond servicing charge to the issue price.

32. Which of the following statements can be made about the underwriting spread charged by Dewey, Cheatham & Howe on the new Tallawhosits City Waterworks bond issue?

   A. The total underwriting spread is larger than the total selling concession.
   B. The total selling concession is larger than the total underwriting spread.
   C. The total reallowance is larger than the total underwriting spread.
   D. The total reallowance is larger than the total selling concession.

33. An intrastate offering is exempt from

   A. federal registration
   B. state registration
   C. blue-sky registration
   D. all registration

34. A prospectus must include

   I. the effective date of the registration
   II. whether the underwriter intends to stabilize the issue if necessary
   III. a statement indicating the SEC has not approved the issue
   IV. disclosure of material information concerning the issuer's financial condition

   A. I, II and IV only
   B. I and IV only
   C. II and III only
   D. I, II, III and IV

◆ Answers & Rationale

1. **D.** Each of the activities listed must be performed prior to the publication of the offering price except the *preparation of legal feasibility documents,* because there are no such legal requirements. (Page 93)

2. **B.** Selling groups provide an opportunity for firms that are not large enough to underwrite an entire issue on their own to take part in larger deals. They also help ensure that the syndicate will be able to place the entire issue. (Page 95)

3. **A.** The managing underwriter can place orders to buy the stock being offered at a given price only until the end of the offering period. (Page 100)

4. **B.** If the underwriter would receive the same amount of money whether the minimum amount or the maximum amount of an issue is sold, the issue is probably being sold under an all-or-none (AON) agreement. The key to understanding this question is to remember that only in an AON underwriting is the minimum that can be sold and the maximum that can be sold the same amount— the entire issue. If any part of an issue is sold (as the question indicates), the entire issue must have been sold and the issuer receives the agreed-upon fee. (Page 95)

5. **D.** The underwriter determines the selling price and communicates it to the members of the selling group. (Page 100)

6. **B.** Of the choices listed, I, II and III are types of underwritings. A fail to receive occurs when a broker-dealer does not receive the securities due it from a buy transaction. The main types of underwritings are:

- Best efforts—when an underwriter will do its best to sell the entire new issue, but will not guarantee success.
- All-or-none—the underwriter will sell the entire issue or none will be sold.

- Firm commitment—the underwriter will guarantee to sell the entire issue.
- Standby—when a corporation will try and sell the new issue itself through a rights offering, but will have an underwriter standing by to sell the unsold shares.

(Page 94)

7. **A.** The underwriting agreements (also known as the *agreement among underwriters*) are separate documents and are not included in a prospectus. (Page 92)

8. **D.** A registered rep is prohibited from sending a research report with either a preliminary or a final prospectus. During the first 90 days of a new issue, printed information discussing the new issue or the company cannot be circulated. (Page 92)

9. **D.** The total spread (the difference between the amount paid to the issuer and the public offering price) is $2.10 plus $.30 expenses per share expenses, or $2.40. Datawaq will receive $27.60 per share from the deal. (Page 100)

10. **A.** $.30 per share for expenses times 1,000,000 shares is $300,000. (Page 100)

11. **B.** Datawaq will receive $2,400,000 in proceeds from the new issue.

$30,000,000	$30 × 1,000,000 shares	
− 2,400,000	$2.40 × 1,000,000 shares	
$27,600,000	Net proceeds	(Page 100)

12. **A.** A syndicate is permitted only to stabilize at or below the bid price in the market. Any other price could artificially inflate the stock's price in the market. (Page 100)

13. **C.** Sales of a new issue can be made only by prospectus. Until the issue is through registration, no orders may be accepted, although indications of interest may be taken. (Page 100)

14. **B.** A best efforts underwriting is one in which any stock that remains unsold is returned to the issuing corporation. (Page 95)

15. **A.** A firm commitment underwriting agreement requires the underwriter to sell the entire issue of stock or to purchase any unsold stock for its own inventory.   (Page 94)

16. **C.** An all-or-none underwriting arrangement requires the underwriter to sell the entire issue of stock or to cancel the offering completely.   (Page 95)

17. **A.** A preliminary prospectus is used to obtain indications of interest from investors.   (Page 92)

18. **B.** The preliminary prospectus includes much important information relevant to the new issue but does not include the public offering price, the date of the offering or the underwriter's spread.   (Page 92)

19. **C.** A standby underwriting arrangement allows a corporation to sell as much of a new issue to current stockholders as possible, backed by the promise of an underwriter to take and sell any unsold shares to the public.   (Page 104)

20. **C.** In order to sell an issue in any state, the broker-dealer, the registered reps and the security itself must each be registered in that state. Registering an issue in a state is known as *blue-skying* the issue.   (Page 97)

21. **A.** In a firm commitment arrangement, any losses incurred will be divided among the underwriters of the issue according to their participation.   (Page 94)

22. **D.** The underwriters of a new issue cannot stabilize the offering during the cooling-off period because the issue is not yet in the hands of investors and therefore cannot be traded in the open market.   (Page 100)

23. **B.** Because TCB's $2,000,000 issue is over $1,500,000, it must file a standard registration statement. If the issue were under the $1,500,000 Regulation A filing limit, it would have to file only an offering circular.   (Page 105)

24. **A.** Because IBS's $1,200,000 issue is under the Regulation A filing limit of $1,500,000, it may file an offering circular.   (Page 105)

25. **D.** Stabilization of new issues during the offering period is permitted if the fact that an underwriter might stabilize an issue is disclosed in the prospectus. Stabilization is also known as *pegging*, and is not permitted once an offering ends.   (Page 100)

26. **C.** A preliminary prospectus is issued before the price is established, and it does not include the eventual offering date or the spread.   (Page 92)

27. **A.** A tombstone advertisement is never required. Tombstones are advertisements that are often placed in the business newspapers to publicize a new issue.   (Page 93)

28. **C.** Even though the shares are being sold to its own employees, those employees are still considered members of the public. The total public offering is for 2,000,000 shares.   (Page 104)

29. **B.** The SEC does not approve, endorse or guarantee the accuracy of a registration statement.   (Page 92)

30. **B.** Stabilizing bids may be placed only at or below the public offering price.   (Page 100)

31. **A.** If a bond issue is priced above par, it is usually because the coupon rate at which the bonds were issued is more than the prevailing rates for other newly issued bonds.   (Page 100)

32. **A.** The underwriting spread is the total difference between the public offering price and the proceeds to the issuer. All expenses incurred and sales concessions paid in an underwriting are deducted from the spread.   (Page 100)

33. **A.** An intrastate offering is limited to companies that do business in one state and sell their securities only to the residents of that state.   (Page 105)

34.   **D.**   Choices I and IV should be obvious. If underwriters intend to engage in activities that are designed to stabilize the price of the security, disclosure in the prospectus is required. The SEC disclaimer is required to appear on every prospectus and states that the SEC has neither approved nor disapproved the issue.   (Page 92)

7 Trading Securities

1. A registered representative observes the following on her quote machine.

XYZP	B 32 1/2	A 32 3/4	Last 32 5/8

   On which exchange and at what price can a customer purchase XYZ?

   I. PSE
   II. PHLX
   III. 32 1/2
   IV. 32 3/4

   A. I and III
   B. I and IV
   C. II and III
   D. II and IV

2. Which of the following statements concerning fill-or-kill orders and all-or-none orders are true?

   I. AON orders must be filled in their entirety.
   II. FOK orders must be filled in their entirety.
   III. AON orders must be canceled if the whole order cannot be executed immediately.
   IV. FOK orders must be canceled if the whole order cannot be executed immediately.

   A. I, II and IV only
   B. I and III only
   C. II and IV only
   D. I, II, III and IV

3. ABC closed at 32 1/2 on a plus tick on the NYSE on September 22nd. September 23rd is the ex-date for a $.28 dividend. What is the lowest price at which you could execute a short sale at the opening of trading September 23rd?

   A. 32
   B. 32 1/8
   C. 32 1/2
   D. 32 5/8

4. Max Leveridge has placed with his broker an open order to buy 1,600 shares of XYZ at $60. XYZ declares a 25% stock dividend. On the ex-date this order will be considered a buy limit order for

   A. 1,600 shares at $45
   B. 1,600 shares at $50
   C. 2,000 shares at $48
   D. 2,000 shares at $60

5. SuperDot is the electronic order system used by which of the following markets for trading common stocks?

   A. New York Stock Exchange
   B. OTC market
   C. Chicago Board Options Exchange
   D. Philadelphia Stock Exchange

6. Lotta Leveridge has her broker enter an order to buy XYZ stock at the opening. Though transmitted promptly, the order does not reach XYZ's trading post in time to be filled at the opening. How is the order handled?

A. The order is canceled.
B. The order is handled as a market order.
C. The order is executed in the day, at a price as close to the opening price as possible.
D. The order automatically becomes an *at-the-open* order the following trading session.

7. Last sale price information is available for National Market System stocks. Which of the following are true concerning the reporting of that information to the system?

I. The trade must be reported within 90 seconds of execution.
II. The trade must be reported immediately after the completion of the transaction.
III. The selling broker-dealer must report the trade.
IV. The buying broker-dealer must report the trade.

A. I and III
B. I and IV
C. II and III
D. II and IV

8. OTC trading practices in corporate securities are subject to the regulation of which of the following regulatory bodies?

I. SIA
II. SEC
III. FOMC
IV. NASD

A. I and II
B. I and IV
C. II, III and IV
D. II and IV

9. An NASD member firm is selling stock to a customer from inventory. The shares sold have been held by the broker-dealer for several months. What price should the dealer use as a basis for a markup?

A. Price at which the securities were purchased
B. Offer price shown in the *Pink Sheets* on the day of the current sale
C. Broker-dealer's own current offer price
D. Best offering price quoted in the inter-dealer market

10. If the following information appeared on your quote machine, how would you respond to a customer inquiry about the current quote on DWAQ stock?

DWAQ					
L	25 3/8	O	25 3/8	C	24 7/8
B	25	H	25 3/8	NC	+ 1/2
A	25 1/2	L	24 7/8	V	424
				T	9:50

A. "The previous close was at 25 3/8."
B. "The stock last traded at 24 7/8."
C. "DWAQ is quoted 24 7/8 bid–25 3/8 ask."
D. "DWAQ is quoted 25 bid–25 1/2 ask."

11. The primary purpose for requiring OTC dealers to provide reports of trades in National Market System securities is to provide

A. regulators with a better audit trail
B. a means of detecting odd lot trading activity
C. investors with information
D. a mechanism for preventing short sales in declining markets

Use the following information to answer questions 12 and 13.

Just prior to the close, a customer enters an order to sell short 200 shares of MCS at 21 3/4 stop limit GTC. The order is not elected on that day. The following trades in MCS occur at the opening of the next trading session.

21 1/2   21 3/8   21 5/8   21 5/8   21 5/8   21 3/4   21 7/8

12. Which transaction elects the order?

A. 21 3/8
B. 21 1/2
C. 21 5/8
D. 21 3/4

13. At what price is the order executed?

A. 21 3/8
B. 21 1/2
C. 21 3/4
D. 21 7/8

14. Which of the following kinds of orders may be turned over to the specialist for execution?

I. Market orders
II. Stop orders
III. Limit orders
IV. Not-held orders

A. I only
B. I and II only
C. I, II and III only
D. I, II, III and IV

15. Which of the following individuals normally trade on the floor of an exchange?

I. Two-dollar broker
II. Commission broker
III. Block trader
IV. Registered representative

A. I and II only
B. I, II and III only
C. II, III and IV only
D. I, II, III and IV

16. When a broker-dealer is making a market, it is acting as a(n)

A. agent
B. principal
C. broker
D. underwriter

17. All of the following are true of the over-the-counter market EXCEPT that

A. it is an auction market
B. typically, bank and insurance company securities trade OTC
C. more issues trade OTC than on the exchanges
D. it handles large block distributions

18. Wholesale corporate bond quotes are found on the

A. *Pink Sheets*
B. *Yellow Sheets*
C. *Blue List*
D. *Green List*

19. The terms "priority," "precedence" and "parity" govern trading at

A. the New York Stock Exchange
B. the over-the-counter market
C. both the exchanges and OTC
D. the third market

20. The Consolidated Tape reported the following transaction:

CWE Pr	T	DWQ
5s26	26	2s91
s		

This means that

A. 26 shares of CWE preferred traded short at 5
B. 50 shares of CWE preferred traded at 26
C. 100 shares of CWE preferred reverse split 5-to-1 and traded at 26
D. 500 shares of CWE preferred traded at 26

21. All of the following are reasons for entering a stop order EXCEPT to

   A. protect established gains in a long position
   B. limit losses in a long position
   C. protect profits in a short position
   D. guarantee execution at a specified price

22. All of the following would appear on the Consolidated A Tape EXCEPT transactions involving

   A. securities listed on the Midwest and Pacific exchanges
   B. options
   C. INSTINET
   D. rights and warrants

23. An open-ended investment company bought preferred utility stock from a bank through INSTINET. This trade took place in the

   A. primary market
   B. secondary market
   C. third market
   D. fourth market

24. All of the following statements about NYSE-listed securities are true EXCEPT that

   A. securities must qualify for listing on the NYSE
   B. securities can be listed on several exchanges at the same time and may sell at different prices on each exchange
   C. all listed securities are marginable
   D. securities can be delisted any time the company's board of directors requests it

25. The bulk of the securities trading over the counter are

   I. listed registered securities
   II. unlisted nonexempt securities
   III. registered nonlisted securities
   IV. unregistered exempt securities

   A. I and II
   B. I and III
   C. II and III
   D. II, III and IV

26. You are a bond trader, and have been given an out-firm with five-minute recall. Forty-five minutes later, the quoting dealer gives you a fill-or-kill. What does this mean?

   A. The five-minute recall is canceled; you must take the securities immediately or lose the trade.
   B. You have placed the order with the quoting dealer, and it is now going to attempt to fill it.
   C. The quoting dealer wants five minutes' advance notice if you fill the trade.
   D. You have five minutes to fill the order or lose the securities.

27. If a client tells you that his company regularly trades securities in the fourth market, this means that it trades

   A. listed securities OTC
   B. unlisted securities OTC
   C. unlisted securities on an exchange
   D. securities directly with other institutional owners

28. If the broker-dealer for which you work lists a quote in the *Pink Sheets*, you know that the firm will be required to

   A. honor that quote for at least one round lot
   B. give a new quote on request
   C. buy or sell one round lot at that price or pay the difference between its quote and that of the next market maker
   D. do nothing because the *Pink Sheets* quotes are expected to be outdated anyway

29. One of your better customers wants you to place an order to sell 200 shares of Magilla Dynamics with an 18 stop when the stock is trading at 18 7/8. Magilla declares a $1.55 dividend. What will happen to your customer's stop order?

   A. Nothing, open sell orders are not adjusted for dividends.
   B. The stop order will be reduced to 16 3/8.
   C. The stop order will be increased to 20.
   D. The stop order will be reduced to 17 1/8.

30. How many firms must be making markets in a stock before that stock can be entered on NASDAQ Level 1?

    A. 1
    B. 2
    C. 5
    D. 10

31. Each of the following types of orders will remain open on the NYSE until certain conditions are met EXCEPT

    A. stop orders
    B. good-till-canceled orders
    C. all-or-none orders
    D. market orders

32. For a client to get immediate execution on an order, the order should be placed as a(n)

    A. stop order
    B. good-till-canceled order
    C. all-or-none order
    D. market order

33. One of your penny-stock customers wants to sell his 25 shares of This Can't Be Sushi, which he heard has appreciated to 9/16ths per share. There is only one TCBS market maker (the one you called when you sold your customer the stock last week), so where would you have to go to get a quote?

    A. *The Blue List*
    B. Your quote machine
    C. *The Pink Sheets*
    D. *The Wall Street Journal*

34. Which of the following activities are NOT part of the function of a specialist on the NYSE?

    A. Setting strike prices for options on the securities he works
    B. Keeping a book of public orders
    C. Guaranteeing an execution price for a trader who requests that the specialist stops stock for him
    D. Buying and selling stock for his own account

35. All of the following actions are prohibited by the NASD when using its Small Order Execution System to trade securities EXCEPT

    A. splitting large customer orders into small ones in order to meet the 1,000-share order-size requirement of SOES
    B. entering riskless and simultaneous transactions
    C. the use of SOES by professional traders who keep their orders under the maximum size limit
    D. entering odd lot orders for execution at next trade

36. Which of the following securities transactions would have to be reported to the Consolidated Tape?

    I. 200 shares of Datawaq bought on the NYSE
    II. 1,200 shares of Microscam sold on the Pacific Stock Exchange
    III. 25 shares of This Can't Be Sushi bought OTC
    IV. 5,000 shares of Consolidated Codfish sold to Microscam by Datawaq's pension account that did not occur through INSTINET

    A. I and II
    B. II, III and IV
    C. III and IV
    D. IV

37. In order to narrow the spread between the bid and the asked of one of his stocks, a specialist could enter an order to buy for his own account. He would be acting in this transaction as a

    A. broker-dealer
    B. broker (or agent)
    C. dealer (or principal)
    D. market maker

38. Your firm, Serendipity Securities, has received an order from one of your customers to buy 300 shares of DWQ at the market. Serendipity goes into the market, buys 300 shares of DWQ from another broker-dealer, and delivers them to the account of your customer. Serendipity's role in this transaction was that of a

    A. broker acting as an agent for a commission
    B. dealer acting as a principal for a profit
    C. broker acting as an agent for a profit
    D. dealer acting as a principal for a commission

39. Your firm, Serendipity Securities, has received an order from one of your customers to buy 300 shares of DWQ at the market. Serendipity goes into the market and buys 300 shares of DWQ from another broker-dealer for its own inventory. It then takes those shares out of inventory and sells them to the account of the customer. Serendipity's role in this transaction is that of a

    A. broker acting as an agent for a commission
    B. dealer acting as a principal for a profit
    C. broker acting as an agent for a profit
    D. dealer acting as a principal for a commission

40. Stock exchanges serve various functions in the trading of securities. Among these functions are

    I.   buying and selling securities for public and institutional customers
    II. establishing the price of securities traded on the floor of the exchange
    III. giving traders permission to use the floor of the exchange to transact orders for customers
    IV. providing access to specialists who maintain markets in specific stocks at trading posts on the floor of the exchange

    A. I, II and III only
    B. II and III only
    C. III and IV only
    D. I, II, III and IV

41. Your firm, Serendipity Securities, has positions in both Datawaq and Microscam. This means that Serendipity

    A. holds shares of both stocks in street name for customers
    B. is a market maker for both stocks
    C. stands ready to buy or sell both stocks on request
    D. could be long or short both stocks in inventory

42. An NASD member that is qualified and registered to transact business in listed securities in over-the-counter transactions must report this type of transaction to the Consolidated Tape within how many seconds of execution?

    A. 30
    B. 60
    C. 90
    D. 120

43. Which of the following statements about transactions in the different securities markets is(are) true?

    I. Transactions in listed securities occur primarily in the exchange markets.
    II. Transactions in unlisted securities occur primarily in the OTC market.
    III. Transactions in listed securities that occur in the OTC market are said to take place in the third market.
    IV. Transactions in listed securities that occur directly between customers or institutions without using broker-dealers as intermediaries are said to take place in the fourth market.

    A. I only
    B. I and II only
    C. I, II and III only
    D. I, II, III and IV

44. A market maker gives a firm quote of 20–20 3/8. The purchasing dealer says, "I'll buy 500 shares at the offering price." The market maker must give

    A. 100 shares at 20
    B. 100 shares at 20 3/8
    C. 500 shares at 20
    D. 500 shares at 20 3/8

45. Which of the following trades occur(s) in the secondary market?

    I. Specialist on the NYSE buying stocks for his own inventory
    II. Municipal bond syndicate selling new issues to the public
    III. Registered representative buying unlisted securities for a client
    IV. Insurance company buying municipal bonds directly from another insurance company

    A. I, II and III
    B. I, III and IV
    C. II and III
    D. IV

46. The Consolidated Tape for the NYSE reads:

ARX	ARC
12.4s11 7/8	29.29 1/8

Which of the following statements is(are) correct?

    I. 40 shares of ARX traded at 11 7/8
    II. 100 shares of ARX traded at 11 7/8
    III. 100 shares of ARX traded at 12
    IV. 400 shares of ARX traded at 11 7/8

    A. I and III
    B. II
    C. III
    D. III and IV

47. Which of the following block sales occurs on the floor and is announced on the Tape prior to execution?

    A. Specialist block purchase
    B. Exchange distribution
    C. Special offering
    D. Secondary distribution

48. A client bought 100 shares of ABC at 20. The stock rose to 30 and she would like to protect her gain. Which of the following orders should be entered?

    A. Sell stop order at 29
    B. Sell limit order at 30
    C. Sell limit order at 30 1/8
    D. Sell stop order at 30 1/8

49. The specialist in IBM tells a floor broker who wants to buy 300 shares of IBM for a customer that the stock is stopped at 120. This means that

    A. trading is temporarily frozen in IBM
    B. the highest offering price is 120
    C. exchange approval is required to buy IBM under 120
    D. the specialist has guaranteed to sell the stock at 120 or lower

50. AT&T common stock has been recently trading between 25 1/4 and 26. Your client would like to buy 500 shares of AT&T at 25. While he would like all 500 shares, he is willing to accept fewer shares at that price. Which of the following orders fulfills his intentions?

   A. Market order to buy 500 shares of T at 25
   B. Limit order to buy 500 shares of T at 25 AON
   C. Limit order to buy 500 shares of T at 25 FOK
   D. Limit order to buy 500 shares of T at 25 immediate or cancel

51. A customer sold 100 shares of XYZ short when the stock was trading at 19. XYZ is now trading at 14 and he would like to protect his gain. What type of order should he place?

   A. Sell stop order at 13 7/8
   B. Sell limit order at 14
   C. Buy limit order at 14
   D. Buy stop order at 14 3/8

52. The Consolidated Tape reported the following:

```
   GAF              DWQ
   40 1/8.1/4       91.91 1/4
```

   Which of the following statements is(are) correct?

   I. The previous order of 100 shares of GAF at 40 1/8 was in error.
   II. 100 shares of GAF sold at 40 1/8.
   III. 100 shares of GAF sold at 40 1/4.
   IV. GAF closed up 1/4 point.

   A. I and III
   B. II
   C. II and III
   D. II and IV

53. Which of the following securities trade on the over-the-counter market?

   I. Government and agency securities
   II. Open-ended investment companies
   III. Large block distributions of listed securities
   IV. Foreign equity securities

   A. I, II and III
   B. I and III
   C. I, III and IV
   D. II and IV

54. An investor enters a day order to buy 200 shares of Honeywell at 63. Three hours later, with Honeywell trading above that price, she calls wanting to change the order to a good-till-canceled order. The registered representative should

   I. cancel the existing order immediately
   II. leave the existing order on the specialist's books
   III. enter a new limit order to buy 200 shares of Honeywell at 63 GTC immediately
   IV. enter a new limit order to buy 200 shares of Honeywell at 63 GTC before the opening of the next day

   A. I and III
   B. I and IV
   C. II and III
   D. II and IV

55. Your client, who has sold 100 shares of PPG short, places a buy stop order at 80. The order is activated when the price of PPG

   A. falls to 80 or below
   B. falls below 80
   C. rises to 80 or above
   D. rises above 80

56. ABC Securities, a broker-dealer that is a member of the NYSE, is a position trader. This means that ABC Securities

   A. makes a market in securities
   B. is in violation of NYSE regulations
   C. is underwriting securities in the primary market
   D. acts as a broker for customers

57. All of the following statements are true of not-held orders EXCEPT that

   A. they are given to a specialist
   B. they give the floor broker discretion over the price and time of execution
   C. the *NH* code is generally used for sizable orders
   D. they may be filled a small portion at a time

58. Ms. Wilcox places an order to buy 300 Digital at 140 stop, but not over 144. This is a

   A. buy stop order
   B. buy limit order
   C. market not-held order
   D. stop limit order

59. The amount of commission must be disclosed on which of the following documents?

   I. Order ticket
   II. Customer confirmation if an agency transaction
   III. Customer confirmation if a principal transaction

   A. I and II
   B. I and III
   C. II
   D. III

60. An over-the-counter dealer has had no activity in the OTC stocks in which it makes a market. When must the market maker report its volume to the NASDAQ?

   A. As soon as the stock begins to trade
   B. Daily
   C. Weekly
   D. Quarterly

61. Xerox has been trading around 70. A customer tells his registered representative that if he can buy 1,000 shares of the stock in one attempt, he'll take it. If not, he's not interested. How should this order be entered?

   A. 1,000 Xerox at 70
   B. 1,000 Xerox FOK
   C. 1,000 Xerox GTC
   D. 1,000 Xerox IOC

62. Your client feels that Pillsbury, currently trading around 39, would be a good buy at 38. Therefore, she places an order to buy 200 Pillsbury at 38 GTC. On the ex-date when the stock splits 2-for-1, her order is still on the specialist's book. How will the order be adjusted on the ex-date?

   A. Buy 100 Pillsbury at 76 GTC
   B. Buy 200 Pillsbury at 19 GTC
   C. Buy 400 Pillsbury at 19 GTC
   D. Buy 400 Pillsbury at 38 GTC

63. Traders must sell on an uptick when selling short on the

   I. exchanges
   II. over-the-counter market
   III. third market

   A. I only
   B. I and II only
   C. II and III only
   D. I, II and III

64. Mr. Smith enters an order to buy Ford at the close. Ford traded between 70 and 71 all day and then, after a last minute rally, closed up 4 1/4 points at 74 1/4. Mr. Smith will receive

   A. the opening price the next morning
   B. the closing price
   C. the same treatment as if he had placed a not-held order
   D. a price as near to the close as possible, at the discretion of the floor broker

65. An order ticket is marked: "Buy 20M Ford Motors 9% Debentures at 95 AON GTC." All of the following statements regarding this order are true EXCEPT that

   A. this is a buy limit order
   B. the order will expire at the end of the day
   C. if executed, the customer will pay $19,000 or less for the bonds
   D. the trade will be filled in its entirety, or not at all

66. The Consolidated Tape reported the following:

GM.SLD	DWQ
70 1/8	91.91 1/4

The symbol *SLD* means that General Motors stock

A. sold short for 70 1/8
B. sold in a special block sale off the floor
C. has stopped trading at 70 1/8
D. was reported out of sequence

67. All of the following statements are true of NASDAQ Level 3 EXCEPT that

A. it shows volume at the end of the day
B. actual interdealer quotes are displayed
C. the quotes are entered by market makers
D. the system displays trades as they occur

68. A new client is interested in buying Aloette, an unlisted security that trades in the national OTC market. The current bid and ask price on Aloette is 9 1/2–9 3/4. Three days from now, the company declares a dividend of $.30. The client wonders if she should wait until the ex-date to buy the stock. What happens to the price of Aloette on the ex-date?

A. Bid 9, ask 9 3/4
B. Bid 9 1/8, ask 9 3/8
C. Bid 9 1/4, ask 9 1/2
D. Bid 9 1/2, ask 9 3/8

69. Ms. Jones is short FFB at 30. When she shorted the stock, she also placed an order to buy 100 shares of FFB at 35 stop GTC. The stock is currently trading at 29. This morning, the board of directors of FFB announced that the company had an outstanding fourth quarter. This announcement caused the stock price to rally, increasing two points in two hours. Ms. Jones tells her registered representative to cover the position immediately at the market. The registered representative should

I. place a market order to buy 100 shares of FFB
II. place a market order to sell 100 shares of FFB
III. place a buy limit order for FFB at 30 GTC
IV. cancel the order to buy 100 FFB at 35 stop GTC

A. I
B. I and IV
C. II
D. III and IV

70. PHH, which closed at 34 3/8–35, will go ex-dividend tomorrow. Which of the following orders in the specialist's book will be reduced on the ex-date?

I. Buy PHH at 36 stop
II. Sell PHH at 34 stop
III. Buy PHH at 34 limit
IV. Sell PHH at 36 limit DNR

A. I, II and III
B. I and III
C. II and III
D. II and IV

71. Which of the following statements are true about buy stop orders?

    I. They can protect against a loss in a short sale.

    II. They become market orders when the stop price is reached.

    III. They do not allow the registered representative discretion as to the time of execution.

    IV. They are always entered above the current market price.

    A. I and II only

    B. I, III and IV only

    C. II and III only

    D. I, II, III and IV

Use the following information to answer questions 72 and 73.

Mr. Jones enters an order to sell short 100 Hewlett Packard at 49 stop limit. Prior to placing the order, HWP was trading at 49 1/4. Subsequent trades are reported on the Tape as follows:

> HWP
> 48 3/4.48 7/8.49.4s49 1/8

72. Which trade triggered the order?

    A. 48 3/4

    B. 48 7/8

    C. 49

    D. 49 1/8

73. Mr. Jones's trade was executed at

    A. 48 3/4

    B. 48 7/8

    C. 49

    D. 49 1/8

74. Consolidated Edison (ED) is trading at 50 5/8. Moishe Hayashi, who owns 100 shares of the stock, places an order to sell ED at 50 1/4 stop limit. The Tape subsequently reports the following trades:

ED	ED.SLD	ED
50 1/2	2s50 1/8	50 1/4.50 1/8

Moishe's order will be executed at

    A. 50 1/8

    B. 50 1/4

    C. 50 1/2

    D. The order is not executed.

Use the following information to answer questions 75 and 76.

These orders for GTE appear in the specialist's book:

Buy	GTE	Sell
200 B-D A	61	
100 B-D B	1/8	
100 B-D B	1/4	
	3/8	
	1/2	
	5/8	100 B-D D
		300 B-D E
	3/4	200 B-D F
	7/8	100 B-D G
	62	

75. What is the size of the market for GTE?

    A. 100 by 100

    B. 100 by 400

    C. 200 by 400

    D. 400 by 700

76. What is the lowest price the specialist can bid for stock for his own account?

    A. 61 1/4

    B. 61 3/8

    C. 61 1/2

    D. 61 5/8

77. A customer entered an order to sell short 100 shares of Valspar. The stock closed on an uptick on Friday at 48. The stock will trade ex-dividend $.55 on Monday. What is the lowest price at which the order can be executed at the opening?

   A. 47 3/8
   B. 47 1/2
   C. 48
   D. 48 1/8

78. Dr. Jack Zwack is short 500 shares of Polaroid at 75. Polaroid is currently trading at 76 3/4. To protect his position, Dr. Zwack enters GTC orders either to buy 500 Polaroid at 70, if it declines, or to buy 500 shares at 80, if it goes up. Polaroid declines to 70, but Dr. Zwack is able to buy only 300 shares. The orders on the specialist's book will be

   A. buy 200 at 70 and buy 200 at 80 stop
   B. buy 200 at 70 and buy 500 at 80 stop
   C. buy 500 at 70 and buy 200 at 80 stop
   D. buy 500 at 70 and buy 500 at 80 stop

79. Dr. Jack Zwack is short 500 shares of Polaroid at 75. Polaroid is currently trading at 76 3/4. To protect his position, Dr. Zwack enters GTC orders either to buy 500 Polaroid at 70, if it declines, or to buy 500 shares at 80, if it goes up. Polaroid goes ex-dividend $1.42 one week later. The open orders of Dr. Zwack will be adjusted to

   A. buy at 68 1/2 and buy at 78 1/2 stop
   B. buy at 68 1/2 and buy at 80 stop
   C. buy at 70 and buy at 78 1/2 stop
   D. buy at 71 1/2 and buy at 80 stop

80. Dealer A has made a firm offer for 30 minutes with recall to Dealer B. What does this mean?

   I.   Dealer A cannot change the price for 30 minutes.
   II. Dealer B must buy the bonds within the next 30 minutes.
   III. Dealer A must call Dealer B before selling the bonds to another dealer.

   A. I only
   B. I and III only
   C. II and III only
   D. I, II and III

81. A company is about to pay a dividend of $.70. On the ex-dividend date, an open order to sell at 46 stop would be automatically adjusted to

   A. 45 1/4 stop
   B. 45 1/2 stop
   C. 45 3/8 stop
   D. 46 stop

82. A customer enters an order to buy 100 shares of ABC at $20 stop. That order becomes a

   A. limit order to buy 100 shares at $20
   B. market order to buy 100 shares before the stock reaches $20
   C. market order to buy 100 shares as soon as the stock reaches $20
   D. market order to buy 100 shares after the stock drops below $20 as long as the execution price is $20 or less

83. A stock that closes at $45 and goes ex-dividend $1.60 the next day will open at

   A. $43
   B. $43 3/8
   C. $43 1/2
   D. $44

◆ Answers & Rationale

1. **B.** The "P" in the quotation is the exchange where the quote originated—the Pacific Stock Exchange. "B" stands for bid; "A" for ask. A customer wanting to buy at the market will pay the ask price. A customer wanting to sell at the market will receive the bid price. (Page 139)

2. **A.** Fill-or-kill (FOK) orders must be executed immediately in their entirety or else canceled. All-or-none (AON) orders must be executed in their entirety but are not canceled if the whole order cannot be executed right away. (Page 127)

3. **B.** Ticks carry forward from day to day. Normally, if a stock closed on a plus tick at 32 1/2, the next day an opening trade of 32 1/2 would be considered a zero-plus tick. Changes in price attributable to the dividend when a stock trades "ex" are ignored for tick purposes. The dividend, expressed in 1/8th increments, must always be rounded to the next highest 1/8th amount. In this case, $.28 is between 1/4th and 3/8ths. It is closer to 1/4th ($.25) but is always rounded to the higher amount, or 3/8ths ($.375). If the stock closed at 32 1/2, on a plus tick, the next day's opening trade at 32 1/8 would be considered a zero-plus tick after the dividend adjustment of 3/8ths is taken into account. Any opening trade lower than 32 1/8 would be a minus tick and therefore would not allow the execution of a short trade. (Page 128)

4. **C.** The order is adjusted on the ex-date. The number of shares increases by the percentage of the stock dividend, and the specified price is reduced to compensate. In this case, the number of shares increased to 2,000 (1,600 + 25%), and the specified price is adjusted to $48 per share. To get the adjusted price, divide the total value of the original market order (1,600 × $60 = $96,000) by the new number of shares ($96,000 ÷ 2,000 = $48). The total market value of the order, $96,000, remains the same. (Page 125)

5. **A.** Many markets have introduced computerized automated order routing and execution systems. An automatic execution system automatically executes market orders or limit orders. The system verifies the execution of the trade back to the broker-dealer and to the market maker with which the trade was executed. An order routing system does not automatically execute transactions but electronically directs orders to the appropriate market location of execution. Confirmation of executed trades are then electronically sent to the firm originating the order. The following order routing and execution systems are used:

- The NYSE uses the Super Designated Order Turnaround system. SuperDot can process market orders for up to 2,099 shares, including odd lot orders.
- The OTC market has two automatic execution systems. The Small Order Execution System (SOES) executes trades for 1,000 or fewer shares of NMS securities or 500 or fewer shares of non-NMS NASDAQ securities. The Computer-Assisted Execution System (CAES) executes trades mostly in listed securities traded OTC and in some NMS securities.
- The Chicago Board Options Exchange uses the Order Routing System (ORS). The ORS sends trades to the appropriate destinations. Market orders and executable limit orders are sent to the Retail Automatic Execution System (RAES), which is part of ORS.
- The Philadelphia Exchange uses PHLX Automated Communication and Execution system (PACE). (Page 129)

6. **A.** An at-the-opening or at-the-opening-only order is to be filled at the opening price or not at all. At-the-opening orders for multiple round lots are to be filled to the extent possible at the opening price. All or any portion of an order not filled at the opening is canceled. An at-the-opening order arriving later must be canceled. It literally missed the opening and, therefore, could not be filled at the opening. If the at-the-opening order is marked GTC (good-till-canceled), it is handled differently. If such an order cannot be filled at one day's

opening, it will be held and attempts will be made to fill the order at the opening in succeeding trading sessions. Do not assume an order is a GTC order unless it is specifically identified as such.
(Page 126)

7.   **A.**   Reported securities are those that report real time sale information (within 90 seconds). This includes NASDAQ National Market System securities. Reporting rules typically require the selling broker-dealer to make a report of the transaction.   (Page 136)

8.   **D.**   The Securities and Exchange Commission (SEC) is responsible for the regulation of nonexempt securities trading throughout the United States. The NASD is the duly authorized SRO for the OTC market. The Securities Industry Association is a trade organization for promoting the interests of the securities business. The Federal Open Market Committee determines the course of open market purchases and sales by the Fed in effecting monetary policy.   (Page 134)

9.   **D.**   NASD rules require that a dealer's markup to a customer be based on the current market rather than the dealer's cost. The dealer's potential loss on inventory is considered to be the risk of making a market.   (Page 137)

10.   **D.**   The "B" represents the bid, the "A" represents the ask price for the security.

DWAQ					
Last	25 3/8	Open	25 3/8	Close	24 7/8
Bid	25	High	25 3/8	Net Change	+1/2
Ask	25 1/2	Low	24 7/8	Volume	424
				Time	9:50

(Page 137)

11.   **C.**   Reporting of trades as they occur (price and volume) in certain over-the-counter securities was initiated by the NASD in order to provide the market (investors) with more detailed and current trading information than had previously been available.   (Page 135)

12.   **B.**   Someone anticipating a downward turn in MCS might use this strategy. This is an order to sell short at 21 3/4 stop limit GTC (good-till-canceled). If MCS trades at or below 21 3/4, the customer will be willing to sell short the stock in anticipation of buying it back at a lower price. This downward move will help verify the customer's expectation that he made a correct decision. A stop limit has been used because the customer wishes to receive at least 21 3/4 per share as the proceeds of his short position. On the day the order was placed, it was not elected (*triggered*) because the stock did not trade at or below the stop price and, therefore, MCS was trading above 21 3/4. Before the order may become a limit order, the stop price must be elected. The opening trade of the next session, 21 1/2, triggers the order because it is lower than 21 3/4.   (Page 123)

13.   **C.**   After being triggered, the order has become a limit order at 21 3/4. The customer will accept no less than this price. Because the customer is selling short, the uptick rule also applies. The uptick requirement is met when the stock trades at 21 5/8 (in fact, each subsequent trade after 21 3/8 happens to be a plus tick or zero-plus tick), and the order then fills at 21 3/4.   (Page 123)

14.   **C.**   A not-held order (NH) is a market order where both price and time discretion have been given to the floor broker by the investor in order to get the best possible execution. This type of order is usually associated with large blocks of stock and is always executed by the floor broker, not the specialist. Limit and stop orders are left with the specialist for execution. Market orders entered before the market opens are also executed by the specialist and set the opening price of a stock for the day. Otherwise, they are executed by the floor broker.   (Page 116)

15.   **A.**   A registered representative may not trade on the floor of the exchange. Only bona fide traders or specialists (members) may trade on the floor.   (Page 113)

16.   **B.**   Making markets is a principal activity. The broker-dealer stands ready, willing and able to buy or sell securities for its own account. A dealer acts as a principal when it owns the securities it is

trading. When the broker-dealer is not acting for its own account, it is acting as a broker or an agent. (Page 134)

17. **A.** The OTC market is a negotiated market; the exchanges are auction markets. (Page 132)

18. **B.** The "yellow sheets" provide dealer-to-dealer quotes for corporate bonds traded over the counter. *The Blue List* is for municipal bonds; the *Pink Sheets* are for OTC stocks. (Page 136)

19. **A.** The auction rules of priority, precedence and parity allow for the efficient execution of orders when several bids or offers are made at the same price at a given time on the floor of the NYSE. *Priority* is the order of first entered. *Precedence* takes place when an entire order can be filled by an opposite order. *Parity* is when two or more orders can fill an opposite order; the brokers match to see who fills the order. The OTC market (including listed securities traded in the third market, over-the-counter) is a negotiated market, not an auction market. (Page 114)

20. **B.** Certain inactive stocks are traded in round lots of less than 100 shares. The symbol ^s_s denotes the trading of a 10-share unit on the NYSE. The "Pr" is an abbreviation for preferred stock. Thus, 50 shares of CWE preferred traded at $26 per share. (Page 140)

21. **D.** Stop (loss) orders are entered to protect a profit or to limit a loss. Because a stop order becomes a market order when the stop price is hit, execution at a specific price can never be guaranteed. (Page 122)

22. **B.** Network A of the Consolidated Tape includes trades on the NYSE and other regional exchanges including the Midwest and Pacific exchanges. Network B prints American Stock Exchange (AMEX) and other transactions. Although many fourth-market trades (institution-to-institution direct trades) are not reported on the Consolidated Tape, INSTINET trades are included. Warrants, rights and preferred stock all trade on the exchanges and thus would appear on the Tape.

Options, however, do not appear on the Tape. (Page 139)

23. **D.** The fourth market consists of direct trades between institutions, pension funds, broker-dealers and others. Many of these trades use IN-STINET. (Page 111)

24. **D.** To be listed on the NYSE, a corporation must satisfy stringent requirements of the Exchange in terms of the total market value of its stock, number of stockholders and earnings. Securities can be listed on several exchanges at once. Because each exchange is independent of all others, what happens on one exchange will not necessarily affect another exchange. All listed securities are marginable under Federal Reserve Board rules. Once a company is listed on the NYSE, it is difficult to become delisted. A request by the board of directors of a company is insufficient cause for the NYSE to grant a delisting. (Page 113)

25. **D.** The SEC governs the securities that are to be traded in the over-the-counter market through registration requirements. Companies with 500 stockholders and $5 million in assets must register with the SEC. Registered securities that are not listed on an exchange constitute the bulk of the volume of trade of OTC equity securities. Municipal bonds and government securities are exempt from SEC registration requirements. The primary market for these securities is the unlisted OTC market. Therefore, the OTC market also facilitates the trading of unregistered, but exempt, securities. (Page 132)

26. **D.** A five-minute recall means that the quoting dealer will hold the securities while you attempt to find a buyer (or seller) at the price the dealer quoted, but it reserves the right to cut the amount of time you have to five minutes if another trader comes in with a firm order. (Page 133)

27. **D.** The fourth market (INSTINET) is transactions between corporations and other large institutions, such as mutual funds and pension plans, that do not involve an intermediary. (Page 111)

28. **B.** Any market maker that lists a quote for a stock in the *Pink Sheets* will not be held to the quote, but must stand ready to give a new quote for one round lot on request.   (Page 136)

29. **B.** Open buy limit orders and open stop orders to sell are reduced on the ex-dividend date. If the dividend cannot be converted exactly into eighths, the amount of reduction will be rounded up to the next eighth.   (Page 124)

30. **B.** A stock must have two active market makers before it can be included on NASDAQ.   (Page 135)

31. **D.** Market orders are executed immediately at the current market price if the stock is trading. A stop order will not be triggered until a set price is hit or passed through. A good-till-canceled order will not be filled until its price is hit or passed through. An all-or-none order will not be filled until the total number of shares specified is bought or sold.   (Page 121)

32. **D.** Market orders are executed immediately at the best available market price if the stock is trading. All of the rest of these orders might have a delayed execution if their conditions are not met.   (Page 121)

33. **C.** Quotes for securities that are inactively traded, have few market makers and are relatively low priced will typically be found in the *Pink Sheets*. The *Pink Sheets* are a publication of the National Quotation Bureau and contain quotes and names of market makers for thousands of thinly traded OTC stocks.   (Page 136)

34. **A.** A specialist may engage in any or all of the listed activities in the performance of his duties as a specialist, except setting option strike prices. That is the prerogative of the Options Clearing Corporation (OCC).   (Page 115)

35. **B.** The NASD's Small Order Execution System was designed to help the small investor trade securities. A riskless and simultaneous transaction is one in which a broker-dealer buys stock in the market for its inventory on the order of a customer, and then immediately uses it to fill the customer's order (and the same on the sell side), a permissible use of SOES.   (Page 131)

36. **A.** The Consolidated Tape reports all transactions involving exchange-listed securities, no matter where they are bought or sold, including fourth market trades done through INSTINET. OTC trades of unlisted securities such as TCBS would not be reported, nor would trades directly between institutions that do not involve broker-dealers and are not done through INSTINET.   (Page 139)

37. **C.** A specialist buying for his own account would be operating as a dealer, which means he is acting as a principal in the transaction and hopes to make a profit.   (Page 116)

38. **A.** Your firm was acting as the customer's agent in acquiring the 300 shares of DWQ. The best way to remember the difference between brokers and dealers is through the letters BAC/DPP. This acronym stands for "Brokers act as Agents for Commissions/Dealers act as Principals for Profits." *Profit* is another way of saying *markup*.   (Page 110)

39. **B.** Your firm was acting as principal in first acquiring the 300 shares of DWQ for its inventory before selling them to the customer. The way to remember the difference between brokers and dealers is through the letters BAC/DPP. This acronym stands for "Brokers act as Agents for Commissions/Dealers act as Principals for Profits." *Profit* is another way of saying *markup*.   (Page 110)

40. **C.** A stock exchange serves as a physical place at which brokers and dealers can conveniently transact business in securities. Specialists add to the efficiency of the system by maintaining a fair and orderly market for certain securities at their trading posts on the floor of the exchange.   (Page 112)

41. **D.** To have (or establish) a position means that your firm is either long the stocks (that is, holds them in its own inventory) or is short the stocks (which it will have to replace at some point in the

future). A firm can even be both long and short a security simultaneously, if this fits its investment strategy at the time. (Page 110)

42. **C.** Registered third-market makers are required to report transactions of listed securities traded over the counter to the Consolidated Tape within 90 seconds of execution. Any late reports (trades reported more than 90 seconds after execution) must be designated as late as they are entered into the system. (Page 139)

43. **D.** Listed securities traded on exchanges compose the exchange market. Unlisted securities traded over the counter are the OTC market. Listed securities traded OTC compose the third market. Securities bought and sold without the aid of a broker-dealer compose the fourth market. INSTINET is a reporting service used by many institutions to locate other parties for fourth-market equity transactions. (Page 111)

44. **B.** The market maker giving the firm quote is only obliged to deliver 100 shares at the asking price of 20 3/8. (Page 134)

45. **B.** Underwriters distribute new issues in the primary market. The secondary market is the trading market. In the trading market, a trade can take place on a stock exchange (the primary market); in the unlisted or over-the-counter market (the secondary market); by trading listed securities in the OTC market (the third market); or in a direct institution-to-institution trade without the services of a brokerage firm (the fourth market).
(Page 111)

46. **D.** The period between "12" and "4s" indicates two trades in ARX. The absence of any volume indication for the first trade means that the 100 shares traded at 12. The "4s" means that 400 shares traded at 11 7/8. (Page 140)

47. **C.** Of the block transactions listed, both specialist blocks and secondary distributions take place off the floor of the exchange. An exchange distribution is a crossing of trades on the floor, which is announced after execution. A special offering and a secondary offering are both announced

on the Tape prior to execution of any orders. When the special offering of a large block is announced on the Tape prior to execution, any interested trader can buy the stock at the *specially offered* price.
(Page 119)

48. **A.** A sell limit order is used to sell out a long position at a higher price (when the market moves up). A sell stop order is used to sell out a long position at a lower price (when the market moves down). To protect against a loss of the gain, a sell stop order would be placed just below where the stock is currently trading. (Page 122)

49. **D.** The specialist has made a firm bid to sell IBM at 120 for a short period of time. The trader is free to attempt to buy from someone else at a better (lower) price. However, if the floor broker finds no offers, he can go back to the specialist to buy at 120. This is stopping stock. It is a courtesy extended to the floor broker by the specialist for a short period of time. It requires no special approval from the exchange and can be done only for public customer orders, not for member firms trading account orders. (Page 117)

50. **D.** Partial execution is permissible on an immediate-or-cancel order. An AON (all-or-none) or FOK (fill-or-kill) order requires execution in full or else the entire order is canceled. Market orders are at the current market price. (Page 126)

51. **D.** A buy limit order is used to buy in a short position at a lower price (when the market moves down). A buy stop order is used to buy in a short position at a higher price (when the market moves up). To protect against the loss of the gain, a buy stop order would be placed just above where the stock is currently trading. (Page 124)

52. **C.** The period indicates that two trades in GAF took place. The absence of any volume indication shows that the trades were for 100 shares at 40 1/8 and then 100 shares at 40 1/4.
(Page 140)

53. **C.** Municipal bonds, government and agency securities and corporate securities all trade in the OTC market. Often, it is easier for institu-

tions to trade large blocks of listed stock off the exchange in a negotiated market, rather than on the exchange, so they also trade OTC. Foreign securities trade in the United States if the companies comply with SEC registration and disclosure requirements. Mutual fund shares (open-end companies) do not trade; they are bought OTC and are redeemed OTC, but there is no trading in the shares. Closed-end investment companies, however, do trade OTC.   (Page 132)

54. **D.** The representative should not cancel the existing order because it would lose priority on the specialist's book. Nor should another GTC order be entered that day because the order could be filled twice. The representative should let the order stay for the day, when it would be canceled automatically if not executed. Then, the representative should enter a GTC order the next morning.   (Page 126)

55. **C.** A buy stop order is always entered at a price above the current offering price. A buy stop order at 80 means that if the market price rises to 80 or above, the order will become a market order to buy and would be filled immediately.   (Page 123)

56. **A.** Position trading is simply trading as principal, or dealer, for the firm's own account. The opposite role is that of a broker (or agent) trading securities in the secondary market for customers.   (Page 110)

57. **A.** In a market not-held order, the client agrees not to hold the broker responsible if he cannot fill the complete order within the time limit given. Such orders allow the floor broker to use his judgment on the best execution strategy. Because specialists cannot accept orders that give them discretion over the execution, they cannot accept market not-held orders.   (Page 127)

58. **D.** Ms. Wilcox has specified a stop limit order. If the stock rises to the stop price of $140, the order is elected and then becomes a buy limit order at 144, meaning an order to buy at $144 or lower.   (Page 124)

59. **C.** The amount of the commission is determined after the trade is executed and, therefore, it is not included on the order ticket. It must be disclosed on the confirmation in the case of agency transactions. There is no commission in a principal transaction, only a markup, which does not have to be disclosed on the customer confirmation.   (Page 138)

60. **B.** Market makers are required to report daily, regardless of the volume of their trading.   (Page 134)

61. **B.** A fill-or-kill order designates that the customer wishes that the order be filled in its entirety in one attempt, or be canceled.   (Page 127)

62. **C.** In a stock split, the number of shares is increased and the price is reduced proportionately on the ex-date. Any orders on a specialist's book that are below the market will also be adjusted. 200 shares times 2 equals 400 shares; the new price will be 38 times 1/2, which is 19.   (Page 124)

63. **A.** A dealer that is making a market in an OTC stock is exempt from the plus tick rule. The short sale rule applies only to trades on an exchange. Even an OTC trade of an exchange-listed stock (a third-market trade) does not fall under the requirement.   (Page 125)

64. **D.** When an order is placed *market at the close,* it will be executed as near to the close as possible, at the discretion of the floor broker. (Remember, specialists cannot accept discretionary orders.)   (Page 126)

65. **B.** The customer has placed a limit order to buy 9% debentures issued by Ford Motors. The limit the customer is willing to pay is 95% of $20,000 worth of bonds, or $19,000 or lower. "AON" means *all-or-none*—either fill the order in its entirety, or do not execute the order. "GTC" is a good-till-canceled order, not a day order.   (Page 127)

66. **D.** "SLD" on the Tape is an indication of a delayed print. This trade was reported out of sequence. (Page 140)

67. **D.** Level 3 of the National Association of Securities Dealers Automated Quotation System (NASDAQ) gives current bid/ask quotes. It also shows volume at the end of the day, but trades are never shown. Level 3 is entered by the market makers that have access to the machines to change quotes. Any change in the quote is reflected across the country in five seconds. (Page 136)

68. **B.** The market price on the ex-dividend date usually drops by an increment big enough to cover the entire dividend. Both the bid and ask prices are affected. A $.30 dividend is covered by 3/8 of a point (.375). Therefore, on the ex-date, the bid price will probably drop to 9 1/8 (9 1/2 − 3/8 = 9 1/8) and the ask price to 9 3/8 (9 3/4 − 3/8 = 9 3/8). (Page 124)

69. **B.** To cut the customer's losses as the stock moves up, the rep should place a buy order at the market to cover the short. The rep should cancel the old buy stop order at 35. (Page 127)

70. **C.** Only open buy limit orders and open sell stop orders are reduced on the specialist's book. These are orders that are placed below the current market price. The "DNR" denotes *do not reduce*. Any order with this designation would not be reduced. (Page 124)

71. **D.** A short sale is profitable if the stock goes down in price. To hedge this position and protect against a possible rise in the price of the stock, a buy stop order can be placed. These orders are always entered above the current market price. Thus, if the stock rises to the stop price, the stop order is automatically activated. It then becomes a market order to buy immediately. The broker has no discretion as to the time of the execution. (Page 123)

72. **A.** A sell stop order is placed below where the stock is currently trading and is triggered when the market moves down. The first trade at 48 3/4

has dropped from the prior trade of 49 1/4 and triggers the order (because the stop was placed at 49). The order now becomes an order to sell short at 49 or better. (Page 123)

73. **C.** Once the trade is triggered, it becomes an order to sell (short) at 49. This requires both a plus tick and a minimum sale price of 49. The next trade at 48 7/8 meets the uptick rule, but not the price requirement. The next trade at 49 meets both requirements. This is where the order will be executed. (Page 123)

74. **D.** The sell stop order is elected (triggered) at 50 1/4 (when the stock trades at or below the stop price of 50 1/4). Now the order becomes a sell limit order at 50 1/4. The order will be executed at that price or higher (the limit placed by the customer). The trade of SLD 50 1/8 is not counted because the trade is out of sequence. The order will be executed at the next trade of 50 1/4 or above, so the order was triggered but not executed. (Page 124)

75. **B.** The size of the market is the number of shares bid and offered just outside the specialist's range of prices. In this case, the size is 100 by 400. (Page 117)

76. **B.** The specialist quote is 61 3/8–1/2. The highest price the specialist can offer his own stock for is 61 1/2. The lowest price the specialist can bid for his own account is 61 3/8. (Page 116)

77. **A.** The security price is adjusted for the dividend at its opening price the next morning. The dividend is rounded to the next highest eighth and subtracted from the closing price. The $.55 dividend is rounded to 5/8; 5/8 is subtracted from the closing price of 48. The stock would open at 47 3/8. Because the stock closed on an uptick, an opening at 47 3/8 would be a zero-plus tick and the customer's short sale can be executed. (Page 124)

78. **A.** The customer has entered an *either-or* order. Thus, if one part of the order is executed, the other portion is adjusted to reflect the execution. In this case, the customer wants to buy either 500 Polaroid at 70 (if it declines) or 500 Polaroid at 80

stop (if it goes up). Of the 500 shares, 300 were bought at $70. Thus, the order will be adjusted to 200 shares—either buy at 70 or buy stop at 80.
(Page 123)

79.   **B.**   Orders entered below the market are reduced for dividends. Only open buy limit and open sell stop and sell stop limit orders are reduced on the ex-dividend date. When calculating the reduction, the dividend is rounded to the next highest 1/8th and then subtracted from the price. Therefore, the open orders in the specialist's book will be changed to buy 500 at 68 1/2 (a buy limit order) and buy 500 at 80 stop (a buy stop order that is not changed).   (Page 124)

80.   **B.**   A firm offer for 30 minutes means that Dealer A cannot change the price for this time period. Dealer A further promises to call Dealer B before selling the bonds to another firm. Dealer B is now assured that it can get the bonds from Dealer A. Therefore, Dealer B is free to try to sell them, even without actually purchasing them from Dealer A; Dealer B does not have to buy the bonds unless it so chooses.   (Page 133)

81.   **A.**   When a stock goes ex-dividend, the price of the stock falls by the amount of the dividend. If the dividends are not equivalent to a round fraction, the shares would be reduced by the next highest fraction. A dividend of $.70 would reduce the stock price by $.75 or 3/4 of a point. The specialist will also reduce open buy limit orders and open sell stop orders by the price of the dividend.   (Page 124)

82.   **C.**   A buy stop order becomes a market order once a transaction occurs at or above the price stated on the stop order.   (Page 122)

83.   **B.**   When a stock goes ex-dividend, the price of the stock is reduced by the amount of the dividend. The dividend is always rounded up to the next 1/8, which for $1.60 is 1 5/8. ($45 − 1 5/8 = $43 3/8.)   (Page 124)

8 Client Accounts

1. Mr. and Ms. Leveridge have a joint margin account with your firm. Ms. Leveridge phones and asks you to sell 300 shares of ABC Inc. and send the check for the proceeds to her. She further requests that the check for the proceeds be made payable to her alone because her husband will be out of the country for more than 30 days on a business trip. What should you do?

   A. Carry out her instructions.
   B. Enter the order to sell the stock but explain to Ms. Leveridge that the check must be made payable to "Mr. and Ms. Leveridge."
   C. Enter the trade but freeze the account and hold all funds long in the account until you receive authorization from Mr. Leveridge.
   D. Refuse to enter the trade.

2. Mr. Brown meets with you at your office and signs the necessary documents to open a margin account with a hypothecation and credit agreement, as well as a consent to loan agreement. All of the following statements are true EXCEPT that

   A. Mr. Brown's stock can be pledged as collateral
   B. Mr. Brown's stock can be provided to other customers who have sold short
   C. Mr. Brown must keep an equity of $2,000 in his account
   D. Mr. Brown's stock will be left long in the account in street name

3. Ms. Black wishes to open a cash account with you. You are the registered representative. Mr. Blue is the branch manager of your office. Who must sign the new account form in order to open this account?

   A. Ms. Black
   B. You
   C. Mr. Blue and you
   D. Ms. Black, Mr. Blue and you

4. Suppose you learn that your client, Mr. Brown, has died. You are the registered representative handling his account. What must you do?

   A. Liquidate the account and send out a check for the proceeds.
   B. Liquidate the account and hold the credit balance in the account until you receive proper authorization to release the funds.
   C. Cancel all open orders and mark the account *deceased*.
   D. Continue to trade in the account as advised by the executor of the estate.

5. A registered representative must follow certain special rules when opening an account for

   A. a 6-year-old child of a clerical employee of a competitive brokerage firm
   B. the wife of an operations manager at another brokerage firm
   C. a registered rep at an affiliated brokerage firm that is owned by the same financial holding company
   D. all of the above

6. Which of the following documents requires a customer's signature in order to establish a discretionary account?

   A. Customer's agreement
   B. Trading authorization
   C. Options agreement
   D. New account form

7. All of the following statements are true about establishing a margin account for a trust EXCEPT that

   A. a principal of the broker-dealer must initial or sign the account documents
   B. minimum account equity requirements are waived
   C. the trust document must specifically permit the use of a margin account
   D. if a corporate trustee has been appointed, a trust officer must sign the account documents

8. Your customer has established an account but has not granted you discretionary authority. As the registered representative, which of the following orders can you accept?

   A. "Buy 500 shares of some computer company."
   B. "Buy as much AT&T as you think I need."
   C. "I've got 330 shares of XYZ in my account; round out my position by either buying 70 or selling 30 shares."
   D. "Buy 300 shares of ABC at the best price you can, sometime this week."

9. As a registered rep, you are assigned to an existing account that was previously handled by another rep who has left your firm. Which of the following should you attend to first?

   A. Suggest the customer buy one of the stocks you are currently recommending.
   B. Liquidate the portfolio for immediate reinvestment in stocks you are currently recommending.
   C. Require that the customer sign a trading authorization naming you as the party with authority.
   D. Verify the account information.

10. Several of your clients have purchased stock in their margin accounts, and one is now asking in whose name his stock is registered. You would tell him it is registered in

    A. his name
    B. your name
    C. the issuing company's name
    D. street name

11. Your aunt would like to open a custodial account for your 7-year-old daughter as a way of contributing towards her education. Your uncle will be the primary donor to the account. Which person's Social Security or tax identification number would you use on the account?

    A. Your daughter's, as the beneficial owner
    B. Your aunt's, as the custodian
    C. Your own, as her parent and legal guardian
    D. Your uncle's, as the donor

12. A third party may NOT be designated to make securities transactions for a

    A. corporation
    B. custodian for a minor
    C. wife
    D. husband

13. All of the following are required on a new account form EXCEPT

A. name
B. date of birth
C. Social Security number
D. occupation

14. In order to establish an account, which of the following would require documentation in addition to the new account form?

I. Corporation
II. Partnership
III. Custodian
IV. Estate

A. I and II
B. I, II and III
C. I, II and IV
D. III and IV

15. A woman wishes to make a gift of securities to her niece's account under the Uniform Gifts to Minors Act. The niece's guardian is opposed to the gift. Under these circumstances, the woman may give the securities

A. only if the niece approves
B. as she desires
C. with the written approval of the guardian
D. only after obtaining the permission of the court

16. All of the following statements are true regarding discretionary accounts EXCEPT that

A. an order may be placed for a discretionary account once the client has guaranteed that the power of attorney is in the mail
B. they must be reviewed on a timely basis
C. they must be approved by an officer, partner, or allied member of the member firm
D. each ticket must show the account to be discretionary

17. An investor calls her registered representative to talk about what she should do with the 500 shares of IBM in her account. She has little investment experience. After a lengthy conversation, she tells the representative, "I'd like you to sell 500 shares of IBM whenever you think the price is right." The representative

A. may accept the order and watch the stock
B. should enter a limit order to sell at slightly above the current market price
C. must get written approval from the branch manager for a discretionary order
D. should assume that this is casual conversation and do nothing at this time

18. Lotta Leveridge signed your firm's loan consent form, hypothecation agreement and credit agreement when she opened her account. This means that

I. your firm will keep all securities in street name
II. her securities can be loaned to other customers with short positions
III. your firm can use securities as collateral for a loan for the brokerage firm
IV. she is required to pay interest on the debit balance

A. I, II and III only
B. II and III only
C. II, III and IV only
D. I, II, III and IV

◆ Answers & Rationale

1. **B.** Because the account is a joint account for the husband and wife, any checks must be drawn in the name of all owners of the account.
(Page 154)

2. **C.** Margined stock must be held in street name to permit easy sale by the broker-dealer should a customer violate margin requirements. The hypothecation agreement allows the stock to be pledged as collateral. The loan consent permits the stock to be loaned to effect short sales by others. The credit agreement indicated the customer would be liable for any interest on funds borrowed to effect margin purchases. The client is not required to maintain a $2,000 equity at all times. For example, through a decline in the stock market, the equity could decline from $2,000 to $1,700 and the account would not be closed.   (Page 150)

3. **C.** The signature of the customer is not required to open a cash account. To open a margin account, the customer's signature must be obtained on the margin agreement. For all accounts, the registered representative signs the new account form, indicating that the information on the form is true and complete. The branch manager serves as the principal and must review and accept the new account by signing the form prior to the opening of the account.   (Page 149)

4. **C.** Upon learning of a client's death, the registered representative must cancel all open orders and mark the account *deceased*. The registered representative must then wait for further instructions from the administrator or executor of the estate before allowing any movement of cash or securities in the account.   (Page 157)

5. **D.** The NYSE, NASD and MSRB all have rules that require broker-dealers to give special attention to accounts opened by certain individuals. This special attention typically involves permission from or written notification to some other broker-dealer regarding the establishment of the account. Accounts opened by the following individuals fall within these rules:

- any employee of any broker-dealer
- the spouse or minor child of any employee of any broker-dealer or
- in certain cases, employees of non-NYSE member financial institutions
(Page 152)

6. **B.** In order to establish a discretionary account, written authorization must be received from the customer(s) in whose name(s) the account has been established. In most cases, this is done by signing a trading authorization allowing another individual permission either only to buy and sell securities in the account (a limited trading authorization) or also to add or remove monies and securities from the account (a full trading authorization). A signed customer's agreement is required when opening a margin account. A signed options agreement is required within 15 days from the date the options account is approved. The customer does not sign the new account form, but the signatures of the RR and the branch manager are required.
(Page 157)

7. **B.** Minimum equity account requirements must be met by anyone opening a margin account. A principal of the firm must initial the form for all new accounts. The trust document must specify that trading on margin is appropriate for the individual(s) being represented. Whoever is the account fiduciary is the individual responsible for signing any supporting account documentation.
(Page 155)

8. **D.** A registered representative who does not have discretionary authority over an account cannot accept any order that does not specify the action to take (whether it is a buy or sell), the specific security involved and the number of shares. The broker is allowed to accept an order specifying all these things at a price and time deemed favorable by the broker, given the investor grants him the power to do so. No written documentation between the client and the broker is required in such an instance.   (Page 157)

9. **D.** You should first verify and update the information you have on the customer. Then you are in a position to make suitable investment recommendations. (Page 148)

10. **D.** Securities held in margin accounts are held in the broker-dealer's name, which is also known as the *street name*, to make transferring the securities easier. (Page 149)

11. **A.** The Social Security or tax identification number of the beneficial owner(s) is normally the one placed on the account. (Page 156)

12. **B.** Only the custodian can effect transactions in a custodian account. (Page 156)

13. **B.** Although the date of birth is normally obtained, it is not required. All that is required is information stating that the customer is of age. (Page 149)

14. **C.** Opening a corporate account requires a properly executed corporate agreement. A partnership account requires a copy of the partnership agreement. An estate account requires a copy of the will appointing the executor. Only a custodian account requires no further documentation. (Page 154)

15. **B.** In a custodian account, any adult, whether related or unrelated, can make gifts. All gifts, however, are irrevocable. (Page 156)

16. **A.** A discretionary account gives the broker full trading authority to buy or sell once written power of attorney has been received by the firm. All trading in this account must be reviewed on a timely basis by a principal or officer of the firm, to check for churning. The principal must also approve, in writing, the opening of each discretionary account. Each discretionary ticket (order memorandum) must be so marked. (Page 157)

17. **A.** This order can be accepted with no written power of attorney required. Discretion as to the time of execution or price does not require a written power. Discretion over picking the stock or the amount of the purchase does require a written power. Essentially, the customer has given the broker a market not-held order. (Page 157)

18. **D.** The forms Lotta signed mean that all the securities are to be held in street name (the account is a margin account), the firm is permitted to use her margin stock as collateral, she must pay interest on any debit balance, and her stock can be loaned for short sales. (Page 150)

9 ◇ Brokerage Office Procedures

1. For delivery of mutilated municipal bonds to be considered good delivery, the certificates must be authenticated. Which of the following entities could validate the mutilated securities?

   I. Issuer
   II. Branch manager
   III. Transfer agent
   IV. Any national bank

   A. I only
   B. I and III only
   C. II and III only
   D. I, II, III and IV

2. Lotta Leveridge wants to place an order to sell 200 shares of ABC stock. She currently has no ABC in her account. As her registered representative, before accepting the order you must try to determine which of the following?

   A. Name of the broker from which the stock was purchased
   B. Where the stock is currently held and whether it can be delivered in five business days
   C. Willingness of Ms. Leveridge to deliver other securities from her account should she fail to deliver the ABC stock
   D. Whether she will pledge her other securities as collateral to secure a stock loan to effect timely delivery

3. Which of the following persons could sign a stock or bond power to effect good delivery of securities sold from an account set up under the Uniform Gifts to Minors Act?

   A. Minor
   B. Parent
   C. Donor
   D. Custodian

4. On February 13th, your customer buys 10M of the 8% Treasury bonds maturing in 1991, for settlement on February 14th. The bonds pay interest on January 1st and July 1st. How many days of accrued interest will be added to the buyer's price?

   A. 14
   B. 43
   C. 44
   D. 45

5. Compute the dollar amount of accrued interest on 10M of an 8% municipal bond bought regular way on March 20, 1987, and maturing on November 1, 1993.

   A. $311.11
   B. $322.22
   C. $324.44
   D. $326.67

6. In which of the following securities do transactions occur with accrued interest added to the price?

   A. Zero-coupon treasury securities
   B. ADRs
   C. Bankers' acceptances
   D. Negotiable certificates of deposit

7. An investor has sold 100 shares of XYZ Company. If he fails to deliver the stock, how many business days may elapse after settlement before the stock must be bought in?

   A.   5
   B.   7
   C.   10
   D.   30

8. One of your clients purchased 100 XRX. He is unable to make payment for these shares and has called to request an extension. Under extraordinary circumstances, Reg T permits a request for the extension of time for payment to be made on or before the

   A.   fifth business day following settlement date
   B.   seventh business day following settlement date
   C.   fifth business day following trade date
   D.   seventh business day following trade date

9. What does the term *and interest* mean in the sale of a corporate bond?

   A.   The buyer must adjust his cost by the amount of interest paid annually.
   B.   The seller must adjust his proceeds by the amount of interest paid annually.
   C.   The buyer must adjust his cost basis and the seller must adjust his proceeds, based on the interest accrued to that point.
   D.   The transaction was done on a net basis and no adjustment is necessary by either party.

10. Which of the following types of information would NOT be disclosed on an OTC confirmation?

    A.   Odd-lot differential
    B.   Principal cost without a markup or markdown
    C.   Number of shares traded
    D.   Agency cost with a commission

Table 9.1 Central Development Corporation — Common $1

Rate – 0.40Q Pd '88 – 1.60 Pd '87 – 1.45

Dividend Amount	Declared	Ex-date	Record Date	Payable
0.30	Nov 16	Nov 30	Dec 6	Jan 12
0.50	Feb 15	Feb 28	Mar 6	Apr 12
0.30	May 24	Jun 6	Jun 12	Jul 12
0.40	Sep 13	Sep 17	Sep 23	Oct 12
0.20	Nov 22	Dec 3	Dec 9	Jan 10 '90

11. Which of the following pieces of information would appear on a confirmation of a when-, as- and if-issued bond trade?

    A.   Settlement date
    B.   Total price
    C.   Accrued interest
    D.   Agent or principal capacity

12. Using Table 9.1, how much in dividends did the board of directors of Central Development Corporation declare on its common stock in 1989?

    A. $1.40
    B. $1.45
    C. $1.50
    D. $1.60

13. Using Table 9.1, how much in dividends did Central Development Corporation pay on its common stock in 1989?

    A. $1.40
    B. $1.45
    C. $1.50
    D. $1.60

14. Using Table 9.2, on what date must you be the holder of record of stock in order to qualify for the $.35 dividend declared by CDC?

    A. October 1st
    B. October 10th
    C. October 16th
    D. October 31st

15. Acme Corporation declared a dividend on March 1st. The record date is Monday, April 9th. What is the ex-dividend date?

    A. Monday, April 2nd
    B. Tuesday, April 3rd
    C. Thursday, April 5th
    D. Friday, April 6th

Table 9.2 Central Development Corporation — Common $1

Rate – 0.40Q Pd '88 – 1.60 Pd '87 – 1.45

Dividend Amount	Declared	Ex-date	Record Date	Payable
0.20	Jan 2	Jan 12	Jan 18	Jan 31
0.20	Apr 2	Apr 9	Apr 13	Apr 30
0.20	Jul 3	Jul 11	Jul 17	Jul 31
0.35	Oct 1	Oct 10	Oct 16	Oct 31

16. An investor sold 100 shares of XYZ on October 31st. The record date for a dividend distribution is November 1st. The registered rep can tell him he is

    I. entitled to the dividend if the trade is done for cash
    II. entitled to the dividend if the trade is done regular way
    III. not entitled to the dividend if the trade is done for cash
    IV. not entitled to the dividend if the trade is done regular way

    A. I and III
    B. I and IV
    C. II and III
    D. II and IV

17. On Wednesday, October 25th, Inxco of Grinnell, Iowa, declared a dividend payable to stockholders of record on Wednesday, November 1st. The record was published in the local paper on October 28th. *The Wall Street Journal* doesn't publish the news until three days later. The ex-dividend date is

    A. October 25th
    B. October 26th
    C. October 27th
    D. October 28th

Use the following information to answer questions 18 through 20.

International Corp.   5:4 stock split:
Record date: April 8th
Payable date: April 30th
Ex-date: May 1st

18. Mr. Jones purchased a round lot of International Corp. on May 4th. How many shares will he receive?

A. 75
B. 100
C. 100 with a due bill for 25 shares
D. 125

19. On May 1st, the price of the stock will be reduced by

A. 15%
B. 20%
C. 25%
D. 50%

20. If the company pays a dividend of $.15 on the new stock, a customer who owned 280 shares before the split will receive how much in dividends?

A. $42.00
B. $48.00
C. $50.00
D. $52.50

21. DWZ Company has just declared a 2:1 stock split payable on October 31st to stockholders of record as of October 9th. The ex-date is Wednesday, November 1st. An investor can buy the stock regular way without receiving a due bill on

A. October 9th
B. October 26th
C. October 31st
D. November 1st

22. Best Buy Company has announced a $.25 dividend payable to stockholders of record on June 1st. An owner of Best Buy stock who sold the stock on May 29th would

A. not be entitled to receive the dividend
B. be entitled to receive the dividend
C. be entitled to receive the dividend only if the stock were delivered before the ex-dividend date
D. receive a due bill from the buyer

23. Best Buy Company has announced a $.25 dividend payable to stockholders of record on June 1st. On what date would all stockholders whose names appear on the record books of Best Buy be entitled to dividends?

A. May 28th
B. May 30th
C. May 31st
D. June 1st

24. The computation for accrued interest on corporate debt obligations is based on

A. actual-day month and actual-day year
B. actual-day month and 360-day year
C. 30-day month and actual-day year
D. 30-day month and 360-day year

25. On July 5, 1985, an investor buys 5M of 9 3/8% Treasury bonds at 88 1/4. The bonds mature on September 1, 1990. If he sells the bonds on February 7, 1986, at 90 7/8, what is the amount of interest he would recognize for federal tax purposes in 1985?

A. $72.60
B. $156.25
C. $220.05
D. $234.50

◆ Answers & Rationale

1. **B.** Mutilated certificates are considered good delivery if validated by the trustee, registrar, transfer agent, paying agent or issuer.

(Page 172)

2. **B.** The rep should ascertain the location of the stock as well as whether the customer can deliver within five business days so the firm can make timely delivery. The broker from which the securities were purchased and the security holdings of the customer are immaterial. (Page 172)

3. **D.** Custodial securities must be signed by the custodian in order to be good delivery. Securities registered in the name of a custodian for the benefit of a minor, for example, are not good delivery if signed by the minor. (Page 172)

4. **C.** Accrued interest for government securities is figured on an *actual days elapsed* basis. The number of days begins with the previous coupon date and continues up to, but not including, the settlement date. For instance, these bonds pay interest on January 1st; the number of days of accrued interest for January equals 31. The bonds settle February 14th; the number of days of accrued interest for February equals 13. Remember, don't count the settlement date (31 + 13 = 44 days).

(Page 170)

5. **C.** Regular way settlement on municipal bonds is five business days. Settlement date on this transaction is March 27th. The bonds pay interest on November 1st and May 1st. Number of days of accrued interest:

Month	Days
November	30 day
December	30 day
January	30 day
February	30 day
March	26 day
Total	146 days (do not count settlement day)

The accrued interest formula for municipal bonds is: Principal × Rate × Time; therefore, $10,000 × 8% × (146 ÷ 360) = $324.44. (Page 169)

6. **D.** Zero-coupon treasuries (also known as *STRIPS*) and bankers' acceptances are issued at a discount and mature at face value; the difference represents interest. Securities like these do not pay interest periodically. Interest does not accrue on them; they trade flat. ADR stands for *American depositary receipt*. ADRs are equity securities and pay dividends, not interest. Some negotiable CDs pay interest at maturity in addition to the face value; such CDs trade with accrued interest.

(Page 168)

7. **C.** If a customer fails to deliver a security he has sold to the broker, the broker must buy in the position on the tenth day after settlement.

(Page 168)

8. **D.** Under Reg T, purchases must be paid for promptly, but no later than seven business days after the trade date. Under extraordinary circumstances, an extension of time for payment may be requested on the seventh day from a national stock exchange or an NASD office, depending on where the stock was traded. (Page 168)

9. **C.** Accrued interest is added to the price the buyer pays and to the price the seller receives.

(Page 168)

10. **A.** There is no odd-lot differential charged in an OTC trade. (Page 166)

11. **D.** When-, as- and if-issued securities are securities for which there will be some amount of delay in delivery. Because their delivery date is not certain, there cannot be a settlement date and accrued interest payable cannot be calculated. Until the accrued interest can be calculated, the total contract price cannot be determined. The firm's capacity in handling the trade is known, however, and can be disclosed on the confirmation.

(Page 167)

12. **A.** In 1989, the total dividends declared were $1.40. (Page 171)

13. **C.**   Dividends paid from January 12, 1989, to October 12, 1989, were $1.50.   (Page 171)

14. **C.**   In order to receive the $.35 dividend, one must be the holder of record of the stock on or before the record date, which, in this example, is October 16th.   (Page 171)

15. **B.**   The ex-dividend date is four business days prior to the record date.   (Page 171)

16. **C.**   If the trade was done the regular way, the investor is entitled to the dividend because he sold it after the ex-dividend date (four days prior to the record date). If the trade was done for cash, the ex-dividend date is the day after the record date.   (Page 171)

17. **B.**   The ex-date is always set four business days prior to the record date, October 26th, in this case. The publication by *The Wall Street Journal* has no bearing on the ex-date.   (Page 171)

18. **B.**   The purchase on May 4th is after the ex-dividend date. Therefore, on May 4th, Mr. Jones will receive 100 shares of stock. If the trade had occurred between April 3rd and April 30th, Mr. Jones would have received 100 shares with a due bill for the 25 shares.   (Page 170)

19. **B.**   The 5-for-4 stock split means that the corporation will issue 5 new shares for 4 old shares, which is 1.25 or 25% more shares. Each share will now be worth 4/5 or .8, which is 80% of an old share. Therefore, the price will be reduced by 20%.   (Page 125)

20. **D.**   The customer has 350 of the new shares. This is calculated by multiplying 5/4 by 280 shares. The 350 shares receive a dividend of $.15 per share ($350 \times .15 = \$52.50$).   (Page 125)

21. **D.**   The ex-date for stock split is the day following the payable date. If the purchase takes place on or after the ex-date, the new owner will receive the correct number of shares. Therefore,

stock sold on November 1st would not require a due bill; the new owner would receive the correct number of shares.

However, if the stock is sold between the record date and the payable date, the new owner must receive a due bill from the seller because the seller (as owner on the record date) will receive the additional shares from the stock split. Therefore, the seller gives the buyer a due bill for the additional shares and the buyer suffers no loss. In this example, if the stock is sold between October 9th and October 31st, a seller would send the buyer a due bill.   (Page 170)

22. **B.**   The record date is June 1st and the ex-dividend date is four business days earlier. Assume June 1st is a Friday; the record date chart would look like this:

25	26	27	28	29	30	31	1
F	S	S	M	T	W	T	F
			Ex-date				Record date

The stock was held beyond the ex-date and the seller would receive the dividend.   (Page 171)

23. **D.**   The record date is June 1st. Holders of stock on that date will receive the dividend.   (Page 171)

24. **D.**   Accrued interest on corporate bonds is computed on a 30-day month, 360-day year.   (Page 169)

25. **A.**   Interest computation is always the same: principal × rate × time. In this example, we know that the bond will pay interest on March 1st and September 1st. March 1st to August 31st equals 184 days. The investor owned the bonds from July 6th to August 31st, or a total of 57 of those 184 days. The rate of interest is divided by two because only half is paid each six months. ($5,000 × [9 3/8% ÷ 2] × [57 ÷ 184] = $72.60)   (Page 170)

10 Margin Accounts

1. Max Leveridge's margin account has available SMA of $10,000. How much would he have to deposit to purchase listed options with premiums totaling $18,000?

   A. $4,000
   B. $6,500
   C. $8,000
   D. $16,000

2. Max Leveridge wants to buy $1,200 worth of stock on margin. He currently has a margin account with open long positions and equity of $600. What will Max's required deposit be on the purchase of $1,200 of securities?

   A. $600
   B. $900
   C. $1,200
   D. $1,400

3. A customer has a margin account with long positions having $20,000 of current market value and a debit balance of $8,000. What is the purchasing power of this customer's account?

   A. $2,000
   B. $4,000
   C. $6,000
   D. $8,000

4. Max Leveridge has a margin account that currently has excess equity. In response to Max's inquiry about future stock purchases, what should you tell him about the relationship between excess equity and purchasing power?

   A. Purchasing power equals 25% of excess equity.
   B. Purchasing power equals 50% of excess equity.
   C. Purchasing power equals 100% of excess equity.
   D. Purchasing power equals 200% of excess equity.

5. Ann Chorsteam is holding long and short positions in different securities in her margin account. Her account records indicate a debit balance of $50,000 and a short credit balance of $35,000. On what amount is the account charged interest?

   A. $0
   B. $15,000
   C. $35,000
   D. $50,000

6. Lenny Kuegel has placed an order to buy 100 shares of ABC stock in his margin account. ABC stock is trading at 50 on a *when-issued* basis. What is Lenny required to deposit?

   A. $0 until the stock is issued
   B. $2,000
   C. $2,500
   D. $5,000

7. Gwinneth Stout is long 200 shares of ABC at 30 and 400 shares of XYZ at 20 in a margin account. The debit balance in the account is $8,000. She sells 200 of the XYZ shares for $4,000. The credit to SMA is

   A. $0
   B. $1,000
   C. $2,000
   D. $4,000

8. A broker-dealer is allowed to extend credit for the purchase of all the following securities EXCEPT

   A. U.S. government securities
   B. exchange-traded stock
   C. options
   D. municipal revenue bonds

9. By how much would SMA increase if a customer bought $22,000 of marginable stock in an existing margin account and fully paid for the transaction?

   A. $0
   B. $5,500
   C. $11,000
   D. $22,000

10. A customer with no other positions in his margin account buys 2,000 shares of ABC at 20 and sells short 1,000 shares of XYZ at 40. If Regulation T is 50%, what is the margin requirement for these transactions?

   A. $0
   B. $4,000
   C. $30,000
   D. $40,000

11. A customer who is long 1,000 shares of XYZ in her margin account with no debit balance sells short 1,000 shares of XYZ at $40 per share. How much can be withdrawn from the account on the settlement date of the short sale?

   A. $0
   B. $20,000
   C. $38,000
   D. $40,000

12. Lotta Leveridge purchased 200 shares of Flibinite, Inc. from you at $60 per share. She gave you a check for the initial requirement. Flibinite announces that it is selling millions of its new Magic Meditation Machine in Japan, and its stock appreciates on the news to $75. How much cash can Lotta withdraw after this market move?

   A. $0
   B. $1,000
   C. $1,500
   D. $3,000

13. For a couple of months now, Max Leveridge has been watching Microscam, Inc. and has decided it is time to short the stock. Max sells short 100 shares at $80 per share. He gives you a cashier's check for the initial requirement. The next day, *The Wall Street Journal* carries an announcement that Microscam just signed a big government contract, and its stock appreciates to $90. How much additional cash does Max have to deposit?

   A. $0
   B. $1,000
   C. $2,400
   D. $2,700

14. Which regulator sets initial margin requirements for nonexempt securities trading in the OTC market?

   A. SEC
   B. FRB
   C. SIA
   D. NASD

15. To purchase a when-issued stock in a cash account, an investor must deposit

   A. the greater of 25% of the purchase price or $2,000 promptly
   B. the greater of 50% of the purchase price or $2,000 promptly
   C. 75% of the purchase price five business days after the trade date
   D. 100% of the purchase price five business days after the trade date

16. Although margin requirements are set by the Federal Reserve Board and the NYSE and NASD, member firms may

    A. increase or decrease these requirements through in-house rules
    B. disregard one set of rules if the other is applicable
    C. increase the requirements through in-house rules
    D. follow requirements that are less stringent

17. The formula for computing equity in a margin account is

    A. long market value − short market value + credit balance + debit balance
    B. long market value − short market value + debit balance − credit balance
    C. long market value + credit balance − short market value − debit balance
    D. long market value + short market value − debit balance + credit balance

18. An individual who sells stock short that he owns is selling

    A. short against long
    B. short against the box
    C. short
    D. none of the above

19. According to Reg T and the NYSE/NASD, initial and maintenance margin requirements for a short account are

    A. 50% initial; 25% maintenance
    B. 50% initial; 30% maintenance
    C. 50% initial; 50% maintenance
    D. 70% initial; 50% maintenance

20. An investor's margin account has the following positions:

Long market value	$50,000
Short market value	$27,000
Debit balance	$12,000
Credit balance	$22,000

    What is the total equity in her account?

    A. $10,000
    B. $15,000
    C. $22,000
    D. $33,000

21. In a new account, what is the initial margin requirement for a customer who sells short 100 shares of Acme at 35?

    A. $1,500
    B. $1,750
    C. $2,000
    D. $3,500

22. An investor will sell stock short to

    A. profit if prices decline
    B. establish a permanent tax loss
    C. defer taxes
    D. liquidate a long stock position

Use the following information to answer questions 23 through 25.

Bob Barker has a margin account with a debit balance of $37,000. He has the following securities in his account:

Company	No. Shares	Market Price
A	100	$110
B	300	$65
C	400	$90

23. The equity in Bob's account is

   A. $22,500
   B. $29,500
   C. $33,250
   D. $37,000

24. Bob's account is restricted. How much would he have to deposit to make it a nonrestricted account?

   A. $0
   B. $2,000
   C. $2,500
   D. $3,750

25. The NYSE minimum margin for Bob's account is

   A. $8,500
   B. $16,625
   C. $29,500
   D. $33,250

26. Which of the following will cause a change in SMA in a long account?

   I. Purchase of stock
   II. Sale of stock
   III. Increase in market value
   IV. Decrease in market value

   A. I and II only
   B. I, II and III only
   C. I and III only
   D. I, II, III and IV

27. An investor purchased $15,000 of stock in a margin account, depositing the Reg T requirement. The account is charged with interest amounting to $100. There has been no other activity in the account. The new debit balance is

   A. $100
   B. $7,400
   C. $7,500
   D. $7,600

28. Which of the following are characteristics of selling short against the box?

   I. Allows a gain on stock to be locked in without selling long
   II. Can be accomplished provided the long position is not liquidated
   III. Turns short-term gains into long-term gains
   IV. Provides general deferral of taxes

   A. I, II and III
   B. I, II and IV
   C. I and III
   D. II and III

29. A customer's debit balance is decreased by all of the following EXCEPT

   A. stock dividends
   B. cash dividends and interest received
   C. deposits of cash
   D. sale of securities

30. An existing margin account with a market value of $20,000 is restricted by $1,200. The account is credited with a $2,100 dividend from one securities position. The customer would like to withdraw cash immediately. What amount can be sent to the customer?

   A. $0
   B. $900
   C. $1,200
   D. $2,100

31. Mr. Smith has a margin account containing securities with a market value of $50,000 and no debit balance. If he sold all his stock, he could withdraw

A. $0
B. $7,500
C. $25,000
D. $50,000

32. Mr. Smith has a margin account containing securities with a market value of $50,000 and no debit balance. How much could he purchase in marginable securities without making a deposit?

A. $7,500
B. $25,000
C. $50,000
D. $100,000

33. Mr. Smith has a margin account containing securities with a market value of $50,000 and no debit balance. How much would the debit balance be if Mr. Smith purchased the maximum amount of securities without depositing additional cash?

A. $0
B. $12,500
C. $25,000
D. $50,000

34. Your employer, Tippecanoe Securities, Inc., was part of the syndicate that underwrote a Central Potato Growers, Inc. stock offering recently. How many days after the end of the offering will you be able to sell CPG to your clients on margin?

A. 30
B. 60
C. 90
D. 180

◆ Answers & Rationale

1. **C.** The options purchases must be fully paid. The customer has available SMA of $10,000, which means $10,000 may be borrowed from the account. The remaining $8,000 must be deposited by the customer. (Page 180)

2. **C.** The $2,000 minimum requirement per account of the NASD and NYSE does not require a deposit greater than 100% of the cost of stock being purchased. Normally one has to deposit only the Reg T requirement when buying marginable stock. However, if an existing account has equity of less than $2,000 and the value of stock to be purchased, plus existing equity, is still less than $2,000, the stock must be paid for in full. (Page 180)

3. **B.** The account has $12,000 of equity. 50% of the market value would be $10,000; therefore, the account has $2,000 of excess equity. When Reg T is 50%, the purchasing power of excess equity is 2 to 1. (Page 183)

4. **D.** Like cash, excess equity buys stock at 2 to 1 (200%). Each $1 of cash or excess equity allows one to buy $2 of marginable securities. (Page 183)

5. **D.** Interest is paid by the customer only on monies loaned by the brokerage firm, meaning the debit balance of $50,000. Although all debits and credits are netted for purposes of calculating equity in a combined margin account, they are maintained separately when determining interest charges to the margin account. (Page 198)

6. **C.** When-issued stock purchased in a margin account is subject to normal margin requirements. Reg T requires 50% and the rules of the NASD and NYSE regarding minimum account requirements ($2,000 and 25%) apply. Because the customer is purchasing $5,000 of securities (100 shares × $50 per share), he must deposit $2,500 ($5,000 × 50%). (Page 181)

7. **C.** Because this account is below 50% margin, the account is restricted ($6,000 equity ÷ $14,000 market value = 42.8% equity). When securities are sold in a restricted account, at least 50% of the proceeds must be retained in the account, with the other 50% released to the customer. If the funds are not withdrawn, the 50% proceeds are noted in the memorandum account, credited to SMA. This means that the funds can be borrowed from the account. Because $4,000 of securities are sold, $2,000 (50%) is credited to SMA. (Page 191)

8. **C.** Credit is extended on the ownership of stocks and bonds. Options have no loan value and credit cannot be extended on their purchase. (Page 180)

9. **C.** Assuming that the customer paid for the securities in full, he would generate $11,000 in SMA. Because the customer need pay only half of the securities' value ($11,000), the additional cash paid ($11,000) would be considered a nonrequired cash deposit and would be credited to the SMA. Another way to look at it is that the customer has fully paid securities with a loan value of 50%, or $11,000. (Page 190)

10. **D.** The margin requirements for both positions must be met. 2,000 shares of ABC at $20 per share requires a margin of $20,000 ($40,000 × 50%). Being short 1,000 shares XYZ at $40 requires a margin of $20,000 ($40,000 × 50%). The sum of these is $40,000. (Page 196)

11. **C.** There is no Reg T requirement when shorting against the box because there is no risk (it is offset by the long position). However, there is a 5% NYSE margin requirement on the long position ($40,000 × 5% = $2,000), so the customer can withdraw only $38,000 ($40,000 − $2,000 NYSE requirement). (Page 197)

12. **C.** Lotta Leveridge could withdraw cash equal to the excess equity. A purchase of 200 shares at $60 per share would require an initial deposit of $6,000 on market value of $12,000. Lotta would have $6,000 in equity and a $6,000 debit. After a rise to $75 a share, the stock's market value would

be $15,000. Lotta's debit balance would remain unchanged at $6,000, but her equity would increase to $9,000 ($15,000 CMV − $6,000 DR). Reg T on $15,000 CMV is $7,500. Lotta's $9,000 equity less the $7,500 Reg T leaves her with $1,500 in excess equity.   (Page 183)

13. **A.** At $80 per share, Max had to deposit 50% of the CMV of the shorted stock. At that point, the account had $8,000 in credit from the sale ($80 × 100 shares) and $4,000 in credit from Max's deposit ($8,000 × 50%) for a total account credit balance of $12,000. Max's equity in the account is the difference between the credit in the account and the CMV of the shorted stock. At a CMV of $80, Max had $4,000 equity ($12,000 − $8,000). At a CMV of $90, Max's equity is $3,000 ($12,000 − $9,000). Required maintenance on a short account is 30% of the CMV of the shorted stock. At a price of $80, the maintenance requirement would be $2,400. At a price of $90, the maintenance requirement would be $2,700. Max will not have to make an additional deposit unless the stock price rises above $92.50, at which point Max's equity would begin to fall short of the maintenance requirement.   (Page 197)

14. **B.** The Federal Reserve Board is responsible for setting margin requirements for all non-exempt securities regardless of where they are traded. Exempt securities are those that are free from FRB margin requirements.   (Page 179)

15. **A.** In a cash account, 100% of the purchase amount must be deposited. However, for when-issued securities, it is not required that payment be made in full until the settlement date, which is set only when the securities are finally issued. Until then, the NASD applies its minimum margin requirement (25% or $2,000, whichever is greater) to the position.   (Page 181)

16. **C.** Firms may set their own margin levels at more stringent levels than the FRB and NYSE/NASD rules. However, they may never go below FRB and NYSE/NASD margin requirements.   (Page 180)

17. **C.** The formula for equity in a long account is the long market value minus the debit balance. The formula for equity in a short account is the credit balance minus the short market value. Together, they equal answer C.   (Page 198)

18. **B.** The question defines selling short against the box.   (Page 196)

19. **B.** Initial Reg T margin is 50% and the maintenance margin is 30% for short accounts.   (Page 196)

20. **D.** The equity in a long account is LMV minus debits ($50,000 − $12,000 = $38,000). The equity in the short account is credits minus SMV ($22,000 − $27,000 = −$5,000). The net equity position is $33,000.   (Page 198)

21. **C.** Reg T requires a 50% margin when selling short. $3,500 times .50 equals $1,750. However, the NYSE requirement that a client deposit a minimum of $2,000 when opening a short account applies. Therefore, C is the correct answer.   (Page 196)

22. **A.** Short sales are used to profit if prices fall.   (Page 196)

23. **B.** LMV minus debit equals equity.

$ 11,000	Company A
+ 19,500	Company B
+ 36,000	Company C
$ 66,500	Total LMV
− 37,000	Debit balance
$ 29,500	Equity

(Page 182)

24. **D.** To be nonrestricted, the account must be at 50% margin. 50% of $66,500 equals $33,250 required equity.

$ 33,250	Required equity
− 29,500	Actual equity
$ 3,750	Equity deficiency

If the $3,750 is deposited, equity would increase to 50% and the account would not be restricted.

(Page 187)

25. **B.** The NYSE minimum margin is the greater of $2,000 or 25% of market value in a long account (.25 × $66,500 = $16,625).   (Page 186)

26. **B.** Once SMA is created in a long account, it is not reduced by a decline in market value. The SMA may still be taken out as long as it will not bring the account below the maintenance level. An increase in market value as well as a sale of stock increases SMA. The purchase of stock decreases available SMA.   (Page 190)

27. **D.** Because the Reg T requirement is 50%, the investor deposits $7,500 and is loaned $7,500 (debit balance) for the $15,000 purchase. If the account is charged with $100 interest expense, the new debit balance is $7,600.   (Page 194)

28. **B.** One cannot use a tax device to convert short-term gains to long-term gains. If an investor sells short against the box on stock that has been held short term, the holding period on the stock is wiped out. Thus, when the short is covered with the delivery of the shares, any gain or loss is always short term. One cannot sell short against the box to lock in a short-term gain and then stretch the gain into a long-term gain.   (Page 196)

29. **A.** Any cash proceeds can be used to reduce a customer's loan. When shares of stock are increased through a stock dividend, the value of each share will be reduced proportionately. There-fore, stock dividends do not decrease the debit balance.   (Page 194)

30. **D.** When dividends are received in a margin account, the proceeds are used to reduce the debit balance and are credited 100% to SMA. These funds can be withdrawn from the account in full for 35 days (which would bring the debit balance back to its original amount). The retention requirement (50%) applies to sales of securities out of a restricted margin account, not to the retention of dividends or interest.   (Page 189)

31. **D.** Because the stock is paid in full, the customer could take all $50,000 if he sold the stock.   (Page 185)

32. **C.** Because there is no loan against the $50,000 stock position, the customer can borrow $25,000 in cash (50%). This would allow the purchase of another $50,000 of stock in the account.   (Page 182)

33. **D.** After the new stock purchase, the account would show:

$ 50,000	Fully paid securities
+ 50,000	New purchase
$100,000	Long market value
− 50,000	Debit balance
$ 50,000	Equity

(Page 182)

34. **A.** A new issue cannot be sold on margin. However, 30 days after issuance, the security can be purchased on margin.   (Page 180)

11 Economics and Analysis

1. The Federal Reserve Board foresees the probability of an overheated economy and the resumption of double-digit inflation. Attempting to avoid the painful results of inflation, the FRB takes actions to slow down the economy, including increasing the discount rate. The likely effects of these moves are a(n)

    I. increase in the prime rate
    II. increase in bond interest and an accompanying decrease in bond prices
    III. slowdown in corporate growth
    IV. decrease in corporate earnings and equity prices

    A. I and II only
    B. I, III and IV only
    C. III and IV only
    D. I, II, III and IV

2. Disintermediation occurs when

    I. money is tight
    II. Reg T eases margin requirements
    III. money-market rates are higher than prevailing bank savings rates
    IV. the FRB reduces the discount rate

    A. I, II and III only
    B. I and III only
    C. II and IV only
    D. I, II, III and IV

3. Which of the following industries would most likely be classed as *cyclical?*

    A. Pharmaceutical
    B. Durable goods
    C. Utilities
    D. Food

4. Which of the following industries would most likely be classed as *defensive?*

    A. Steel
    B. Automotive
    C. Airline
    D. Clothing

5. Which of the following industries would be most adversely affected by increases in interest rates?

    A. Pharmaceutical
    B. Durable goods
    C. Utilities
    D. Automobile

6. Which of the following is a coincident indicator?

    A. Stock market
    B. Machine tool orders
    C. Industrial production
    D. Employment

7. Which of the following is a leading indicator?

    A. Stock market
    B. Gross national product
    C. Unemployment
    D. Industrial production

8. Which of the following is considered the most accurate method of measuring GNP?

    A. Actual dollars
    B. Constant dollars
    C. Eurodollars
    D. M1 dollars

9. The FOMC is purchasing T bills in the open market. Which two of the following scenarios are likely to occur?

   I. Secondary bond prices will rise.
   II. Secondary bond prices will fall.
   III. Interest rates will rise.
   IV. Interest rates will fall.

   A. I and III
   B. I and IV
   C. II and III
   D. II and IV

10. What happens to outstanding fixed-income securities when the rate of inflation slows?

    A. Yields go up.
    B. Coupon rates go up.
    C. Prices go up.
    D. Short-term fixed-income securities are affected most.

11. In order to calculate constant dollars, domestic GNP is adjusted

    A. to match foreign GNP
    B. for inflation
    C. to include bank reserves
    D. downward by the balance of payments

12. Which of the following is considered a lagging indicator?

    A. S&P 500
    B. Housing permits issued
    C. Loans outstanding
    D. Hours worked

13. To determine the amount of change in the GNP from one year to another, both years should be converted into

    A. the exchange value of the dollar, as compared with major foreign currencies
    B. international depositary receipts
    C. constant dollars
    D. the current dollar price of gold bullion

14. If inflation momentum is decreasing, the value of fixed-income securities would be

    A. stable
    B. increasing
    C. decreasing
    D. fluctuating

15. Federal Open Market Committee activities are closely monitored by Wall Street because of the effect of its decisions on all of the following EXCEPT

    A. money supply
    B. interest rates
    C. exchange rates
    D. money velocity

16. If the Federal Reserve Board decided that it was necessary to change the money supply, which of the following instruments would it NOT use?

    A. Bank reserve requirements
    B. Open market operations
    C. Tax rate
    D. Discount rate

17. Which organization or governmental unit sets fiscal policy?

    A. Federal Reserve Board
    B. Government Economic Board
    C. Congress
    D. Secretary of the Treasury

18. In its attempt to increase the money supply, the Federal Open Market Committee is purchasing T bills. This action should cause the yield on T bills to

    A. increase
    B. decrease
    C. fluctuate
    D. stabilize

19. Arrange the following economic phases in the normal order in which they occur.

    I. Contraction
    II. Expansion
    III. Peak
    IV. Trough

    A. I, II, III, IV
    B. II, III, I, IV
    C. III, II, I, IV
    D. IV, I, III, II

20. Arrange the following economic phases in the normal order in which they occur.

    I. Recovery
    II. Trough
    III. Recession
    IV. Prosperity

    A. I, IV, III, II
    B. II, I, III, IV
    C. III, IV, I, II
    D. IV, III, I, II

21. Which of the following economists is(was) a supporter of supply-side economics?

    A. Adam Smith
    B. John Maynard Keynes
    C. Arthur Laffer
    D. Milton Friedman

22. Which of the following economists is(was) a supporter of demand-side economics?

    A. Adam Smith
    B. John Maynard Keynes
    C. Arthur Laffer
    D. Milton Friedman

23. According to Keynesian economic theory, an economy's health can be ensured if the government

    A. cuts taxes for businesses and the wealthy
    B. increases aggregate demand
    C. increases the money supply
    D. does not interfere

24. According to supply-side economic theory, an economy's health can be ensured if the government

    A. cuts taxes for businesses and the wealthy
    B. increases aggregate demand
    C. increases the money supply
    D. does not interfere

25. What kind of economists would encourage a government to spend money to move the economy into an expansionary phase?

    A. Classical
    B. Keynesian
    C. Supply side
    D. Monetarist

26. What kind of economists would encourage a government to cut business taxes to move the economy into an expansionary phase?

    A. Classical
    B. Keynesian
    C. Supply side
    D. Monetarist

27. Which of the following is considered a lagging economic indicator?

    A. Ratio of consumer credit to consumer income
    B. Building permits and housing starts
    C. Nonagricultural employment
    D. Dow Jones industrial average

28. What term do economists use to describe a downturn in the economy that lasts more than two consecutive quarters?

    A. Inflation
    B. Stagflation
    C. Depression
    D. Recession

29. What term do economists use to describe a downturn in the economy that is characterized by both unemployment and rising prices?

    A. Inflation
    B. Stagflation
    C. Depression
    D. Recession

30. Which of the following situations could cause a fall in the value of the U.S. dollar in relationship to the Japanese yen?

    I. Japanese investors buying U.S. Treasury securities
    II. U.S. investors buying Japanese corporations
    III. Increase in Japan's trade surplus over that of the United States
    IV. General decrease in U.S. interest rates

    A. I, II and III
    B. I and III
    C. II and III
    D. II, III and IV

31. If the Federal Open Market Committee has decided that the rate of inflation is too high, it is most likely to

    I. tighten the money supply
    II. loosen the money supply
    III. lower the discount rate
    IV. raise the discount rate

    A. I and III
    B. I and IV
    C. II and III
    D. II and IV

32. Which of the following is considered a lagging economic indicator?

    A. Duration of unemployment
    B. Personal income
    C. Money supply
    D. Orders for durable goods

33. New orders for durable goods is what kind of economic indicator?

    A. Leading
    B. Coincident
    C. Coterminous
    D. Lagging

34. A slowdown in deliveries is what kind of economic indicator?

    A. Leading
    B. Coincident
    C. Coterminous
    D. Lagging

35. Industrial production is what kind of economic indicator?

    A. Leading
    B. Coincident
    C. Coterminous
    D. Lagging

36. A reduction in the reserve requirement by the FRB will have what sort of effect on total bank deposits?

    I. Decrease
    II. Increase
    III. Multiplier
    IV. Logarithmic

    A. I and III
    B. I and IV
    C. II and III
    D. II and IV

37. An increase in the reserve requirement by the FRB will have what sort of effect on total bank deposits?

    I. Decrease
    II. Increase
    III. Multiplier
    IV. Logarithmic

    A. I and III
    B. I and IV
    C. II and III
    D. II and IV

38. The open market operations of the Fed are intended to cause direct changes in

    A. interest rates
    B. exchange rates
    C. money velocity
    D. the money supply

39. According to technical analysis, when the market is consolidating a chart showing the market trendline would appear to be moving

    A. upwards to reach a new peak
    B. downwards to reach a new low
    C. downwards with sporadic upswings
    D. sideways within a narrow range

40. Four of the best known indexes and averages are listed below. How would they rank from the broadest measure of the market to the fewest number of issues in the index?

    I.   Dow Jones industrial average
    II. NYSE Composite Index
    III. Standard & Poor's 500
    IV. Wilshire 5,000 Index

    A. I, IV, III, II
    B. II, III, I, IV
    C. III, II, IV, I
    D. IV, II, III, I

41. The Dow Jones industrial average is a(n)

    A. price-weighted average of 30 primarily industrial stocks
    B. price-weighted average of 300 primarily industrial stocks
    C. unweighted average of 30 primarily transportation stocks
    D. unweighted average of 300 primarily transportation stocks

42. One of your customers noticed that the monthly reports of total short interest of the NYSE have been showing an increase in the number of shares sold short. When he asks you for an interpretation, you should tell him that this signals a

    A. bullish market
    B. bearish market
    C. period of stability in the market
    D. period of volatility in the market

43. In the analysis of a company's stock, a technical analyst would take into consideration all of the following EXCEPT

    A. market price
    B. history
    C. volume
    D. earnings

44. A fundamental analyst would most likely use the same techniques as a technical analyst to determine

    I.   timing
    II. price
    III. industry selection
    IV. company selection

    A. I
    B. I and II
    C. III
    D. III and IV

45. Proponents of which technical theory assume that small investors are usually wrong?

    A. Breadth of market theory
    B. Short interest theory
    C. Volume of trading theory
    D. Odd lot theory

46. According to the Dow theory, reversal of a primary bullish trend must be confirmed by

    A. the duration of the secondary movements
    B. the advance/decline line
    C. the Dow Jones industrial and transportation averages
    D. all of the above

47. If your firm wanted to measure the credit risk of ABC Corporation, it would use the

    A. ratio of total debt to total assets
    B. ratio of total debt to net tangible assets
    C. current ratio
    D. price-earnings ratio

48. ABC Inc. is preparing to report its net income for the past year. An increase in which of the following will cause a decrease in the reported net income?

    I. Tax rate
    II. Cash dividend
    III. Allowance for bad debts

    A. I
    B. I and II
    C. I and III
    D. II

49. Using Table 11.1, what is the approximate earnings per share for Time?

    A. $1.00
    B. $1.40
    C. $5.10
    D. $6.36

50. Using Table 11.1, the closing price for Time on the preceding trading day was

    A. 69 3/8
    B. 69 7/8
    C. 70 1/4
    D. 71

Table 11.1

NEW YORK STOCK EXCHANGE COMPOSITE TRANSACTIONS
Tuesday, September 13, 1998

52 Weeks					P-E	Sales				Net
High	Low	Stock	Div	Yld %	Ratio	100s	High	Low	Close	Chg.
91 3/8	57 1/2	Time	1.00	1.4	11	5106	70 5/8	69	69 7/8	-3/8

Use the following choices to answer questions 51 through 55.

    I. Current assets
    II. Current liabilities
    III. Working capital
    IV. Total assets
    V. Total liabilities
    VI. Net worth

51. Which balance sheet items would be affected by a corporation's purchase of a printing press for cash?

    A. I and III
    B. I, III, IV and V
    C. I, V and VI
    D. IV and V

52. Which balance sheet items would be affected when a corporation declares a cash dividend?

    A. I and II
    B. I, II, IV and V
    C. I and VI
    D. II, III, V and VI

53. Which balance sheet items would be affected when a corporation pays a cash dividend?

    A. I and II
    B. I, II, IV and V
    C. I and VI
    D. II, III and VI

54. Which balance sheet items would be affected when the holders of a corporation's convertible bonds convert into common stock?

    A. I and III
    B. I, IV and VI
    C. II, III and V
    D. V and VI

55. Which balance sheet items would be affected when a corporation redeems a bond at par several years before maturity?

    A. I and V
    B. I, III, IV and V
    C. II, III, V and VI
    D. IV and V

Use the following information to answer questions 56 through 60.

XYZ Corporation Financial Statement as of December 31, 1995

Long-term Debt	
10% debentures	
convertible at $25	$10,000,000
Net Worth	
6% preferred stock	$2,000,000
Common stock	
($1 per share par value)	$2,000,000
Paid-in surplus	$18,000,000
Retained earnings	$18,000,000
Depreciation	$2,500,000
Earnings before	
interest and taxes	$4,000,000
Tax bracket	34%
Market price of common stock	18 5/8
Market price of perferred stock	$90

56. What is XYZ Corporation's nondiluted earnings per share?

    A. $.93
    B. $.99
    C. $1.26
    D. $2.00

57. What is XYZ Corporation's return on common shareholder's equity?

    A. 4.89%
    B. 5.21%
    C. 9.30%
    D. 10.52%

58. What is XYZ Corporation's earnings per share on a fully diluted basis?

    A. $.85
    B. $1.05
    C. $1.10
    D. $1.26

59. What is the current rate of return on XYZ's preferred stock?

    A. 3.22%
    B. 6.00%
    C. 6.67%
    D. 7.76%

60. What is the common stock ratio for XYZ Corporation?

    A. 4%
    B. 40%
    C. 72%
    D. 76%

61. How would you determine a company's margin of profit?

    A. Determine the gross profits per share earned during the fiscal year.
    B. Determine earnings in excess of net income.
    C. Calculate the gross profit retained in business.
    D. Calculate the ratio of gross profit to net sales.

Use the following information to answer questions 62 through 64.

Flibinite, Inc. Financial Statement as of December 31, 1995

5.5% convertible (at $20) debentures outstanding	$10,000,000
8% preferred stock outstanding ($100 par)	$5,000,000
500,000 shares common stock outstanding ($10 par)	$5,000,000
Operating income before taxes and interest	$3,000,000
Tax bracket	34%
Current market value of Flibinite preferred	$40
Current market value of Flibinite common	$20

62. What is the earnings per share of Flibinite, Inc.?

    A. $2.21
    B. $2.43
    C. $3.23
    D. $4.90

63. What is the approximate bond interest ratio of Flibinite, Inc.?

    A. 1.5
    B. 3.5
    C. 5.5
    D. 7.5

64. What is the current return on Flibinite, Inc. preferred stock?

    A. 5%
    B. 12%
    C. 18%
    D. 20%

65. A fundamental analyst would be concerned with all of the following EXCEPT

    A. historical earnings trends
    B. inflation rates
    C. capitalization
    D. trading volumes

66. Which of the following are responsibilities of the Federal Reserve Board?

    I.   Acting as an agent for the U.S. Treasury
    II. Regulating credit
    III. Serving as the nation's central bank
    IV. Setting the prime rate

    A. I, II and III only
    B. I and III only
    C. II and IV only
    D. I, II, III and IV

67. The balance sheet equation is

    A. assets + liabilities = net worth
    B. shareholder's equity = assets – liabilities
    C. assets = liabilities – net worth
    D. equity – assets = liabilities

68. The common stock of all of the following corporations would be considered defensive stock EXCEPT

    A. Boeing Corporation, an airplane manufacturer
    B. Super Valu, a retail grocery chain
    C. Commonwealth Edison, a utility
    D. Sintex, a pharmaceutical company

Use the following balance sheet information to answer questions 69 and 70.

CUTTER INDUSTRIES
Balance Sheet

Assets		Liabilities	
$ 100,000	Cash	$ 250,000	Taxes payable
400,000	Accounts receivable	100,000	Accounts payable
500,000	inventories	150,000	Notes payable
1,000,000	Machinery/equipment	1,500,000	Long-term notes
2,000,000	Plants/bldgs/land	1,000,000	Debentures
100,000	Goodwill		
$4,100,000		$3,000,000	
		$1,100,000	Shareholders' equity

69. What is the net working capital of Cutter Industries?

    A. $250,000
    B. $500,000
    C. $600,000
    D. $1,100,000

70. What is the current ratio for Cutter Industries?

    A. 1:1
    B. 1.33:1
    C. 1.36:1
    D. 2:1

71. The open market operations of the FOMC affect all of the following EXCEPT

    A. bank excess reserves
    B. the national debt
    C. the amount of money in circulation
    D. interest rates

72. A technical analyst would be concerned with all of the following trends EXCEPT

    A. a reversal
    B. support levels
    C. PE ratios
    D. changes in the DJIA

73. Statistics from which of the following industries are considered a leading indicator of economic growth?

    A. Natural gas
    B. New housing
    C. Automotive
    D. High technology

74. Which of the following is part of M2 but not of M1?

    A. Currency in circulation
    B. Demand deposits at S&Ls
    C. Money-market mutual funds
    D. Checking accounts at commercial banks

75. Which of the following indexes or averages is based on the prices of only 65 stocks (30 industrials, 20 transportation and 15 utilities)?

    A. S&P Composite Index
    B. *Value Line*
    C. Dow Jones composite average
    D. Wilshire 5,000 Index

76. During the past two quarters, the GNP declined by 3%, unemployment rose by .7% and the Consumer Price Index fell off by 1.3%. This economic condition is called

    A. inflation
    B. depression
    C. stagflation
    D. recession

77. Reducing the allowance for bad debts will

    A. increase current assets
    B. decrease current liabilities
    C. increase long-term debt
    D. decrease fixed assets

78. An increase in inventories is a sign of

    A. increasing consumer demand
    B. deteriorating economic conditions
    C. an expansion of the GNP
    D. increased industrial production

79. For the past seven months, prices have been rising and analysts are predicting continued upward price movement. Under these conditions, FIFO accounting will cause a corporation to have

    A. higher profits
    B. higher costs of sales
    C. lower costs of inventory on the balance sheet
    D. reduced taxes

80. Additional paid-in capital is

    A. also called *earned surplus*
    B. the total of all residual claims that stockholders have against the assets of a corporation
    C. the difference between the total dollar amount of common stock and par value
    D. the total of all earnings since the corporation was formed, less dividends

81. The Fed has just increased the discount rate. Which of the following is MOST likely to be adversely affected by this action?

    A. Cyclical industries
    B. Defensive industries
    C. Heavy industries like steel
    D. Utilities

82. All of the following are characteristics of extraordinary items on financial statements EXCEPT that

    A. they include nonrecurring expenses
    B. they appear on the balance sheet
    C. the SEC requires them to be listed separately
    D. they include unusual sources of income

83. Through its open market operations, the Federal Reserve trades all of the following EXCEPT

    A. Ginnie Maes
    B. Treasury notes
    C. project notes
    D. FICB securities

84. For the past year, disposable personal income has fallen steadily. Which of the following is MOST likely to be affected?

    A. Defense industry
    B. Automotive industry
    C. Tobacco industry
    D. Firm that produces nondurable consumer goods

85. The balance sheet for Winter Enterprises Inc. shows that its assets increased over the last quarter while its equity remained the same. Which of the following statements is(are) true of Winter Enterprises?

    I. Net worth increased.
    II. Total liabilities increased.
    III. Accrued expenses decreased.
    IV. Debt remained the same.

    A. I
    B. I and IV
    C. II
    D. II and III

86. The federal funds rate has fallen to an all-time low. All of the following statements are true EXCEPT that

    A. the Fed is trying to expand credit
    B. the prime rate will rise
    C. banks will have no difficulty borrowing short-term moneys
    D. the money supply will increase

Use the following information to answer questions 87 and 88.

	ABC	DEF	GHI	JKL
Earnings per share	$1.10	$1.25	$1.50	$1.90
Dividends	0	.25	.75	1.33
Retained earnings ratio	100%	80%	50%	30%

87. Which of the following four corporations is MOST likely a growth company?

    A. ABC
    B. DEF
    C. GHI
    D. JKL

88. Which of the following four corporations is MOST likely a utility company?

    A. ABC
    B. DEF
    C. GHI
    D. JKL

89. Disintermediation is MOST likely to occur when

    A. money is tight
    B. interest rates are low
    C. margin requirements are high
    D. the interest ceilings on certificates of deposit have been raised

90. Industrial stocks are the largest component of which of the following indexes and averages?

    I.   Dow Jones Composite
    II. NYSE Composite
    III. Standard & Poor's 500

    A. I only
    B. I and III only
    C. II only
    D. I, II and III

91. For the past two years, Swanson Printing, Inc. has increased its cash dividend payments, although its earnings have not increased during the period. How would this action affect the balance sheet for Swanson Printing?

    A. Reduce shareholder's equity
    B. Increase assets
    C. Decrease liabilities
    D. Increase retained earnings

92. Which of the following conditions might cause the Federal Reserve Board to expand credit?

    I.   Decline in the unemployment rate
    II. Falling bond prices
    III. Drop in the GNP
    IV. Increase in the money supply

    A. I, II and IV only
    B. I and III only
    C. II and III only
    D. I, II, III and IV

93. Growth companies tend to have all of the following characteristics EXCEPT

    A. low PE ratios
    B. low dividend payout ratios
    C. high retained earnings ratios
    D. potential investment return from capital gains rather than income

94. Sadler Corporation declared a stock dividend. Which of the following balance sheet items will be affected?

    I.   Shareholder's equity
    II. Liabilities
    III. Assets
    IV. Retained earnings

    A. I, II and III
    B. I and IV
    C. III and IV
    D. IV

95. To tighten credit during inflationary periods, the Federal Reserve Board can take any of the following actions EXCEPT

    A. raise reserve requirements
    B. change the amount of U.S. government debt held by institutions
    C. sell securities in the open market
    D. lower taxes

96. The common stock ratio is

    A. long-term debt ÷ total capitalization
    B. total liabilities ÷ total assets
    C. total liabilities ÷ total shareholder's equity
    D. (common at par + capital in excess of par + retained earnings) ÷ total capitalization

97. A highly leveraged company has the smallest percentage of its total capitalization in

    A. common stock
    B. preferred stock
    C. earned surplus
    D. long-term debts

Table 11.2   Central Development Corporation — Common $1

Rate – 0.40Q Pd '88 – 1.60 Pd '87 – 1.45

Dividend Amount	Declared	Ex-date	Record Date	Payable
0.20	Dec 2	Dec 12	Dec 18	Jan 1
0.20	Mar 2	Mar 7	Mar 13	Apr 1
0.20	Jun 3	Jun 11	Jun 17	Jul 1
0.35	Sep 1	Sep 10	Sep 16	Oct 1

98. Using Table 11.2, if Central Development Corporation had earnings of $2.00 per share this year, what was its dividend payout ratio on its common stock?

   A. 21.1%
   B. 26.7%
   C. 37.5%
   D. 47.5%

99. The board of Acme Sweatsocks has voted to pay a $.32 dividend to holders of its common stock. These dividends will be paid from

   A. net income
   B. retained earnings
   C. debt service
   D. new stock issues

100. The total assets of CCC Corporation amount to $780,000. $260,000 represents current assets. Its total liabilities are $370,000, of which $200,000 is considered long-term or other liabilities. What is the working capital for CCC Corporation?

   A. $60,000
   B. $90,000
   C. $110,000
   D. $410,000

101. The total assets of CCC Corporation amount to $780,000. $260,000 represents current assets. Its total liabilities are $370,000, of which $200,000 is considered long-term or other liabilities. What is the shareholder's equity of CCC Corporation?

   A. $170,000
   B. $410,000
   C. $980,000
   D. $1.15 million

102. A corporation has a net income after taxes of $5.2 million. There are 4 million shares of common stock outstanding. The earnings per share is

   A. $.80
   B. $1.30
   C. $1.78
   D. $5.20

◆ Answers & Rationale

1. D. Attempts of the FRB to slow down the economy will decrease the supply of money with a corresponding increase in interest rates. When interest rates go up, the prime rate increases, bond yields go up and bond prices drop. Higher interest rates have a tendency to slow down corporate growth with a resulting slowdown in earnings. Thus, stock prices tend to fall. All of these occur in approximately the sequence listed in the question. (Page 215)

2. B. Disintermediation is the withdrawal of time deposits from banks for investment in other securities. This occurs when market interest rates rise substantially above the legal interest rate limits set for banks by the Federal Reserve Board. (Page 217)

3. B. The production of durable goods depends upon whether the economy is in an expansion or a contraction phase. Pharmaceuticals, utilities and food are necessary all the time. (Page 225)

4. D. Steel, automotive and airline industries are involved in the production of capital goods. Clothing is a necessary item of personal consumption and is not influenced by business cycles (other than luxury items). (Page 225)

5. C. Utilities borrow significantly so that the total capitalization of a utility has a larger amount of long-term debt than would be found in a pharmaceutical, durable goods or automobile concern. As a result, changes in interest rates will significantly affect current income of these highly leveraged companies. (Page 225)

6. C. Industrial production is a coincident indicator. The stock market anticipates the economy. Employment is a lagging indicator because it is not influenced until expansion or contraction periods have begun. (Page 208)

7. A. The stock market anticipates the economy and is a leading indicator. (Page 208)

8. B. Constant dollars are mathematically adjusted to remove the effects of inflation, so that when comparing the GNP of one period to another economic activity, rather than inflation, is measured. (Page 206)

9. B. When the Federal Open Market Committee purchases T bills in the open market, it pays for the transaction by increasing the reserve accounts of member banks, the net effect of which will increase the total money supply and signal a period of relatively easier credit conditions. Easier credit means interest rates will decline and the price for existing bonds will rise. (Page 215)

10. C. When the rate of inflation slows, and it is expected to remain stable in the foreseeable future, the coupons on new issue bonds will decline to offer declining yields. The price of outstanding bonds will rise to adjust to the lower yields on bonds of comparable quality. (Page 217)

11. B. By adjusting GNP by inflation, one is able to measure economic activity with less distortion. After adjustment, the GNP will be set in constant dollars. (Page 206)

12. C. Both the S&P 500 and housing permits are leading indicators. The measure of hours worked is a coincident indicator as it reflects levels of employment during the current period of time. Loans outstanding would be the lagging indicator. (Page 208)

13. C. In order to compare GNP from one year to another, and thus compare the amount of real economic activity by comparison, constant dollars must be used to eliminate distortions caused by inflation. (Page 206)

14. B. When the rate of inflation is declining, the coupon rate of new issue bonds will be less and yields will decline. The price of outstanding bonds will rise to adjust their yield. (Page 217)

15. **C.** The FOMC is one of the most influential committees in the Federal Reserve System. Its decisions affect money supplies, interest rates and the speed at which dollars turn over (money velocity). The foreign exchange rate is set in the interbank market.   (Page 215)

16. **C.** The Federal Reserve Board has several tools at its disposal that could be used to change the money supply, including bank reserve requirements, open market operations (trading government securities) and the discount rate. (Page 214)

17. **C.** Congress sets fiscal policy, while the FRB sets monetary policy.   (Page 212)

18. **B.** The purpose of the FOMC purchase is to increase the attractiveness (market price) of T bills. Because the price will be driven up by an increased market demand and a decreased supply, yields should decrease.   (Page 215)

19. **B.** Economists consider expansion (recovery) as the beginning of the business cycle, followed by the peak (prosperity), contraction (recession or deflation) and the trough.
(Page 205)

20. **A.** Economists consider expansion (recovery) as the beginning of the business cycle, followed by the peak (prosperity), contraction (recession or deflation) and the trough.
(Page 205)

21. **C.** Professor Arthur Laffer has been a proponent of supply-side economics since the 1970s; he believes that tax cuts for businesses and the wealthy would help the economy as a whole.
(Page 211)

22. **B.** John Maynard Keynes was the first demand-side economist; he believed that by increasing the income available for spending and saving a government could increase demand and improve the country's economic well-being.   (Page 209)

23. **B.** Keynesians theorize that government efforts to increase aggregate demand by increasing its own purchases of goods and services will result in the healthiest economy.   (Page 209)

24. **A.** Supply-siders believe that cutting taxes for businesses and the wealthy will result in the healthiest economy.   (Page 211)

25. **B.** Keynesians advocate government intervention in the workings of the economy through increased government spending, which in turn increases aggregate demand.   (Page 210)

26. **C.** Supply-siders advocate government intervention in the workings of the economy through tax cuts for businesses and the wealthy, which in turn provides increased supplies of goods.
(Page 211)

27. **A.** Consumers tend to borrow more after the economy improves and interest rates go down, and pay back loans after the economy contracts and interest rates go up.   (Page 208)

28. **D.** An economic downturn that lasts for more than two consecutive quarters (six months) is known as a *recession*.   (Page 205)

29. **B.** *Stagflation* is the term used to describe the unusual combination of inflation and unemployment (stagnation).   (Page 207)

30. **A.** A general decrease in U.S. interest rates would probably indicate a stable, healthy U.S. economy, and would support the value of the U.S. dollar.   (Page 217)

31. **B.** If the FOMC decides that it is in the economy's interest to lower the inflation rate, it can encourage this to occur by raising the discount rate, which in turn will decrease (tighten) the money supply.   (Page 215)

32. **A.** The average time it takes an unemployed person to find a new job is a lagging indicator. Employment is usually one of the last things

to pick up as the economy enters a period of expansion. Layoffs are one of the last resorts for companies when the economy turns down.　(Page 208)

33.　**A.**　New orders for durable goods is a leading economic indicator.　(Page 208)

34.　**A.**　Slowdowns in deliveries is a leading economic indicator.　(Page 208)

35.　**B.**　Industrial production is a coincident economic indicator.　(Page 208)

36.　**C.**　If the FRB lowers the reserve requirement, total bank deposits will increase because of the multiplier effect. With a lower requirement, the banks will have more money available to lend.　(Page 214)

37.　**A.**　If the FRB raises the reserve requirement, total bank deposits will decrease because of the multiplier effect. With a higher requirement, the banks will have less money available to lend.　(Page 214)

38.　**D.**　The open market transactions of the FOMC have a direct and powerful effect on M1, the largest component of the money supply.　(Page 215)

39.　**D.**　A consolidating market is one that is staying within a narrow price range. When viewed on a graph, the trendline is horizontal and is said to be moving *sideways,* meaning neither up nor down.　(Page 221)

40.　**D.**　Of the indexes and averages listed, the Wilshire 5,000 Index is the broadest measure of the market—it contains 5,000 issues (NYSE, AMEX and OTC securities). The NYSE Composite Index is based on the prices of all the common stocks listed on the exchange. The S&P 500, as the name implies, is based on the prices of 500 stocks—400 industrials, 20 transportation, 40 financial and 40 utility. The index recording the least number of issues is the DJIA—only 30 industrial stocks.　(Page 220)

41.　**A.**　The DJIA, published by Dow Jones & Company, is a price-weighted average of 30 stocks. These stocks represent primarily industrial corporations, but also include AT&T and American Express.　(Page 220)

42.　**A.**　Even though short interest represents the number of people who expect the stock market to take a downward turn, it is considered a bullish indicator by many investors. Each share that has been sold short has to be replaced (covered) at some point. In order to replace the stock shorted, the investor will have to go into the market to buy that stock. When all of those short sellers have to buy back stock they shorted, it puts upward pressure on the price of those stocks.　(Page 224)

43.　**D.**　A market technician (technical analyst) deals primarily with timing of activity and market trends, while a fundamental analyst centers on a particular industry or company within an industry and its relative health and market potential.　(Page 219)

44.　**B.**　A fundamental analyst would look over the health and positioning of a company, but might use technical analysis of timing and price to reinforce a decision to buy.　(Page 225)

45.　**D.**　Odd lots are usually traded by small investors. Some analysts believe small investors are usually wrong.　(Page 223)

46.　**C.**　Charted price trends can be deceptive, so a trend must be confirmed by the Dow Jones industrial and transportation averages.　(Page 223)

47.　**B.**　Credit risk is the danger of default by the issuer. Of the ratios given, the most relevant measure of credit risk is the ratio of total debt to net tangible assets.　(Page 237)

48.　**C.**　Dividends are paid out of retained earnings and have no effect on the net income reported by the company.　(Page 235)

49.　**D.**　Price divided by earnings per share equals PE ratio. From the display price, you see that the closing price of Time was 69 7/8 and the PE ratio was 11. This tells you that the price of 69 7/8 is 11 times the amount of the earnings per share. So, you divide 69 7/8 by 11 to get $6.36, which is the approximate earnings per share.   (Page 240)

50.   C.   The close shown is 69 7/8, down 3/8, which means that the previous day's close was 3/8 higher, or 70 1/4.   (Page 142)

51.   A.   Cash (a current asset) decreases, while fixed (noncurrent) assets such as machinery (e.g., a printing press) increase. This leaves total assets unchanged but reduces current assets. Therefore, working capital (current assets minus current liabilities) also decreases.   (Page 229)

52.   D.   When a cash dividend is first *declared,* current liabilities (a part of total liabilities) immediately increase by the amount of dividends payable. Retained earnings, a component of net worth, decreases. Working capital decreases because current liabilities have increased and current assets remain unchanged.   (Page 229)

53.   B.   When the dividend is actually *paid,* current assets (cash) and current liabilities (dividends payable) both decrease equally. Both total assets and total liabilities decrease as well.   (Page 229)

54.   D.   When bondholders convert to common stock, long-term debt (liabilities) decreases because the debt is converted to equity. Shareholder's equity, part of net worth, increases by the amount of debt converted to equity.   (Page 230)

55.   B.   When bonds are redeemed at par, the corporation pays off its obligation to bondholders thus reducing long-term debt liability. This payment is made in cash and therefore reduces current assets and working capital.   (Page 229)

56.   A.   Nondiluted earnings per share is calculated without taking into account the potential diluted effects of convertible securities present in a corporation's capital structure; it is calculated by dividing the earnings available to common by the number of common shares ousanding.

$ 4,000,000	Earnings before interest and taxes
– 1,000,000	Interest (10% debentures)
$ 3,000,000	Taxable income
– 1,020,000	Taxes (34%)
$ 1,980,000	Net income (after taxes)
– 120,000	Preferred dividend (6% × $2,000,000)
$ 1,860,000	Earnings available to common

Number of common shares outstanding =

$$\frac{\$2,000,000}{\$1.00 \text{ par value per share}} = 2,000,000 \text{ shares}$$

$$\frac{\$1,860,000}{2,000,000} = \$.93 \text{ earnings per share}$$

(Page 241)

57.   A.   Return on equity equals earnings available to common divided by common shareholder's equity. In this case, earnings available to common is $1,860,000.

$ 2,000,000	Common stock (at par)
+ 18,000,000	Paid-in surplus
+ 18,000,000	Retained earnings
$ 38,000,000	Common shareholder's equity

$$\frac{\$1,860,000}{\$38,000,000} = 4.89\% \text{ return on equity}$$

(Page 239)

58.   B.   In order to calculate earnings per share on a fully diluted basis, pretend that all convertible security holders converted to common stock at the beginning of the year. Determine earnings available to common by omitting the interest expense on any convertible debt, and omitting the preferred dividend on any convertible preferred. The preferred stock in this particular question is not convertible.

$ 4,000,000	Earnings before interest and taxes
– 0	Interest
$ 4,000,000	Taxable income
– 1,360,000	Taxes (34%)
$ 2,640,000	Net income (after taxes)
– 120,000	Preferred dividend
$ 2,520,000	Earnings available to common

Now determine the number of common shares that would be outstanding assuming all convertible security holders have converted to common. $10,000,000 debentures convertible at $25 equals 400,000 shares ($10,000,000 ÷ 25).

$$
\begin{array}{rl}
400,000 & \text{Additional shares} \\
+\ 2,000,000 & \text{Shares outstanding} \\
\hline
2,400,000 & \text{Total}
\end{array}
$$

$$\frac{\$\,2,520,000}{2,400,000} = \$1.05 \text{ fully diluted EPS}$$

Although it is relatively unusual for fully diluted earnings per share to be greater than nondiluted earnings per share, it is not impossible. Do not assume that fully diluted EPS is always lower.

(Page 241)

59.   **C.**   Current rate of return, also known as current yield on common or preferred stock, is calculated as dividends per year divided by current market price. The par value per share of the preferred stock is not given in the question so assume it is $100 per share.

6% dividend rate × $100 par value = $6 per share

Current market price is $90.

$$\frac{\$6}{\$90} = 6.67\%$$

(Page 25)

60.   **D.**   The common stock ratio is defined as common shareholder's equity divided by total capitalization.
   Common shareholders' equity was determined to be $38,000,000 (common stock at par plus paid-in surplus plus retained earnings). Total capitalization is:

$$
\begin{array}{rl}
\$\ 38,000,000 & \text{Common shareholder's equity} \\
+\ 2,000,000 & \text{Preferred stock} \\
+\ 10,000,000 & \text{Long-term debt} \\
\hline
\$\ 50,000,000 & \text{Total capitalization}
\end{array}
$$

$$\frac{\$38,000,000}{\$50,000,000} = 76\% \text{ common stock ratio}$$

(Page 237)

61.   **D.**   The margin of profit for a company is a measure of the company's gross profit in comparison with net sales. To calculate margin of profit,

subtract cost of goods sold (COGS) from net sales to obtain the ratio known as gross margin, or margin of profit.

(Page 239)

62.   **B.**   Earnings per share (EPS) is calculated as follows:

$$
\begin{array}{rl}
\$\ 3,000,000 & \text{Operating income} \\
-\ 550,000 & \text{Interest} \\
\hline
\$\ 2,450,000 & \text{Pretax income} \\
-\ 833,000 & \text{Taxes (34\%)} \\
\hline
\$\ 1,617,000 & \text{Aftertax income} \\
-\ 400,000 & \text{Preferred dividend} \\
\hline
\$\ 1,217,000 & \text{Income to common shares} \\
\div\ 500,000 & \text{Common shares} \\
\hline
\$\quad 2.43 & \text{Earnings per share}
\end{array}
$$

(Page 240)

63.   **C.** $3,000,000 operating income divided by $550,000 interest equals 5.45 coverage.

(Page 242)

64.   **D.** $8 preferred dividend divided by $40 preferred market value equals 20% yield (return).

(Page 241)

65.   **D.**   A fundamental analyst is concerned with the fundamental qualities of an issuer. This would include information such as the economic climate, inflation rate, how the industry is performing, the historical earnings trends for the company, how it is capitalized, and its product lines, management and balance sheet ratios. A technical analyst would be concerned with trading volumes or primary market trends.

(Page 225)

66.   **A.**   The Fed is the nation's independent monetary authority and central bank. It acts as the fiscal agent for the Treasury and attempts to maintain monetary stability and regulate credit. The prime rate is set by commercial banks, not by the Federal Reserve.

(Page 214)

67.   **B.**   On a balance sheet, assets always equal total liabilities plus shareholder's equity (or net worth). Another way of saying the same thing is: assets − liabilities = shareholder's equity.

(Page 227)

68.   **A.**   Defensive stocks tend not to be volatile. Firms that produce nondurable consumer goods (tobacco, food, drugs, energy) are more immune to the business cycles than other industries and are sometimes called *defensive* industries. This term has nothing to do with the defense industry that supplies the Pentagon with goods and services.
(Page 225)

69.   **B.**   Working capital equals current assets minus current liabilities. The total current assets are $1,000,000 (cash + accounts receivable + inventories). Total current liabilities are $500,000 (notes payable + taxes payable + accounts payable). Therefore, working capital is $500,000.
(Page 230)

70.   **D.**   The current ratio equals:

$$\frac{\text{Current assets}}{\text{Current liabilities}} = \frac{\$1,000,000}{\$500,000} = 2 \text{ to } 1$$
(Page 238)

71.   **B.**   When the Fed buys and sells securities on the open market, it is attempting to expand or contract the amount of money in circulation. When the Fed buys, bank excess reserves go up; when the Fed sells, bank excess reserves go down. This, in turn, affects the money supply, credit and, therefore, interest rates. The national debt is affected only when the government issues and redeems T bills, not when it is trading them in the market.
(Page 215)

72.   **C.**   Technical analysts are more interested in forecasting market trends and securities prices than in studying individual corporations. Therefore, they are concerned with market prices, trading volumes, changes in the Dow Jones industrial average, reversals, support and resistance levels, advance/decline lines, short interest and many other factors that might help them time a buying or selling decision. Fundamental analysts, on the other hand, concentrate on the intrinsic quality of the stock. Therefore, fundamental analysts are concerned with PE ratios and earnings per share.
(Page 219)

73.   **B.**   A leading indicator is one that predicts future growth trends. The usual indicators involve increases in basic productive processes, which means that more people will be hired and more disposable income will then be available. Such indicators include steel shipments and housing starts.
(Page 208)

74.   **C.**   Money-market funds are part of M2 but not M1. M2 includes everything in M1, plus time deposits and money-market funds.
(Page 213)

75.   **C.**   The most widely quoted and oldest measures of changes in stock prices are the Dow Jones averages. They are also the smallest in terms of the number of stocks included in the averages. The composite Dow Jones has only 65 stocks.
(Page 220)

76.   **D.**   Two consecutive quarters or more of decline is termed a *recession*.
(Page 205)

77.   **A.**   Reducing the allowance for bad debts increases accounts receivable (a current asset). Therefore, this action increases current assets.
(Page 229)

78.   **B.**   Increasing inventories mean that consumer demand is slackening. Thus, disposable income is dropping and economic conditions are deteriorating. Increased consumer demand, a rising GNP and increased industrial production are all positive economic signs.
(Page 208)

79.   **A.**   In a period of rising costs, FIFO (first-in, first-out) will show greater profits than the alternative LIFO (last-in, first-out) method of inventory valuation. Under FIFO, the cheaper-to-produce "older" inventory is depleted first, resulting in lower cost of sales and hence higher profits. Therefore, taxes are probably higher with FIFO. Because the remaining inventory is valued at the latest price paid, in an inflationary economy FIFO results in increasing the cost of inventory carried on the balance sheet. Under LIFO, the more-expensive-to-produce "newer" inventory is depleted first, resulting in higher costs of sales and hence lower profits.
(Page 234)

80.   **C.**   Paid-in capital (often called *paid-in surplus*) is shareholder's equity that has not been

generated through the retained earnings of the corporation. It is the difference between the dollar amount received from the sale of stock and the par value of the stock. Earned surplus is another name for retained earnings, which are defined by answer D. Answer B is the definition of shareholder's equity.   (Page 230)

81. **D.** If the discount rate increases, all other interest rates are likely to follow. Because utilities are typically the most highly leveraged of all industries, an increase in interest rates could substantially increase their debt service cost and thus reduce earnings.   (Page 215)

82. **B.** Extraordinary items are items of income or expense that will not recur year after year. An example might be the sale of land held for expansion or the sale of a part of the business. These items will not occur in the following year because the transaction has already taken place. The SEC requires registered corporations to list these items separately and not commingle them with operating expenses and revenue. These transactions appear on the income statement after operating income and expenses.   (Page 232)

83. **C.** The Federal Open Market Committee (FOMC) trades U.S. government and agency securities in the secondary market. The FOMC will buy securities to inject reserves into the banks and will sell securities to drain reserves from the banks. This includes securities that are fully backed by the U.S. government, such as Treasury notes and GNMA certificates, and agency securities, such as those issued by the Federal Intermediate Credit Banks (FICBs). The Fed does not conduct open market operations with municipal securities.   (Page 215)

84. **B.** If disposable income is falling, consumers will cut back on purchases. First to be cut are durable goods purchases—automobiles, home appliances, etc. Firms that produce nondurable consumer goods, such as cigarettes, bread and aspirin, are less affected by business cycles and, therefore, are sometimes called *defensive* industries.   (Page 207)

85. **C.** The formula for the balance sheet is: assets = liabilities + net worth. If assets increase while net worth (equity) remains the same, then total liabilities (debt) must increase. Accrued expenses are liabilities.   (Page 227)

86. **B.** The federal funds market involves short-term loans (sometimes overnight) to one bank from another member bank that has excess reserves. If the funds rate is falling, short-term interest rates are low and banks will have no difficulty borrowing required reserves; therefore, the money supply will expand. These conditions could be the result of deliberate actions on the part of the Fed to expand credit. The prime rate, which is the rate that commercial banks charge their best customers, will undoubtedly fall also.   (Page 215)

87. **A.** A growth company will pay out very little in dividends and retain most of its earnings to fund future growth. ABC Corporation has the highest retained earnings ratio and is most likely to be a growth company.   (Page 241)

88. **D.** A utility pays out most of its earnings as dividends and will retain very little savings. Therefore, JKL Corporation, with a low retained earnings ratio, is the most likely to be a utility.   (Page 241)

89. **A.** Disintermediation is the flow of deposits out of banks and savings and loans into alternative, higher paying investments. It occurs when money is tight and interest rates are high because these alternative investments may then offer higher yields than S&Ls and banks can offer. However, when interest rates are low, investors may prefer to keep their money in banks and S&Ls.   (Page 217)

90. **D.** The industrial sector is the largest component of all three indexes. Therefore, the values of the indexes are most likely to be affected by a change in industrial stocks.   (Page 220)

91. **A.** Dividends are paid out of the retained earnings of the corporation. If earnings stay the same but the directors decide to increase dividend payments, the retained earnings must decrease.

This reduces the shareholder's equity (net worth) of the corporation. When cash dividends are declared, the company's liabilities increase until they are paid. Paying dividends reduces the firm's assets and eliminates the liability for the dividends.
(Page 241)

92. **C.** If economic conditions are deteriorating, the Fed might loosen the money supply to stimulate credit. A decline in the GNP indicates that the economy is deteriorating. Falling bond prices means that interest rates are rising; therefore, the Fed may have to expand credit. A decline in the unemployment rate, on the other hand, is a positive sign of improving economic conditions. If the money supply is already increased, the Fed may have to tighten, not loosen, credit.   (Page 216)

93. **A.** Growth companies have high PE ratios, low dividend payout ratios and high retained earnings ratios. Growth company market prices are bid up by investors anticipating that fast growth will increase the PE ratio. Such firms retain most earnings (high retained earnings ratios) to fund future growth. Investors select growth companies for growth (capital gain potential), not for investment income.   (Page 241)

94. **D.** Stock dividends are a distribution of additional shares to the shareholders in proportion to their existing holdings. When a stock dividend is declared, retained earnings are reduced because the dividend is paid out of retained earnings. At the same time, common at par and capital in excess of par are increased by the same amount. Thus, net worth does not change, nor do current assets or liabilities because no money is paid out.
(Page 235)

95. **D.** To curb inflation, the Fed can sell securities in the open market (thus changing the amount of U.S. government debt held by institutions). It can also raise the reserve requirements, the discount rate or the margin requirements. The Fed has no control over taxes, which are changed by Congress.   (Page 216)

96. **D.** This is the common stock ratio. Total capitalization is total long-term capital (total long-

term liabilities plus shareholder's equity). Answer A is the bond ratio (also known as the *debt ratio*). Answer B is the debt to asset ratio. Answer C is the debt to equity ratio.   (Page 237)

97. **A.** The total capitalization of a company consists of its long-term capital. This includes long-term debt plus net worth: capital stock (common and preferred), paid-in capital (also called paid-in surplus) and earned surplus (or retained earnings). By definition, a highly leveraged company has the smallest portion of its capitalization in common stock. Utility companies tend to be highly leveraged.   (Page 237)

98. **D.** The dividends payout ratio is: annual dividends paid divided by earnings per share, or $.95 divided by $2.00, which equals .475 (or 47.5%).   (Page 241)

99. **B.** Cash dividends are typically paid from retained earnings; stock dividends from treasury stock.   (Page 235)

100. **B.** Current liabilities equals total liabilities minus long-term and other liabilities.

$ 370,000	Total liabilities
– 200,000	Long-term liabilities
$ 170,000	Current liabilities

Working capital equals current assets minus current liabilities.

$ 260,000	Current assets
– 170,000	Current liabilities
$ 90,000	Working capital

(Page 230)

101. **B.** Total assets equals total liabilities plus shareholder's equity.

$780,000 = $370,000 + Shareholder's equity

Shareholder's equity = $410,000   (Page 230)

102. **B.** Earnings per share equals net income (less preferred dividends) divided by number of common shares outstanding. Thus,

$$EPS = \frac{\$5.2 \text{ million}}{4 \text{ million}} = \$1.30$$

(Page 240)

12 Investment Recommendations and Taxation

1. Which of the following taxes are known as *progressive taxes*?

   I. Sales
   II. Gasoline
   III. Income
   IV. Gift
   V. Estate

   A. I and II only
   B. II and IV only
   C. III, IV and V only
   D. I, II, III, IV and V

2. An investor has effected the following transactions in her account:

   Bought 100 ABC at 40 on June 15, 1995.
   Bought 100 ABC at 32 on November 30, 1995.
   Sold 100 ABC at 35 on December 20, 1995.

   What is the tax consequence of these transactions?

   A. Loss of $100
   B. Gain of $300
   C. Loss of $500
   D. No gain or loss

3. A corporation in a 34% tax bracket reports operating income of $4,000,000 for the year. The firm also received $200,000 in preferred dividends. Assuming no other items of income or expense, what is the company's tax liability?

   A. $1,360,000
   B. $1,370,200
   C. $1,380,400
   D. $1,420,800

4. An investor in a 28% tax bracket has a $5,000 loss after netting all capital gains and losses realized. How much may the investor deduct from income that year?

   A. $0
   B. $2,500
   C. $3,000
   D. $5,000

5. An investor in a 28% tax bracket has a $5,000 loss after netting all capital gains and losses realized. The following year this investor has a $1,000 capital gain. After netting his gains and losses, what will be his tax situation that second year?

   A. He will have a $1,000 gain.
   B. He will have a $1,000 loss to carry over to the next year.
   C. He will offset $1,000 ordinary income this year.
   D. There will be no tax consequences.

6. Lotta purchased 1,000 shares of XYZ at the offering at $10 per share in March 1992. By November 1995, the stock rose to $30. At present, Lotta believes the stock is overvalued and would like to take a profit. However, she also believes that her tax bracket will be lower next year due to new tax legislation. Because she wants to pay minimum tax on maximum profit, you should recommend that she

   A. sell the stock immediately before her tax bracket changes
   B. sell short against the box now (1995) and close the position in 1996
   C. put a sell stop at 29 and cancel the order if the tax bill does not pass
   D. write a covered call that expires in 1996

7. Max Leveridge bought a $100,000 7 3/8% Exxon bond at 94 and paid 60 days' accrued interest on the purchase. What was his cost basis?

   A. $708
   B. $5,000
   C. $94,000
   D. $94,000 plus interest

8. Which of the following groups of taxpayers would be most affected by a regressive tax?

   A. Low income
   B. Middle income
   C. High income
   D. Passive income

9. Which of the following taxes would be considered *regressive*?

   A. Income
   B. Sales
   C. Inheritance
   D. Estate

10. Max Leveridge is calculating his income taxes and goes through the alternative minimum tax calculations as well. He has both numbers, but doesn't know what they mean. You should tell him that

    A. the alternative minimum tax is added to the regular tax
    B. he pays the greater of the regular tax or the alternative tax
    C. the excess of the alternative tax over the regular tax is added to his regular tax
    D. he pays the lesser of the regular tax or the alternative tax

11. Mini Leveridge has not followed your investment advice and now has net capital losses of $10,000 for the year. How much of these losses can she offset against her non-passive income for the year?

    A. $1,500
    B. $3,000
    C. $6,000
    D. $10,000

12. Maye Morrow, retired and in the 15% tax bracket, has a long-term capital gain of $3,000. What percentage of this gain will be paid as tax?

    A. 15%
    B. 20%
    C. 28%
    D. 40%

13. David Stone, in the 28% tax bracket, bought 100 shares of ABC common at 50 and 19 months later sold the shares at 70. What is his maximum tax liability on this investment?

    A. $224
    B. $400
    C. $560
    D. $2,000

14. Your customer bought an original issue discount bond issued by General Electric Credit Corporation. How is the discount on this bond taxed?

    A. As capital gains upon maturity or the sale of debenture
    B. As income upon maturity or the sale of debenture
    C. It is accreted and reported as interest income during the life of the bond
    D. It is tax-exempt

15. A customer owns 10M of 7% U.S. Treasury bonds. She is in the 28% federal tax bracket and the 10% state tax bracket. What is her annual tax liability on these bonds?

    A. $70
    B. $98
    C. $196
    D. $266

16. Your client is following a constant dollar investment plan. The market value of his equity portfolio has increased from $100,000 to $120,000. To maintain his investment plan, he should

    A. transfer $20,000 from his equity portfolio to his bond portfolio
    B. increase his bond portfolio so it will also have a market value of $120,000
    C. continue to invest a fixed dollar amount each month in specific equity securities
    D. continue to invest a fixed dollar amount in both equity and debt securities

17. Johnson Cleaners is in the maximum corporate tax bracket. It will be allowed to exclude from taxation 70% of income earned on investments in

    A. government and agency securities
    B. municipal bonds from the same state the corporation is located in
    C. corporate common and preferred stock
    D. industrial development bonds

18. A client in the highest tax bracket wants to minimize her tax burden. The interest on which of the following securities is exempt from federal, state and local taxes?

    A. City of New York general obligation bonds
    B. GNMA pass-through certificates
    C. Treasury bills
    D. Bonds issued by the Commonwealth of Puerto Rico

19. A married couple who file jointly have a $5,000 long-term capital loss with no offsetting capital gains. Which of the following statements is NOT true of the tax treatment of this loss?

    A. The maximum they can deduct this year is $3,000.
    B. They can carry forward $2,000 to future years.
    C. Capital losses can only be used to offset capital gains.
    D. Capital losses can be deducted dollar-for-dollar.

20. Lucille Jasinski owns AT&T stock and wants to continue holding the security. The stock has fallen from 26 when she bought it on February 2nd to a 52-week low of 20 7/8. She sells the stock on December 1st at the low and repurchases it at the same price on December 15th. What are the tax consequences of this investment?

    A. Lucille has a capital loss.
    B. By repurchasing the investment at the same price, she keeps the same cost basis.
    C. The holding period for the stock was wiped out.
    D. The tax loss is not allowed.

21. If a customer is concerned about interest rate risk, which of the following securities would you NOT recommend?

    A. Treasury bills
    B. Project notes
    C. 10-year corporate bonds
    D. 18-year municipal bonds

22. You have a convertible corporate bond available that has an 8% coupon, is yielding 7.1%, but may be called some time this year. Which feature of this bond would probably be LEAST attractive to your client?

    A. Convertibility
    B. Coupon yield
    C. Current yield
    D. Near-term call

23. To open a new account, the registered representative must obtain information about the client's

    I. financial needs
    II. investment objectives
    III. financial condition

    A. I and II only
    B. I and III only
    C. II and III only
    D. I, II and III

24. Which of the following statements are true about Treasury STRIPS?

    I. They are not subject to reinvestment risk.
    II. They generate taxable interest income to owners each year the STRIPS are held.
    III. Their prices are less sensitive to interest rate changes than prices of coupon bonds with comparable maturities.
    IV. The investor receives only the face value at maturity.

    A. I and II
    B. I, II and IV
    C. II and III
    D. III and IV

25. An investor purchasing a Treasury STRIP could be assured of

    I. a locked-in rate of return
    II. a lump-sum payment of the face amount (which includes interest) at maturity
    III. lower taxes because the returns would be taxed at the lower capital gains rate
    IV. little or no reinvestment risk

    A. I
    B. I, II and III
    C. I, II and IV
    D. I and IV

26. Your clients would like to have $40,000 set aside when their child starts college, but do not want to invest in anything that could endanger their principal. In this situation, you should recommend

    A. zero-coupon bonds or Treasury STRIPS
    B. corporate bonds with a high rate of interest payment
    C. municipal bonds for their long-term tax benefits
    D. Treasury bills

27. Changing any of the following characteristics of the stocks and bonds in an investor's portfolio would probably add diversification to the investor's holdings EXCEPT changes made strictly according to the

    A. geographic location of the issuer
    B. relative prices of the securities
    C. industries in which investment is being made
    D. types of securities

◆ Answers & Rationale

1. C. With a progressive tax, the amount of tax (percentage) increases with an increase in the taxable amount such as income, estates and gifts (taxes are paid by the donor). Gasoline and sales taxes are considered to be regressive taxes because all persons pay the same percentage tax regardless of their wealth. (Page 258)

2. D. The 30-day wash sale rule of the IRS states that the purchase of substantially identical securities within 30 days of a securities transaction at a loss will result in the loss being disallowed for tax purposes. The 30-day time period is considered to be either before or after the sale date. The wash sale rule supersedes the investor's ability to identify the specific securities sold. The purchase of 100 shares of ABC on November 30, 1995, is within 30 days of the sale on December 20, 1995. (Page 263)

3. C. The corporation's $4,000,000 operating income will be taxed at the corporate maximum tax rate of 34%. For tax purposes, corporations can exclude 70% of all dividends received from domestic common and preferred stocks. Thus, 30% of the $200,000 received from preferred dividends will be taxed at the 34% tax rate. $200,000 times 30% is $60,000. The $4,000,000 in income plus $60,000 received in taxable dividends equals $4,060,000. $4,060,000 multiplied by a 34% tax rate equals taxes of $1,380,400. (Page 267)

4. C. The maximum deduction of capital losses in any one year is $3,000. Any remaining losses can be carried forward into the next year. (Page 260)

5. C. The losses carried forward from the previous year are $2,000. These losses are netted against the gain of $1,000 for a net loss of $1,000. That $1,000 loss can be used to offset $1,000 of ordinary income. In other words, the net $1,000 loss is deducted from the investor's income. No further loss remains to carry forward. (Page 260)

6. B. Note that answer A would not produce the minimum tax consequences while answers C and D might not maximize profits. (Page 264)

7. C. Accrued interest is not counted in establishing the cost basis of a bond for tax purposes. (Page 261)

8. A. A regressive tax is one that takes a larger percentage from a person with a low income than it does from a person with a high income. (Page 258)

9. B. All of the other taxes listed are progressive. Income taxes, inheritance taxes and estate taxes all take a larger bite from a person with a high income than from a person with a low income. Sales tax takes a proportionately higher part of the income from a low-income family. (Page 258)

10. C. The excess is added to the regular tax. (Page 266)

11. B. Net capital losses are deductible against earned (nonpassive) income to a maximum of $3,000 per year. The balance of such losses can be carried forward to the next year. (Page 260)

12. A. Both long-term and short-term capital gains are currently taxed at ordinary income rates. Because Maye is in the 15% tax bracket, this percentage is the maximum she will pay on the gain. (Page 260)

13. C. The sale of securities held over 12 months results in a long-term capital gain or loss. The tax break for long-term capital gains was repealed by the Tax Reform Act of 1986. Under current tax law, both long-term and short-term gains are taxed at ordinary tax rates. In this case, the investor bought 100 shares at $50 ($5,000) and sold at $70 ($7,000), resulting in a $2,000 capital gain. 28% times $2,000 equals a $560 tax liability. (Page 260)

14. C. Under IRS rules, owners of original issue discount bonds are required to accrete the discount over the life of the bond. Because this is a corporate bond, the discount is accreted and taxed annually. (Page 264)

15.   **C.** $5,000 times 7% equals $350 annual interest per bond. $350 times 2 equals $700 annual interest, which is taxable only by the federal government. $700 times 28% equals $196 tax liability. (Page 261)

16.   **A.**   In a constant dollar plan, an investor keeps a constant dollar amount of his portfolio in equity securities. If the market value of the equities rises, then the excess is transferred to fixed income securities. If the market value of the equities falls, then the debt is liquidated and the equity position restored to its constant value. This procedure serves to balance an investor's portfolio. (Page 256)

17.   **C.**   Corporate ownership of another company's stock allows the owner to exclude 70% of the dividends from taxation. (Page 267)

18.   **D.**   Bond issues by protectorates of the United States (Guam, Puerto Rico and the Virgin Islands) are triple tax-exempt: federal, state and local. Interest income from municipal bonds is federal tax exempt, but is not state tax exempt unless the bondholder is a resident of the state where the bonds are issued. Interest from Treasury bills and most other government and agency securities is state tax exempt, but is subject to federal taxes. Exceptions are GNMA and FNMA securities, which are taxed on all levels. (Page 259)

19.   **C.**   Capital losses are deducted from ordinary income and so reduce tax liability. The maximum individuals or married couples can deduct is $3,000 annually. If the long-term capital loss exceeds the maximum, the excess losses are carried forward to future years (up to the $3,000 limit) until the loss is exhausted. Under current IRS regulations, $1 of losses results in $1 of deductions. (Page 260)

20.   **D.**   The IRS will not allow the loss. Lucille is in the same position (holding the same security) and, therefore, has not made a true transaction; thus, the IRS will disallow the paper loss. It would have been allowed had Lucille bought it back after 30 days; this is the wash sale rule. Note that the loss will be allowed when the new shares are ultimately sold. (Page 263)

21.   **D.**   Interest rate risk is the danger that interest rates will change over the life of the debt instrument. This risk is greatest for long-term bonds. (Page 251)

22.   **D.**   The near-term call would mean that no matter how attractive the bond's other features, the client may not have very long to enjoy them. (Page 252)

23.   **D.**   Under Rule 405 (the NYSE's *Know Your Customer* Rule), all of this information is considered essential before opening an account. (Page 246)

24.   **B.**   Zero-coupon securities are not subject to reinvestment risk because there are no periodic interest payments to be reinvested. Even though the interest they pay is received by holders only when the securities mature, accretion of the discount is required to be reported as income each year. (Page 251)

25.   **C.**   Even though an investment in a Treasury STRIP does not yield a regular cash flow, paying all of its interest at maturity, the difference between the purchase price and the mature value is still taxed as ordinary income and must be accrued on a yearly basis. (Page 251)

26.   **A.**   Zero-coupon bonds represent the lowest risk coupled with the highest return of all the investments listed. They offer no current income. (Page 248)

27.   **B.**   Diversification of a portfolio is rarely done by price alone. (Page 255)

13 U.S. Government Rules and Regulations

1. Historically, what is the most common method for an investor to acquire *restricted stock*?

   A. Mergers or acquisitions
   B. Private placements
   C. Standby underwritings
   D. Employee profit-sharing plans

2. Under the Securities Act of 1933, an *accredited investor* is defined as one having a(n)

   I. annual income of at least $1,000,000
   II. annual income of at least $200,000
   III. net worth of $200,000
   IV. net worth of $1,000,000

   A. I or III
   B. I or IV
   C. II or III
   D. II or IV

3. Blue-sky laws pertain to all of the following EXCEPT

   A. registration of securities within a state
   B. regulation of securities trading in other states
   C. regulation of securities trading in a state
   D. registration of securities salespersons in a state

4. All of the following are exempt securities EXCEPT

   A. commercial paper
   B. BAs
   C. CDs
   D. ADRs

5. If his firm is in the process of underwriting a stock issue that is currently in registration, a registered representative is allowed to

   A. accept an order
   B. promise a specific number of shares
   C. perform a private transaction for a customer
   D. accept an indication of interest

6. Under the provisions of Rule 144, what is the percentage of outstanding stock allowed to be sold every 90 days?

   A. 1%
   B. 3%
   C. 4%
   D. 5%

7. To which securities market does the Securities Act of 1933 apply?

   A. Primary
   B. Secondary
   C. Third
   D. Fourth

8. All of the following are exempt from registration under the Securities Act of 1933 EXCEPT

   A. small business investment companies
   B. chartered commercial banks
   C. U.S. government issues
   D. utility companies

9. In connection with the sale of a new issue and prior to filing a registration statement for that issue, a registered representative is prohibited from

    I.   soliciting indications of interest for the security
    II. soliciting orders
    III. confirming the sale of the security to a customer

    A. I only
    B. II only
    C. II and III only
    D. I, II and III

10. Which of the following is(are) regulated or mandated by the Securities Exchange Act of 1934?

    I.   Full and fair disclosure on new offerings
    II. Creation of the SEC
    III. Manipulation of the market
    IV. Margin requirements on securities

    A. I
    B. I, II and III
    C. II
    D. II, III and IV

11. All of the following are covered under blue-sky laws EXCEPT the

    I.   registration of nonexempt securities
    II. registration of state-chartered bank issues
    III. registration of government securities
    IV. licensing of registered representatives

    A. I, II and III
    B. I and III
    C. I and IV
    D. II and III

12. A broker-dealer may hold fully paid customer securities under which of the following conditions?

    A. Only if the securities are in a cash account
    B. If requested by the customer in writing
    C. If segregated by the broker-dealer
    D. Under no circumstances

13. A stock offering to a limited number of non-qualified investors, without SEC registration, is a(n)

    A. private placement
    B. Rule 144 offering
    C. intrastate offering
    D. secondary offering

14. Your client wishes to buy securities that are not registered in his state of residence. You can purchase securities for this client's account if the security

    I.   has been traded for at least 12 months
    II. is exempt from registration
    III. is listed on the NYSE
    IV. is listed on the Canadian Stock Exchange

    A. I and II
    B. I, II and IV
    C. II and III
    D. III and IV

15. Which of the following governs an insider selling stock under Rule 144?

    A. Investment Company Act of 1940
    B. Maloney Act
    C. Securities Act of 1933
    D. Securities Exchange Act of 1934

16. A prospectus for a primary public offering of a NASDAQ stock must be sent to customers for how many days after the effective date?

    A. 25
    B. 40
    C. 90
    D. 120

17. Blue-sky laws require the registration of

    I. small business investment companies
    II. real estate investment trusts
    III. registered representatives
    IV. U.S. government securities

    A. I and II
    B. I, II and III
    C. II and III
    D. III and IV

18. In reviewing prospectuses and registration statements, the SEC

    A. guarantees the adequacy of the disclosures made in a prospectus
    B. guarantees the accuracy of the disclosures made in a prospectus
    C. passes on the merits of a particular security covered by the registration statement
    D. does not approve securities registered with it and offered for sale

19. Which of the following is(are) a concern of state securities laws?

    I. Provisions set by the Securities Act of 1933
    II. Adherence to the laws of each state governing the sale of new issues
    III. Revocation of the broker-dealer's registration

    A. I
    B. I and III
    C. II
    D. II and III

20. Which of the following is protected by the Securities Investor Protection Corporation?

    A. Broker-dealer failure
    B. Fraudulent transaction
    C. Issuer default
    D. Market risk

21. ABC Company makes a new offering to accredited investors of stock not registered with the SEC. This type of offering is called a(n)

    A. secondary offering
    B. Rule 144 offering
    C. intrastate offering
    D. private placement

22. The Securities Act of 1933 covers all of the following EXCEPT

    A. due diligence
    B. prospectus requirements
    C. full and fair disclosure
    D. blue-sky laws

23. The extension of credit in customer accounts is governed by Regulation T and covers the

    I. initial margin requirement of 50% for purchases of eligible stock in margin accounts
    II. initial payment requirement of 100% for purchases in a cash account
    III. minimum equity requirement of $2,000 for all margin accounts
    IV. time limit for payment in a cash account of seven business days

    A. I and II
    B. I, II and IV
    C. II, III and IV
    D. III and IV

24. Which of the following statements about blue-sky laws is NOT true?

    A. They attempt to protect the public from fraudulent sale of securities within a particular state.
    B. A state securities division has the power to revoke the license of a broker-dealer and the license of any securities salesperson for violation of its laws.
    C. An issuer that intends to offer securities for sale in several states must comply with the provisions of the Securities Act of 1933 and all securities laws of the appropriate states.
    D. The Securities Act of 1933 sets forth certain standard provisions that must appear in all blue-sky laws.

25. Which of the following provisions govern the offering of restricted shares to the public without filing a Form 144?

    I.   The dollar amount is $1,000,000 or less.
    II. 100,000 shares or less are sold.
    III. 500 shares or less are sold.
    IV. The dollar amount is $10,000 or less.

    A. I and II
    B. I and III
    C. II and IV
    D. III and IV

26. Under the Securities Exchange Act of 1934, insiders include

    I.   the attorney who wrote the offering circular for the company
    II. a bookkeeper in the accounting department of the company
    III. the wife of the president of the company
    IV. a brother of the president of the company

    A. I only
    B. II only
    C. II, III and IV only
    D. I, II, III and IV

Use the following information to answer questions 27 and 28.

On Tuesday, October 3rd, a customer tells you that she wants to sell some Rule 144 stock she holds in ALFAtronics. ALFA has 16,500,000 shares outstanding. Trading volume in ALFA shares for the last few weeks has been as follows:

Week ending:	Shares traded:
Sept. 31	160,000
Sept. 24	170,000
Sept. 17	160,000
Sept. 10	165,000
Sept. 3	170,000
Aug. 27	162,000

27. Assuming all other requirements for Rule 144 are met, what is the maximum number of shares the customer can sell during the next 90 days?

    A. 135,000
    B. 162,000
    C. 165,000
    D. 170,000

28. What would be the maximum permissible sale during the next 90 days if the customer had filed a Form 144 one week ago?

    A. 162,000
    B. 165,000
    C. 166,250
    D. 170,000

29. A Regulation A filing covers

    A. an offering of $1,500,000 or less in 12 months
    B. an offering of letter stock
    C. a private offering
    D. an offering of $1,500,000 or more in 12 months

30. An investor and his father own 20% and 5%, respectively, of the outstanding shares of the same corporation. The father wants to sell the holding. According to Rule 144, the father

    I. must file Form 144 to sell the shares
    II. does not have to file a Form 144 to sell the shares
    III. is considered an *affiliated person*
    IV. is not considered an *affiliated person*

    A. I and III
    B. I and IV
    C. II and III
    D. II and IV

31. If a brokerage firm goes bankrupt, the dollar amount of insurance coverage applicable to a customer's special cash account with a balance of $100,000 is

    A. $0
    B. $100,000
    C. $200,000
    D. $500,000

32. The Securities Act of 1933 exempts all of the following securities EXCEPT

    A. municipal issues
    B. savings and loan issues
    C. real estate investment trusts
    D. U.S. government issues

33. Corporations are required to issue annual reports by the

    A. Investment Company Act of 1940
    B. Trust Indenture Act of 1939
    C. Securities Exchange Act of 1934
    D. Securities Act of 1933

34. The Securities Exchange Act of 1934 covers which of the following?

    I. Trading of government securities
    II. Trading of corporate securities
    III. Issuance of financial reports by corporations
    IV. Issuance of government securities

    A. I, II and III
    B. I, II and IV
    C. I and III
    D. II and IV

35. The federal regulation that prohibits insider trading is the

    A. Securities Act Amendments of 1975
    B. Trust Indenture Act of 1939
    C. Securities Exchange Act of 1934
    D. Securities Act of 1933

36. Most blue-sky laws have provisions for all of the following EXCEPT

    A. revoking a registration or license when a state securities division determines that a broker-dealer or salesperson has violated any part of the blue-sky laws
    B. registering all broker-dealers and their salespeople in each state in which they do business
    C. selling securities issued in other states
    D. comparably compensating salespeople registered in more than one state

37. Under Reg D, all of the following parties would be considered accredited investors EXCEPT a(n)

    A. institutional investor
    B. executive officer of a unit investment trust
    C. individual with $250,000 net worth, or $350,000 in combination with her spouse
    D. private development investment company

38. Investors most commonly acquire restricted stock through

    A. rights offerings
    B. corporate takeovers
    C. private placements
    D. exchange purchases

39. In the event of the bankruptcy of a broker-dealer, the Securities Investor Protection Corporation covers

    A. $100,000 per separate customer
    B. $100,000 per account
    C. $500,000 per separate customer
    D. $500,000 per account

40. The Chinese Wall prohibitions refer to which of the following situations?

    A. Difficulties a U.S. client would encounter in attempting to trade foreign stocks directly instead of using ADRs
    B. Registered rep calling the corporate finance department of his firm to get information about a company it is helping underwrite a new issue of stock
    C. Affirmative action program originally created on Wall Street to expand the brokerage network in California
    D. Refusal of traders on the Tokyo Stock Exchange to recognize Taiwanese securities

◆ Answers & Rationale

1. **B.** A private placement is an exempt transaction under the Securities Act of 1933, which means that the security issued is not registered with the SEC. The transfer of unregistered securities is restricted and it is known as a *restricted security*. Private placements are the most common way in which restricted securities are acquired. Business merger and acquisition activity occasionally result in the issuance of restricted securities. A standby underwriting is used during a rights offering and is a public distribution of a fully registered security. Profit-sharing plans normally are funded with a share of profits, not stock.   (Page 274)

2. **D.** In order to qualify as an accredited investor under Regulation D of the Securities Act of 1933, one must meet one or more of the following: have a net worth of $1,000,000; have an income of $200,000 for each of the past two years with expectations of the same this year; be an institutional investor; or be an insider.   (Page 274)

3. **B.** Blue-sky laws are developed within a state for control of security trading within that state.   (Page 285)

4. **D.** An ADR is an American depositary receipt. It is used to facilitate the trading of foreign securities by U.S. citizens.   (Page 273)

5. **D.** When an issue is in registration (in the cooling-off period) there can be no advertising or sale. The registered representative may, however, distribute preliminary prospectuses and may accept indications of interest from customers. A registered representative may never engage in private securities transactions.   (Page 271)

6. **A.** Rule 144 (sale of restricted or control stock) allows for the sale of 1% of the outstanding shares or the weekly average of the last four weeks' trading volume, whichever is greater, every 90 days.   (Page 275)

7. **A.** The Securities Act of 1933 covers the registration and disclosure requirements regarding new issues. The new issue market is the primary market. The trading markets are covered under the Securities Exchange Act of 1934.   (Page 270)

8. **D.** Utility companies are not exempted from the Securities Act of 1933. Government issues, small business investment companies and small chartered commercial banks are all exempt under the act.   (Page 273)

9. **D.** Before the registration statement is filed, there can be no sale of the issue and no soliciting of orders or indications of interest in the issue. Once the registration statement is filed, the issue is in the 20-day cooling-off period. Again, there can be no sale of the issue, nor can orders be solicited. Now, however, it is permissible to accept indications of interest. Once the registration is effective, all three activities are permitted.
          (Page 270)

10. **D.** The Securities Exchange Act of 1934 set up the SEC and regulates the market. The Securities Act of 1933 requires full and fair disclosure.   (Page 276)

11. **D.** Blue-sky registration laws apply to the licensing of agents (RRs) and registration of securities in each state. States require the registration of nonexempt securities. Securities that are exempt, including government issues and state-chartered bank issues, need not be registered in the state.   (Page 285)

12. **C.** Fully paid customer securities may be held by broker-dealers, but must be segregated and put into safekeeping.   (Page 281)

13. **A.** An offering to a limited number of investors (35 nonaccredited investors or less) is a private placement.   (Page 274)

14. **C.** To be sold in a given state, a security must be registered in that state, unless the security is exempt from registration. Most states exempt listed securities from state registration (a *blue chip*

exemption). In addition, exempt securities under the act of 1933 are also usually exempt from state registration.   (Page 285)

15. **C.** The Securities Act of 1933 encompasses Rule 144, the sale of restricted (unregistered) or control stock.   (Page 274)

16. **A.** The SEC requires that a prospectus be sent to investors for 25 days after a primary public offering of an exchange- or NASDAQ-listed stock.   (Page 271)

17. **C.** Blue-sky laws require state registration of sales representatives and nonexempt securities. Securities that are exempt from registration under the act of 1933 are generally exempt from registration under blue-sky laws. Because U.S. government securities and small business investment companies are exempt under the act of 1933, they are automatically exempt from registration under the blue-sky laws.   (Page 285)

18. **D.** The SEC requires full disclosure regarding a new issue so that the investor can make an informed decision on the security. It does not, however, guarantee the accuracy or adequacy of the disclosure, nor does it approve or disapprove of an issue.   (Page 270)

19. **D.** Blue-sky laws cover the registration requirements for broker-dealers and new issues in each state. Only choices II and III are true regarding the blue-sky laws. The Securities Act of 1933 is a federal statute and, as such, does not apply to regulations within a state. The 1933 act applies only to interstate issues and trading.   (Page 285)

20. **A.** SIPC protects customer accounts against broker-dealer failure.   (Page 284)

21. **D.** A private placement (which is exempt from registration with the SEC) is an offering of a new issue to an unlimited number of accredited investors and a maximum of 35 nonaccredited investors.   (Page 273)

22. **D.** Blue-sky laws are state laws and are not covered under the federal securities act.   (Page 285)

23. **B.** Reg T sets initial margin at 50% for margin accounts and requires 100% deposit for purchases in cash accounts. Reg T also requires that payment in all accounts be made promptly but no later than seven business days after that trade date. Reg T does not set minimum maintenance margin requirements; these are set by the NYSE and NASD.   (Page 277)

24. **D.** The Securities Act of 1933 is a federal statute and the federal government does not dictate state law. Blue-sky laws protect the public from securities fraud in each state and must be complied with by issuers and broker-dealers.   (Page 285)

25. **D.** Under Rule 144, a Form 144 need not be filed if fewer than 500 shares are sold and the dollar amount is less than $10,000.   (Page 274)

26. **D.** While the act of 1934 defines an insider as an officer, director or 10% stockholder of the company, the courts have broadened the definition to include anyone who has inside information.   (Page 277)

27. **C.** Under Rule 144, the maximum sale every 90 days is the greater of 1% of the outstanding shares or the weekly average of the last four weeks' trading volume. 1% of 16,500,000 is 165,000. The average of the last four weeks is $(160,000 + 170,000 + 160,000 + 165,000) \div 4$, which is 163,750. The greater amount is 165,000 shares.   (Page 275)

28. **C.** The average of the four previous weeks' trading volume now becomes $(170,000 + 160,000 + 165,000 + 170,000) \div 4$, which is 166,250. This is greater than 1% of the outstanding shares, or 165,000.   (Page 275)

29. **A.** A Regulation A filing under the Securities Act of 1933 exempts the security from registration and is limited to offerings of $1,500,000 or less within 12 months.   (Page 273)

30. **A.** Under Rule 144, an *affiliate* is a person who is in a control relationship with the issuer. Because the investor owns more than 10% of the stock, he is a control person under Rule 144 and must sell his holding in compliance with the rule. His father is also considered an affiliate because he is also in a control relationship. Rule 144 includes relatives of control persons and makes a sale of restricted securities by these persons subject to the conditions of the rule (such as filing Form 144).
(Page 274)

31. **B.** Coverage is $500,000 maximum with cash not to exceed $100,000. An individual with $100,000 of securities is covered for $100,000.
(Page 284)

32. **C.** REITs are registered nonexempt securities. U.S. government, municipal and savings and loan issues are exempt.
(Page 273)

33. **C.** The Securities Exchange Act of 1934 mandates that companies file annual reports with the SEC.
(Page 277)

34. **A.** The Securities Exchange Act of 1934 regulates secondary trading or trading markets, while the Securities Act of 1933 regulates the primary, or new issue, market. Trading of corporates and governments would therefore fall under the 1934 act, as does corporate financial reporting. The 1933 act covers the issuance of new securities. Governments are exempt securities under the 1933 act.
(Page 276)

35. **C.** The 1934 act prohibits insider trading.
(Page 277)

36. **D.** The typical blue-sky laws have provisions for revoking the license of a broker-dealer or salesperson. The provisions require the registration of all broker-dealers, salespeople and provisions for the sale of securities issued in other states (they need to be registered in that state). By process of elimination, you can conclude that there are provisions for everything except comparable compensation for salespeople registered in more than one state. The blue-sky laws do not tell a brokerage firm how to compensate people.
(Page 285)

37. **C.** Under Regulation D, all of the parties listed would qualify as accredited investors except for the individual with a net worth of $250,000. An individual must have a net worth exceeding $1,000,000 or an annual income exceeding $200,000.
(Page 274)

38. **C.** Investors most commonly acquire restricted stock either directly or indirectly from issuers in transactions that do not involve public offerings.
(Page 274)

39. **C.** Coverage under SIPC amounts to $500,000 per separate customer, with no more than $100,000 of that amount going to cover cash and cash equivalents.
(Page 285)

40. **B.** The Chinese Wall rules were designed to prevent the sharing of insider information between the corporate finance section of a broker-dealer and the retail sales department. Much of the information obtained when the corporate finance department helps an issuer underwrite a new issue of securities could, if it wasn't public knowledge, be used to affect unfairly the stock price.
(Page 279)

14 Self-regulatory Organizations Rules and Regulations

1. Binding arbitration is required in all the following disputes EXCEPT

   A. broker-dealer against broker-dealer
   B. customer against broker-dealer
   C. broker-dealer against customer
   D. broker-dealer against associated person

2. Which of the following means of settling disputes is attractive to broker-dealers because of its relatively low cost?

   A. Litigation
   B. Coterminous defeasance
   C. Repatriation
   D. Arbitration

3. The NASD's rules on freeriding and withholding govern purchases of hot issues by family members of broker-dealer personnel. Which of the following are considered in determining whether such purchases are a violation?

   I. Number of shares purchased
   II. Suitability of the investment
   III. Buyer's investment history

   A. I and II only
   B. I and III only
   C. II and III only
   D. I, II and III

4. Under NYSE rules, duplicate confirmations must be sent to an account owner's employer (and other special actions taken) when establishing a margin account for which of the following?

   I. Employee of a bank
   II. Employee of another NYSE broker-dealer
   III. Independent insurance agent
   IV. Officer of another NYSE broker-dealer

   A. I and II
   B. I and III
   C. II and IV
   D. III and IV

5. Which of the following must be approved by a supervisory analyst?

   A. Research reports
   B. Market letters
   C. Personal appearances
   D. Television advertising

6. Which of the following individuals would be permitted to purchase 200 shares of a bio-engineering company's $8,000,000 hot issue under certain circumstances?

    I.   Employee of a member firm
    II. Investment advisor for an advisory account
    III. Bank president
    IV. Officer of a member firm

    A. I and II
    B. I and IV
    C. II and III
    D. II, III and IV

7. Of the following statements, which two are correct regarding an NASD Form DK?

    I.   It is sent to the customer.
    II. It is sent to the NASD or NYSE.
    III. It is sent to the contra broker.
    IV. It is used to report an unmatched trade.

    A. I and III
    B. II and III
    C. II and IV
    D. III and IV

8. Under NYSE rules, which of the following communications with the public requires approval of a supervisory analyst?

    A. Market letter
    B. Television interview
    C. Research report
    D. Seminar

9. The president of a local bank opens a margin account with an NYSE member firm. All the following documentation will be required EXCEPT a

    A. new account form
    B. hypothecation agreement
    C. margin agreement
    D. written authorization from the bank's board of directors

10. Under NYSE rules, permission of the employer is required to open a margin account for which of the following persons?

    I.   Bank teller
    II. Independent insurance agent of an insurance company
    III. Bank officer
    IV. Insurance company receptionist

    A. I, II and IV only
    B. I and III only
    C. I and IV only
    D. I, II, III and IV

11. Under NYSE rules, all of the following must be recorded in a log concerning a public lecture or seminar EXCEPT the name(s) of the

    A. speaker
    B. sponsor
    C. persons attending
    D. seminar or lecture

12. Over-the-counter transactions are governed by the NASD 5% markup policy to

    A. limit each customer trade to 5% of the customer's total portfolio value
    B. ensure fair and reasonable customer transactions
    C. set agency commissions at 5% on OTC transactions
    D. set principal markups at 5% on OTC transactions

13. Marginable OTC stocks are determined by which of the following?

    A. FRB
    B. SEC
    C. NASD
    D. MSRB

14. Under the NASD rules for OTC dealers, in an agency transaction commissions are determined by all of the following EXCEPT the

   A. availability of the security
   B. dollar value of the security
   C. costs involved in executing the trade
   D. cost price of the securities held in inventory by the dealer

15. Under the NASD Rules of Fair Practice, freeriding and withholding applies to

   I. debt issued under a prospectus
   II. new equity issues
   III. secondary distributions and Regulation A filings

   A. I only
   B. I and III only
   C. II only
   D. I, II and III

16. The NASD 5% markup policy applies to dealers trading in

   A. shares of a registered secondary offering requiring a prospectus
   B. open-end investment companies
   C. securities trading in the OTC market by a dealer
   D. all of the above

17. Listing requirements that must be met by a corporation for the NYSE include

   I. a national interest in trading the stock
   II. voting by stockholders through the solicitation of proxies
   III. 4,000 stockholders of 100 stocks or more
   IV. 2,000 stockholders of 100 shares or more

   A. I and II
   B. I, II and III
   C. I, II and IV
   D. III and IV

18. Under NYSE rules, the term "discretionary" refers to an

   A. account in which someone has been given power of attorney over another individual's account
   B. account in which the customer has power of attorney over an incompetent individual's account
   C. order that specifies the size of the security, but leaves the choice of time and price up to the account executive
   D. account where the broker has the power to decide which security and whether to buy or sell without customer authorization for those specific trades

19. A research report distributed by a member firm must disclose that the member firm

   I. is a market maker in the issue
   II. holds call options on the issue
   III. was a selling group member in an underwriting of the company's stock within the past two years
   IV. was a managing underwriter of the company's stock within the past three years

   A. I and II
   B. I, II and III
   C. I, II and IV
   D. III and IV

20. Under NYSE rules, prior approval of sales literature and research reports must be given by a(n)

   I. chartered financial analyst
   II. supervisory analyst
   III. allied member
   IV. individual member

   A. I
   B. I, III and IV
   C. II and III
   D. II, III or IV

21. All of the following are considered advertising or sales literature EXCEPT

    A. market letters
    B. research reports
    C. prospectuses
    D. telephone directory listings

22. Under NYSE rules, which of the following would be considered the LEAST important in setting up a new account?

    A. Education
    B. Citizenship
    C. Income
    D. Investment objectives

23. Under the NASD Rules of Fair Practice, all of the following are prohibited EXCEPT a

    A. mutual fund sponsor gives a $50 gift to a registered rep
    B. mutual fund sponsor gives a $99 gift to a registered rep
    C. discount from the offering price not stated in the prospectus is given
    D. wholesale override stated in the prospectus is given

24. Records of seminars must be kept by brokerage firms and must include all of the following EXCEPT the

    A. sponsor
    B. name of the individual who gives the seminar
    C. names of the individuals who attend the seminar
    D. nature of the topic

25. Which of the following can result in the delisting of a stock listed on the NYSE?

    I. The company does not mail out proxies.
    II. Public interest in the stock declines considerably.
    III. The company files for bankruptcy.
    IV. The company issues nonvoting common stock.

    A. I and III only
    B. II and IV only
    C. III and IV only
    D. I, II, III and IV

26. The NASD Rules of Fair Practice govern the actions of its members. All of the following are considered violations of the rules EXCEPT

    A. churning accounts
    B. the blanket recommending of low-price speculative stocks
    C. using discretionary authority
    D. guaranteeing the customer against loss

27. The NASD freeriding and withholding policy prohibits (except for specified situations) which of the following from buying a hot issue at the public offering price?

    I. Officer of the underwriters in the syndicate
    II. Employee of the firms in the syndicate offering the new issue
    III. Bank officer with a long-standing relationship with the underwriter
    IV. Finder of the firm being underwritten

    A. I and III only
    B. I and IV only
    C. II, III and IV only
    D. I, II, III and IV

28. A written record of speaking engagements must be kept for

    A. 6 months
    B. 1 year
    C. 3 years
    D. 6 years

29. Under the NASD 5% markup policy, an OTC firm that is a market maker in ABC common stock will consider which of the following to determine a markup to a customer?

I. Cost of services provided by the firm
II. Price of the security
III. Amount of the purchase
IV. Profit or loss to the firm on that specific transaction

A. I, II and III
B. I, III and IV
C. I and IV
D. II and III

30. The NASD 5% markup policy applies to

A. principal OTC trades
B. mutual funds
C. new issues
D. all of the above

31. Under NASD rules, a simultaneous trade in the OTC market is

A. permitted and must conform to the NASD 5% markup policy
B. permitted and must conform to the 8 1/2% guideline
C. permitted only when acting as dealer
D. not permitted

32. The NASD adopted the 5% markup policy for OTC transactions in order to

A. limit each customer trade to 5% of the customer's total portfolio value
B. ensure fair and reasonable customer transaction costs
C. set principal markups at 5% on OTC transactions
D. set agency commissions at 5% on OTC transactions

33. All of the following situations require member firms of the NYSE to notify employers of customers EXCEPT when opening a(n)

A. account for an employee of an NYSE firm
B. margin account for a bank teller
C. margin account for an employee of an NYSE firm
D. margin account for the president of an insurance firm

34. Riskless or simultaneous transactions

A. require disclosure of the markup by the firm executing the transactions
B. are illegal transactions under NASD rules
C. do not require application of the NASD 5% markup policy
D. do not require disclosure of the markup by the firm executing the transactions

35. Under NYSE rules, prior to a registered representative taking a second job written permission must be granted by the

A. registered rep's employer
B. NYSE
C. SEC
D. NASD

36. In a proceeds transaction for a customer where the proceeds from the liquidation of one OTC stock are used to purchase another OTC stock, the NASD 5% markup policy applies to

A. each side of the transaction separately
B. the combined profit of both the buy side and the sell side
C. the profit on the buy side only
D. the profit on the sell side only

37. Under the requirements of the NYSE, a bank vice-president who opens a cash account must

    A. have duplicates of confirmations and statements sent to his employer
    B. sign the credit agreement
    C. receive the written consent of his employer
    D. fill out a new account form

38. The Consolidated Tape erroneously reported the execution of 100 shares of ABC at 29 1/2. The brokerage firm confirmed the price to the customer. The firm later finds that the actual price was 29 3/4. What price will the customer pay for the shares?

    A. 29 1/2
    B. 29 5/8, with the difference split between the firm and the customer
    C. 29 3/4
    D. He has the option of canceling the order.

◆ Answers & Rationale

1. **C.** In disputes involving a broker-dealer against a broker-dealer, a customer against a broker-dealer and a broker-dealer against an associated person, all must submit to binding arbitration. In the case of a broker-dealer against a customer, the customer is not compelled to submit to arbitration. He may *elect* to arbitrate, and in signing documentation to that effect the customer is bound to the decision of the Board of Arbitration. (Page 297)

2. **D.** Arbitration is a system for resolving disputes between parties by submitting the disagreement to an impartial panel, consisting of one, three or five people. Arbitration expedites binding decisions involving disputes and avoids costly litigation. The words *coterminous defeasance* are nonsense. Taken separately, coterminous applies to overlapping debt while defeasance refers to an action taken by a corporation to reduce its debt on its balance sheet. Repatriation also has no bearing on the question. (Page 297)

3. **B.** The Rules of Fair Practice require a member participating in the distribution of a new issue to make a bona fide public offering at the public offering price. Failure to do so is considered freeriding and withholding, which usually occurs when hot issues are being distributed. It is a violation to withhold any securities for the member's account, or sell securities to an employee of a member or to his immediate family. There are exceptions. A member may sell securities to a nonsupported person in the immediate family of an employee of a member if: (1) the securities were sold to such persons in accordance with their normal investment practice with the member; (2) the amount withheld and sold to such accounts is insubstantial and not disproportionate in amount as compared to sales to the public. *Suitability of the investment* has nothing to do with freeriding and withholding. (Page 293)

4. **C.** According to NYSE and MSRB rules, when an employee of a member firm opens an account with another member broker-dealer, dupli-

cate confirmations must be sent to the employer. An officer of a broker-dealer is considered an employee and needs permission from another officer to open the account. The NASD requires duplicate confirmations only upon the request of the employee's firm. Duplicate confirmations are not required to be sent to bank and insurance employers (choices I and III) when employees open accounts. Prior permission is needed for these people only when opening margin accounts.   (Page 301)

5. **A.** Research reports must be prepared or approved by a supervisory analyst acceptable to the NYSE. Advertisements and market letters must be approved by a member, allied member or authorized delegate prior to their release. Member organizations must also establish specific written supervisory procedures applicable to members, allied members and employees who engage in presenting speeches, writing newspaper or magazine articles or making radio or TV appearances. (Page 300)

6. **C.** The bank president is considered an *officer* of the bank, and so is not included in the prohibitions against selling a hot issue to an *employee* of a bank. Investment advisors may purchase shares of a hot issue if they meet certain restrictions. Employees and officers of member firms may never purchase hot issues of securities. (Page 293)

7. **D.** DK stands for a *Don't Know* notice. This notice is used in interdealer trades if one of the dealers does not receive a confirmation of a trade it did with a contra dealer. The unconfirmed dealer sends a DK notice, which says, in effect, "Don't you know this trade? Our records indicate we did it with you." (Page 297)

8. **C.** The firm would be liable for the accuracy and content of the research report because it would be prepared by the firm and would supposedly have the firm's name and reputation behind it. All the other pieces are prepared on a more individualized, local basis and would not fall under the jurisdiction of the supervisory analyst. (Page 300)

9. **D.** The board of directors would not become involved in the day-to-day operations and activities of its employees.   (Page 301)

10. **C.** Independent agents and officers of the corporation are not considered employees under NYSE rules.   (Page 301)

11. **C.** It would be impractical to record and retain the names of all attendees at each function; but the names of the speaker, the topic and the sponsor must be kept.   (Page 300)

12. **B.** The NASD 5% markup policy states that the over-the-counter markups and commissions to customers must be fair and reasonable. Five percent is a guideline, not a rule.   (Page 294)

13. **A.** The Federal Reserve Board determines whether any security is marginable.   (Page 305)

14. **D.** Under the NASD 5% markup policy, the factors to be taken into consideration when determining a markup commission include: dollar amount of the trade, size of the trade, difficulty, any special costs incurred, etc. The relevant price from which to mark up the security is the current market price—not the actual cost of the shares in inventory.   (Page 294)

15. **D.** Freeriding and withholding rules state that a broker cannot withhold a hot issue from sale to the public and ride the price up itself (take a free ride). The policy applies to all new securities (not only equities) that are hot.   (Page 293)

16. **C.** The NASD 5% markup policy applies to all over-the-counter trades except those where a prospectus is required. Mutual fund sales require delivery of a prospectus, as do registered offerings.   (Page 294)

17. **C.** To be NYSE listed, a corporation must have at least 2,000 stockholders, allow stockholders to vote, have a national interest in trading the stock and meet minimum earnings and asset tests.   (Page 304)

18. **D.** An order is *discretionary* when it is placed by the member firm or its representative for a customer's account, without the customer's express authorization for that order. Additionally, for the order to be considered discretionary, the firm must choose more than merely the price and time of execution (e.g., the size or the security must be chosen by the firm).   (Page 301)

19. **C.** In its research report on a company, the member firm must disclose if it has any financial interest in the company (e.g., owning the company's stock, owning call options, or having acted as an underwriter in an offering of the company's stock). However, the member firm need not disclose that it was a selling group member in an underwriting of the company's stock. (Page 300)

20. **D.** The NYSE rules require that all sales literature and research reports be approved by a member, allied member or supervisory analyst prior to use. A chartered financial analyst is not qualified to approve reports.   (Page 300)

21. **C.** Advertising is any communication to the general public. The other three answers fit this definition. Prospectuses are not considered advertising.   (Page 292)

22. **A.** Answers B, C and D are all required when opening a new account. It is not necessary to ascertain a customer's educational background.   (Page 300)

23. **A.** The NASD rules allow a maximum gift of $50 from a mutual fund sponsor to a registered representative.   (Page 295)

24. **C.** A firm need not keep records of the names of individuals attending a seminar. The requirement is that for a three-year period the firm must keep a record of the date, the nature of the discussion, the location and the name of the individual giving the seminar.   (Page 300)

25. **D.** The NYSE considers many factors when determining whether a company should be delisted. Among the factors are all the choices given.   (Page 304)

26.   **C.**   Use of discretionary authority is not a violation of the Rules of Fair Practice, but abuse of that authority by excessive trading and the misuse of a customer's funds or securities is. Answers A, B and D are clear violations. Recommendations should be based on the customer's financial status and objectives. Low-priced stocks may result in a higher percentage of commission. Brokers that make a practice of selling low-priced stocks are often called *penny brokers*.   (Page 301)

27.   **D.**   The freeriding and withholding policy categorically prohibits NASD member firms, their officers and their employees from buying a hot issue at the public offering price. It also states that the immediate families of employees of member firms, institutional accounts, officers of institutions and finders (persons who introduce a corporation that wants to be underwritten to the underwriter) cannot be given shares of a hot issue at the public offering price unless they buy an *insubstantial* amount and have demonstrated a history of buying new issues.   (Page 293)

28.   **C.**   Generally speaking, most records must be kept for three years.   (Page 300)

29.   **A.**   Any inventory profit or loss is not considered under the NASD 5% markup policy.   (Page 294)

30.   **A.**   The NASD 5% markup policy applies to agency and principal OTC transactions; it does not apply to prospectus offerings (mutual funds and new issues).   (Page 294)

31.   **A.**   In a normal agency trade, the broker goes to a market maker to buy for a customer and would charge a commission. In a riskless or simultaneous trade, the broker is performing the exact same transaction except that it is accounted for in a different manner. The broker-dealer will buy the security into its inventory account and simultaneously sell the same security out of that account to the customer; this procedure is permissible under NASD rules. The markup or commission that is charged must be fair and reasonable under the 5% policy.   (Page 294)

32.   **B.**   The NASD 5% markup policy states that OTC markups and commissions to customers must be fair and reasonable. The 5% policy is a guideline, not a rule.   (Page 294)

33.   **D.**   NYSE rules require that if an NYSE employee or an employee of a member firm opens either a cash or a margin account at another member firm, the employer must be notified in writing. If an employee of an institution wishes to open a margin account, the employer must also be notified in writing. An officer of an institution, however, is not an employee, so no written notification is required for this individual to open a margin account.   (Page 301)

34.   **A.**   Broker-dealers must disclose the markup in a riskless or simultaneous transaction of any security in which they make a market and in all transactions involving NASDAQ NMS securities.   (Page 294)

35.   **A.**   In order to take a second job, a registered representative must get prior written permission from his employer.   (Page 299)

36.   **B.**   In a proceeds transaction (sell one position; take the proceeds and buy another), the NASD 5% markup policy allows a combined markup or commission representing both sides of the trade.   (Page 294)

37.   **D.**   The vice-president of a bank may open a cash account at a brokerage house merely by filling out a new account form. Because he is an officer of an institution, he does not need the consent of his employer, nor is it necessary to send duplicate confirmations or statements to his employer.   (Page 301)

38.   **C.**   If the actual price was 29 3/4, the customer must accept the trade at that price even though the trade was erroneously confirmed at a different price.   (Page 302)

15   Municipal Securities

1. The MSRB rule entitled "Quotations Relating to Municipal Securities" applies to the distribution or publication of which of the following?

   I. Quotations
   II. Requests for offers
   III. Bids or offers
   IV. Indications of bid wanted

   A. I and II only
   B. I, III and IV only
   C. II and IV only
   D. I, II, III and IV

2. According to MSRB rules, a municipal security dealer is prohibited from

   I. responding to quote inquiries with nominal quotations that are clearly indicated as such at the time
   II. providing quotes, while participating in a joint account, that indicate more than one market for the securities that are the subject of the account
   III. selling a quantity of bonds exceeding its participation in a joint account

   A. II only
   B. II and III only
   C. III only
   D. I, II and III

3. A municipal dealer is immediately reoffering 7% bonds it has purchased at par. Which of the following quotes would indicate prices nearest the recent purchase at par and therefore are most likely to be considered bona fide quotes under MSRB rules?

   I. 6.8 less 1/2
   II. 108 1/4
   III. 101 1/8
   IV. 4.95 net

   A. I, II and III
   B. I and III
   C. II, III and IV
   D. II and IV

4. A registered representative is trying to close a large municipal bond sale, but the customer voices concern about price risks due to a potential increase in interest rates. Which of the following actions by the registered rep would be prohibited by MSRB rules?

   I. Selling him a bond put or entering into a repurchase agreement in the transaction
   II. Guaranteeing the customer against any loss
   III. Offering to share in profits or losses resulting from the transaction
   IV. Personally offering to repurchase the bonds at a specified price and date

   A. I and III only
   B. II, III and IV only
   C. II and IV only
   D. I, II, III and IV

5. A municipal securities dealer has made no investment in the account of a nonrelated customer. Under what circumstances is the dealer allowed to share in the profits or losses of the account?

   A. When a written instrument is created and included with the confirmation of all transactions
   B. When the customer requests it in writing
   C. Under no circumstances
   D. Either when a written instrument is created and included with the confirmation of all transactions, or when the customer requests it in writing

6. Under MSRB rules, a control relationship with respect to a municipal security exists in which of the following situations?

   I. Officers or employees of a broker-dealer hold positions of authority over the municipal issuer.
   II. Officials of the municipal issuer hold policymaking positions at the broker-dealer.
   III. The municipal issuer is a public finance client of the broker-dealer.
   IV. An employee of the broker-dealer lives in the issuer's municipality.

   A. I and II only
   B. I, II and III only
   C. II and III only
   D. I, II, III and IV

7. MSRB rules prohibit which of the following during the apprenticeship period of a new registered representative?

   I. Being compensated on a per transaction basis
   II. Conducting municipal securities business with the public
   III. Conducting municipal securities business with other dealers
   IV. Performing any of the duties of a municipal securities representative

   A. I and II
   B. II and III
   C. II and IV
   D. III and IV

8. MSRB rules requiring certain books and records to be kept for specific lengths of time apply to which of the following?

   I. Records of all principal and agency transactions
   II. Written customer complaints
   III. Official statements
   IV. Client account records

   A. I, II and IV only
   B. I and IV only
   C. II and III only
   D. I, II, III and IV

9. When acting as an agent for a customer, the MSRB rules require a reasonable effort on the part of the broker to obtain which two of the following?

   I. A fair price in relation to prevailing market conditions
   II. The best price
   III. A reasonable price in relation to prevailing market conditions
   IV. Quotes from at least three municipal dealers or one broker's broker

   A. I and II
   B. I and III
   C. II and III
   D. II and IV

10. According to MSRB rules, which of the following would be allowed to approve municipal securities advertising?

   I. General securities principal
   II. Municipal securities principal
   III. Financial and operations principal
   IV. The MSRB

   A. I and II
   B. II, III and IV
   C. II and IV
   D. III and IV

11. The MSRB rule on quotations applies to which of the following?

   I. Providing a bid or an offer
   II. Asking for a bid or an offer
   III. Providing nominal quotes

   A. I only
   B. I and III only
   C. III only
   D. I, II and III

12. What would be included on the confirmation of a municipal bond that is offered *when, as and if issued*?

   I. Number of bonds
   II. Settlement date
   III. Yield to maturity
   IV. Total dollar amount

   A. I and III
   B. I and IV
   C. II and III
   D. II and IV

13. Under MSRB rules, which of the following call provisions could affect the yield required to be shown on a customer's municipal bond confirmation?

   A. Sinking fund
   B. Catastrophe
   C. In-whole
   D. Extraordinary

14. Ms. Nelson purchases a municipal bond from your firm. According to MSRB rules, her confirmation must disclose

   I. where your firm acquired the bonds
   II. whether your firm acted as agent or principal
   III. your firm's telephone number
   IV. the price your firm paid for the bonds

   A. I and III
   B. I and IV
   C. II and III
   D. II and IV

15. The requirement that a broker-dealer must disclose control relationships under MSRB rules is

   A. required for new issues only
   B. required in all customer transactions
   C. required for secondary market transactions only
   D. not required

16. Under MSRB rules, which of the following is necessary for a bond to be considered good delivery?

   A. Five days any way
   B. Hand-delivered in five days
   C. Notice sent in five days
   D. Endorsed with legal opinion attached

17. Under MSRB rules, if a municipal securities dealer has a financial advisory relationship with an issuer, which of the following statements is FALSE?

   A. The contract must be in writing.
   B. The contract must set forth the basis of compensation.
   C. The relationship must be disclosed to purchasing customers.
   D. The relationship must be confidential and need not be disclosed.

18. Under MSRB rules, required customer account information includes

    I.   whether the customer is of legal age
    II. the name and address of the customer's employer
    III. the signature of the representative introducing the account
    IV. the customer's tax identification number

    A. I and IV only
    B. II and III only
    C. III and IV only
    D. I, II, III and IV

19. Under MSRB rules, unless otherwise agreed, good delivery of a municipal bond trade between dealers would include all of the following EXCEPT the

    A. properly endorsed bond certificates
    B. legal opinion of the issuer's bond counsel
    C. delivery receipt
    D. check for accrued interest

20. The Securities Acts Amendments of 1975 authorized the MSRB to adopt rules concerning all of the following EXCEPT the

    A. form and content of price quotations
    B. sale of new issues to related portfolios
    C. information to be provided by corporate issuers
    D. records to be maintained by municipal dealers

21. MSRB rules regulate which of the following quotes?

    I.   Asking for a bid
    II. Asking for an asked
    III. Giving a bid
    IV. Giving an asked

    A. I and II only
    B. II and III only
    C. III and IV only
    D. I, II, III and IV

22. In connection with an account opened by the RR of a municipal securities dealer for an employee of another municipal securities dealer, under MSRB rules the municipal dealer opening the account must

    A. send written notice to the employer
    B. send copies of confirmations on all account trades to the employer
    C. follow any written instructions from the employer regarding the account
    D. do all of the above

23. A representative wishes to execute an order for the discretionary account of a customer. The municipal dealer has a control relationship with the issuer of the security to be purchased. Under MSRB rules, the representative

    A. may not execute the order
    B. must have specific authorization from the customer
    C. may wait until the firm terminates the control relationship
    D. may refer the customer to a firm that has no control relationship

24. Broker-dealer B has received a mutilated bond from Broker-dealer A. The bond was accompanied by a bond power and a legal opinion. To be considered good delivery under MSRB rules, authentication is required from the

    A. delivering dealer
    B. principal of the delivering dealer
    C. transfer agent
    D. delivering registered representative

25. Under MSRB rules, a dealer selling a new issue to a customer must provide all of the following EXCEPT

    A. final confirmation of the transaction, showing the amount due
    B. a copy of the official statement
    C. the CUSIP number (if any)
    D. a copy of the agreement among underwriters

26. Special procedures must be used whenever a dealer opens a municipal securities account for

    A. a clerical employee of another dealer
    B. the spouse of a trader employed by another dealer
    C. the minor child of an operations supervisor employed by another dealer
    D. all of the above

27. If a municipal dealer maintains an account for the employee of another municipal dealer and the employing dealer has not sent any written instructions, which of the following must be sent to the employing dealer?

    I. Monthly statement of all transactions in the account
    II. Written notice of a security recommended for account purchase
    III. Duplicate confirmations of all securities purchased for the account

    A. I only
    B. I and III only
    C. III only
    D. I, II and III

28. Under MSRB rules, which of the following is required in order to execute orders in a customer's discretionary account?

    I. The customer must authorize each transaction in writing.
    II. The transactions must be in accordance with the discretionary authorization.
    III. The transaction prices must be fair and equitable.
    IV. The orders must be filled from the best available market.

    A. I
    B. I, II and IV
    C. II and III
    D. II, III and IV

29. Under MSRB rules, a municipal representative opening a new customer account must have all of the following prior to settlement of the first order EXCEPT

    A. signatures of the representative and accepting principal
    B. customer's name and residence or principal business address
    C. tax identification or Social Security number
    D. written customer authorization if it is in a discretionary account

30. Under MSRB rules, which of the following would indicate that a control relationship exists between a municipal dealer and an issuer?

    A. The dealer has an employee involved in distributing the municipal issue.
    B. The principal of the dealer lives within the municipality.
    C. The dealer was an underwriter of the municipality's last issue.
    D. The dealer also acts as a paying agent for the municipality.

31. Which of the following classifies municipal securities based on market factors rather than credit considerations?

    A. White's Tax-Exempt Bond Rating Service
    B. Standard & Poor's Corporation
    C. Moody's Investors Service
    D. Fitch Investors Service, Inc.

32. Which of the following securities would MOST likely be assigned a Moody's MIG rating?

    A. Special tax bonds
    B. Special assessment bonds
    C. Project notes
    D. TANs and BANs

33. Which of the following have an impact on the marketability of municipal bonds?

    I.   Price and date of call provisions
    II.   Quantity and quality of the bonds in the block available
    III. Length of time until the bonds mature
    IV.   Dated date of the bonds in the block

    A. I, II and III only
    B. I and III only
    C. II and IV only
    D. I, II, III and IV

34. In addition to regularly collected property taxes, which of the following are sources of money that a municipality can tap into in order to service bonds backed by that municipality's full faith and credit?

    I.   Delinquent ad valorem tax collections
    II.   Fines and penalties for late tax payments
    III. Tax increases

    A. I only
    B. I and II only
    C. III only
    D. I, II and III

35. Which of the following is considered a double-barreled bond?

    A. Public Housing Authority bond
    B. Bridge authority revenue bond guaranteed by the full faith and credit of a city
    C. Moral obligation bond
    D. Dome stadium bond with provisions for emergency ceiling support

36. How do municipal bond analysts view an increase in tax rates and assessed values of property?

    A. Both are negative events.
    B. Both are positive events.
    C. An increase in tax rates is a positive event.
    D. An increase in assessed values is not considered a negative event.

37. Which of the following are considered sources of debt service for revenue bonds but not for general obligation bonds?

    I.   Ad valorem property taxes
    II.   License taxes paid by businesses
    III. Special liquor and tobacco taxes

    A. I
    B. I and II
    C. II
    D. II and III

38. Which of the following taxes are considered sources of debt service for special tax bonds?

    I.   Business license
    II.   Alcohol
    III. Gasoline
    IV.   Ad valorem

    A. I, II and III only
    B. I and III only
    C. II and IV only
    D. I, II, III and IV

39. The provision in a revenue bond indenture specifying that any bonds issued at a later date with an equal claim on project revenues (parity bonds) can only be issued if debt service coverage is adequate is known as the

    A. additional bonds test
    B. rate covenant
    C. nondiscrimination covenant
    D. MSRB covenant

40. User-charge revenue bonds typically contain a rate covenant requiring the issuer to set rates sufficiently high to meet the requirements for all of the following EXCEPT

    A. optional call provisions
    B. expenses incurred for operation and maintenance of the facility
    C. debt service requirements
    D. renewal and replacement fund payments

41. The City of Cedar Rapids, Iowa, recently issued municipal revenue bonds to finance a new regional business center. During the subsequent operation, revenues from the project are inadvertently commingled with other city revenues and attributed to other revenue sources. What is the impact of this on the business center bonds?

    A. Lower debt service coverage ratio, lower price, and higher yield
    B. Higher debt service coverage ratio, higher price, and lower yield
    C. Lower debt service coverage ratio, lower price, and lower yield
    D. Higher debt service coverage ratio, higher price, and higher yield

42. Who has the final responsibility for debt service on an industrial revenue bond?

    A. A municipal authority established by the issuer
    B. The MSRB
    C. The corporation leasing the facility
    D. The municipal issuer of the bonds

43. The primary obligor defaults on a moral obligation bond. If funds are to be appropriated to make debt service payments, which of the following parties would take action?

    A. Governor
    B. Municipal Securities Regulatory Board
    C. State supreme court
    D. Legislative branch of the state government

44. If bonds are currently trading at a basis of 8%, which of the following bonds would MOST likely be refunded by the issuer?

    A. 6 1/2% bond maturing in 2018, callable at 100
    B. 7 1/2% bond maturing in 2017, callable at 102
    C. 8% bond maturing in 2018, callable at 102
    D. 8 1/2% bond maturing in 2024, callable at 100

45. A callable municipal bond maturing in 30 years is purchased at 102. The bond is callable at par in 15 years. If the bond is called at the first call date, the effective yield earned on the bond is

    A. lower than the yield to maturity
    B. the same as the yield to maturity
    C. higher than the yield to maturity
    D. not determinable

46. A municipal dealer gives a 3% basis quote for three municipal bonds with the same maturity date and coupon rates of 4%, 4.3% and 5%. The 4% bond is selling at $102, while the 5% bond is selling at $105. What is the price of the 4.3% bond?

    A. 102.9
    B. 103.5
    C. 103.9
    D. 104.1

47. An investor in the 28% income tax bracket is considering purchasing either an 8% municipal bond or a 10.5% corporate bond. Which of the following is true about the aftertax yields of the two bonds?

    A. The yields on the two bonds are equivalent.
    B. The corporate yield is higher than the municipal yield.
    C. The municipal yield is higher than the corporate yield.
    D. The yield difference cannot be determined.

48. Two 15-year municipal bonds are issued at par. Both have a 6% coupon rate. One is callable at par in five years and the other is callable at par in ten years. If interest rates decline to 4.8%, which bond will be expected to appreciate the most?

   A. The bond callable in five years will appreciate the most.
   B. The bond callable in ten years will appreciate the most.
   C. Both bonds will appreciate by the same amount.
   D. There is not enough information to determine which will appreciate the most.

49. In municipal bond language, what is a *workable indication*?

   A. Likely bid
   B. Likely offer
   C. Indication that the issuer will probably award the winning bid to your underwriting syndicate
   D. Indication that the managing underwriter will probably award your firm the number of bonds that it has requested

50. Which of the following is(are) a normal activity of a municipal bond dealer?

   I. Underwriting new issues of municipal bonds
   II. Acting as a principal in effecting transactions in the secondary market
   III. Taking short positions in municipal bonds to accommodate a customer or achieve an orderly market

   A. I only
   B. I and II only
   C. II only
   D. I, II and III

51. In the municipal bond business, the function of a broker's broker is to

   I. help sell municipal bonds that a syndicate has been unable to sell
   II. protect the identity of the firm on whose behalf the broker's broker is acting
   III. help prepare bids for an underwriting syndicate
   IV. serve as a wholesaler, offering bonds at a discount from the current bid and offer

   A. I
   B. I and II
   C. III
   D. III and IV

52. You sell James Odegaard a municipal bond that has been advance refunded. It will be called at 102 four years from now. On the confirmation, the yield that must be stated is the yield to

   A. maturity
   B. maturity or yield to call, whichever is lower
   C. maturity or yield to call, whichever is higher
   D. call

53. The City of Mudlickit, Idaho, has issued an 8 1/2% puttable general obligation bond. Which of the following statements are true of this bond?

   I. The issuer's approval is required to exercise the put option.
   II. The issuer's approval is not required to exercise the put option.
   III. The option is more likely to be exercised if interest rates fall.
   IV. The option is more likely to be exercised if interest rates rise.

   A. I and III
   B. I and IV
   C. II and III
   D. II and IV

54. Ms. Sundberg buys a municipal bond from you on Monday, December 15th. This bond is a J & J 15. Which of the following statements is true?

    A. The bond settles on December 16th.
    B. Ms. Sundberg will receive accrued interest on December 15th.
    C. Ms. Sundberg will receive accrued interest on the settlement date.
    D. Ms. Sundberg will pay accrued interest when the trade is settled.

55. When Mr. Lund purchases a new municipal bond, the accrued interest is calculated

    I. from the trade date
    II. from the dated date
    III. to the interest payment date
    IV. up to, but not including, the settlement date

    A. I and III
    B. I and IV
    C. II and III
    D. II and IV

56. If Mr. Lund were to purchase a bond in the secondary market, which of the following would be a factor in calculating the price that he would pay for the bond?

    I. Settlement date
    II. Dated date
    III. Coupon
    IV. Scale

    A. I and III
    B. I and IV
    C. II and III
    D. II and IV

57. Which of the following would insure payment of principal and interest on the outstanding debt of a municipal bond issue if the issuer experiences financial difficulty?

    I. MBIA
    II. FDIC
    III. FRB
    IV. AMBAC

    A. I and II only
    B. I and IV only
    C. II, III and IV only
    D. I, II, III and IV

58. A qualified legal opinion rendered by the issuer's bond counsel may reflect which of the following?

    A. The bonds are not qualified for sale in other states.
    B. The bond counsel is qualified to judge the validity of the issue.
    C. The bond qualifies for an investment-grade credit rating.
    D. The authority to issue bonds for this type of project is in doubt.

59. All of the following should be evaluated when considering the purchase of a municipal revenue bond EXCEPT

    A. the existence of competitive facilities
    B. a project feasibility study
    C. a legal opinion signed by a qualified bond counsel
    D. the municipality's operating budget

60. The manager of ABC Municipal Securities is interested in bidding on some general obligation bond issues that will be available in the coming months. Where would the manager look to find information about these forthcoming issues?

    A. *The Blue List*
    B. Standard & Poor's *Bond Guide*
    C. *The Wall Street Journal*
    D. *The Bond Buyer*

61. Mr. Lilligren is interested in buying a new municipal bond that is about to be issued. Which of the following would be his best source of information for details on that bond?

    A. *The Wall Street Journal*
    B. *The Bond Buyer*
    C. The official statement
    D. *The Blue List*

62. Your manager notifies you that a new municipal bond issue that you have been working on has been oversubscribed. How is the priority for acceptance of orders for this issue determined?

    A. On a first-come, first-served basis
    B. As outlined in the official statement
    C. As outlined in the official notice of sale
    D. As outlined in the agreement among underwriters

63. Who signs the agreement among underwriters for a municipal bond issue?

    A. Managing underwriter and the issuer
    B. Managing underwriter and the trustee
    C. Managing underwriter and the bond counsel
    D. All members of the underwriting syndicate

64. Your firm is interested in submitting a bid on a forthcoming general obligation municipal bond issue. Your firm could obtain the appropriate bid worksheets through a service provided by

    A. *The Blue List*
    B. *The Bond Buyer*
    C. the MSRB
    D. Standard & Poor's

65. Ms. Olson asks you about the creditworthiness of a forthcoming municipal bond issue. What would be the best source of information for you to use in order to give Ms. Olson an opinion?

    A. *The Wall Street Journal*
    B. Legal opinion
    C. Official statement
    D. Official notice of sale

66. Which of the following would be found in the agreement among underwriters for a municipal bond offering?

    I. Legal opinion
    II. Amount of the concession
    III. Appointment of the bond counsel
    IV. Establishment of the takedown

    A. I and III
    B. I and IV
    C. II and III
    D. II and IV

67. Which of the following would a bond counsel review in writing a legal opinion on a forthcoming municipal bond issue?

    I. Validity of the signatures of the representatives of the issuer
    II. Minutes of the meetings between the issuer and the managing underwriter
    III. Agreement among underwriters
    IV. Internal Revenue Code

    A. I and III
    B. I and IV
    C. II and III
    D. II and IV

68. Which of the following are terms that refer to municipal bond underwritings?

    I. Standby
    II. Best efforts
    III. Preliminary prospectus
    IV. Firm commitment

    A. I and III
    B. I and IV
    C. II and III
    D. II and IV

69. In a municipal underwriting, the scale is

    A. the first thing that is determined by the underwriting syndicate in calculating its bid
    B. the yield at which the syndicate plans to reoffer the bonds to the public
    C. both A and B
    D. neither A nor B

70. Your firm is a member of an underwriting syndicate for an issue of municipal bonds. The municipal syndicate release terms letter states that the bonds are being offered net, with a 1/2-point concession and a 2-point additional takedown. If your firm sells $100,000 of these bonds, it will receive a credit of

    A. $500
    B. $2,000
    C. $2,500
    D. $100,000

71. The Village of Codfish has decided to pre-refund a bond issue that still has several years remaining to maturity. What will be the effect of this action on outstanding bonds?

    A. Outstanding bonds should experience an increase in marketability and rating.
    B. Prerefunding will effectively cancel any call protection the bonds had.
    C. Bondholders can petition the company for immediate tender.
    D. Remaining bondholders will experience an increase in current yield.

72. Which of the following securities trade flat?

    I.   Treasury bills
    II. Zero-coupon bonds
    III. Municipal GO bonds
    IV. Defaulted bonds

    A. I and II only
    B. I, II and IV only
    C. IV only
    D. I, II, III and IV

73. Which of the following pay interest monthly?

    A. T bills
    B. Commercial paper
    C. Municipal general obligation bonds
    D. GNMA pass-through certificates

74. Disclosure of control relationships is required in which of the following types of transactions?

    A. All types of transactions
    B. Principal transactions
    C. Agency transactions
    D. Primary distributions

75. As a member of the syndicate selling a new issue of Tallawhosits City Waterworks bonds, Dewey, Cheatham & Howe received a 1/2 point takedown on the bonds. You place 20 of those bonds with a customer at par. What is DCH's profit per bond?

    A. $.50
    B. $5
    C. $10
    D. $50

◆ Answers & Rationale

1. **D.** MSRB Rule G-13 requires municipal brokers and dealers to give bona fide bids and offers for municipal securities, and allows requests for bids (BW—bids wanted) and requests for offers (OW—offers wanted). (Page 334)

2. **A.** Nominal quotes for informational purposes are allowed as long as they are clearly indicated as such at the time they are given. Dealers participating in a joint account (either syndicate or secondary) are not allowed to distribute quotes relating to the securities in the account that indicate more than one market for the same securities. Selling more than your participation is allowed. Joint accounts are undivided as to selling.

(Page 334)

3. **B.** Under MSRB rules, markups that a dealer charges on bonds must be fair and reasonable, with the dealer considering the security's availability, the current market and the fact that it is entitled to a profit on the trade. The MSRB does *not* define specifically what markups are *fair and reasonable*. This question asks you to make a judgment regarding the fairness of markups. Of the quotes given, two represent small markups and two are very large markups. Because the bonds were bought at par, a quote of 101 1/8 is a substantially smaller markup than a quote of 108 1/4. Because the bonds are 7% coupon, a quote of 6.8% less 1/2 (point) is less of a markup than a quote of 4.95% net. The smaller markups are the *fairest* quotes.

(Page 334)

4. **B.** MSRB rules specifically prohibit associated persons of a municipal securities dealer from guaranteeing a customer against loss or promising to repurchase customer securities at a set price for their own account. MSRB rules specifically permit the sale of bona fide put options or repurchase agreements to customers by municipal securities dealers. Sharing in any profits or losses is also prohibited. (Page 336)

5. **C.** MSRB rules state that municipal security dealers and their associated persons may not share in the profits or losses of a customer's account or transaction. (Page 336)

6. **A.** MSRB rules state that a control relationship exists when a broker-dealer controls, is controlled by, or is under common control with the issuer of the security. In choice I the broker-dealer *controls* the issuer. In choice II the issuer controls the broker-dealer. In choice IV the employee does not vote, so no control exists. (Page 353)

7. **A.** MSRB Rule G-3 states that during the 90-day apprentice period, a municipal securities representative may function in a representative capacity provided the person does not conduct business with any member of the public. Also, he may not be compensated for transactions during this time. Securities dealers are not considered to be members of the public. (Page 349)

8. **A.** The MSRB, NASD and NYSE each requires retention of broker-dealer records for specific periods. Offering documents, such as official statements and prospectuses, are issuer documents and not considered broker-dealer records.

(Page 350)

9. **B.** MSRB rules require only that municipal securities dealers effect trades for customers that are fair and reasonable in light of current market conditions. (Page 334)

10. **A.** Either a general securities principal or a municipal securities principal must approve municipal securities advertising prior to the first use. Municipal securities advertising includes any material designed for use by, or disseminated to, the public. This advertising includes items such as reports, market letters and other promotional materials. Financial and operations principals supervise anyone who deals with the receipt or sending of cash or securities whether these are the customer's or the firm's assets. These principals do not have any authority over the sales process; thus, they may not approve municipal securities advertising. The Municipal Securities Rulemaking Board is the self-regulatory organization responsi-

ble for municipal securities. It does not have the responsibility for approving municipal securities advertising. (Page 353)

11. **D.** MSRB Rule G-13 applies to all quotations on municipal securities that are distributed or published. This includes both providing and requesting bids and offers. Dealers will often ask for "bid wanted" in *The Blue List* and will publish both "bid wanted" and "offer wanted" in *Munifacts*. These bids and offers must be bona fide quotations. Nominal quotes are informational only. (Page 334)

12. **A.** On a new municipal bond offering, where the customer receives a *when, as and if issued* confirmation, the final settlement date is not known; therefore, the amount of accrued interest is unknown (because it is payable until settlement). Thus, the dollar amount is unknown (because it includes accrued interest). Also, MSRB rules state that the extended principal amount (meaning total dollar amount for the bonds excluding accrued interest and any other charges) need not be included. Note that all of these items would be included on the final confirmation sent to the customer once the settlement date is announced. (Page 351)

13. **C.** MSRB rules require customer confirmations to disclose the lowest of yield to maturity, yield to premium call or yield to par option. (Par option is a call provision at par.) The rules distinguish between *in-whole* and *in-part* call provisions. Sinking fund calls are *in-part* calls. Only *in-whole* calls are used to calculate a yield to call. Extraordinary optional redemptions (call of the bonds when the property is prepaid) or extraordinary mandatory redemptions (*catastrophe call* when the facility is destroyed by fire) are not used when calculating yield to call. (Page 311)

14. **C.** Customer trade confirmations must make explicit disclosures regarding numerous aspects of each transaction, particularly those related to the terms of the transaction and the parties involved. The broker-dealer must always disclose the capacity in which it acted (i.e., principal or agent). The confirmation must show the name of the person for whom the trade was executed (i.e., the customer).

The name, the address and even the telephone number of the broker-dealer must be shown to enable the customer to contact the firm easily. The settlement date is also required. The broker-dealer is not required to disclose where it acquired the bonds or the price it paid. (Page 352)

15. **B.** MSRB rules require disclosure to clients of any control relationship that exists between the broker-dealer and the issuer. For example, if a broker-dealer owns any part of an industrial firm that is involved in the issuance of industrial revenue or pollution control revenue bonds, the client of the broker-dealer must be informed of that relationship. (Page 353)

16. **D.** MSRB arbitration rules, like the NASD's rules, generally do not cover *procedural* items. The time allowed for delivery would be considered procedural, while the condition of the certificate would not. (Page 172)

17. **D.** Whenever a fiduciary relationship exists, it must be disclosed to clients and certain other parties—especially if there is any communication about the issue with the general public. (Page 331)

18. **D.** All of the information listed is required under MSRB rules. (Page 350)

19. **D.** It would be highly impractical to require each firm continually to draft checks for accrued interest. (Page 172)

20. **C.** The registration of non-exempt securities by their issuers falls under the jurisdiction of the SEC, not the SROs. (Page 285)

21. **D.** All of the combinations of giving and obtaining quotes are regulated by the MSRB. (Page 334)

22. **D.** These procedures were designed to prevent the employee or dealer from using funds it does not own. Such procedures provide a system of checks and balances that help ensure the integrity of client accounts. (Page 153)

23. **B.** Even in a discretionary account, a registered rep may not exercise discretion when a control relationship exists between the issuer and the dealer. (Page 336)

24. **C.** For MSRB purposes, good delivery means an attached and signed bond power, an attached legal opinion and authentication by the transfer agent. (Page 351)

25. **D.** The agreement among underwriters is a private, nonpublic contractual agreement that the underwriters are not required to disclose. (Page 323)

26. **D.** Special procedures must be followed whenever an account is opened for the employee of another broker-dealer. The firm opening the account must give the employing broker-dealer written notice that the account is being opened. Duplicate copies of all confirmations must be sent to the employer. (Page 153)

27. **C.** Unless instructed otherwise, in writing, only duplicate confirmation statements need be sent. (Page 153)

28. **D.** The customer who has given discretionary authority in writing to another individual does not have to give him written consent for each transaction. (Page 157)

29. **C.** For MSRB purposes, a tax identification (or Social Security) number is not necessary prior to opening a new account or entering the first trade. (Page 350)

30. **D.** Acting as a paying agent for a municipality is an example of a control relationship. (Page 353)

31. **A.** White's ratings ranks the yields for 20-year bonds of municipal issuers. A highly secure bond is ranked against a benchmark of 100. If the bond should trade .05% in yield higher than the benchmark bond, it is rated 99. If it trades .10% in yield higher, it is rated 98; .15% higher, 97, etc.

This service uses trading market activity, rather than credit rating, as the basis for ranking issues. Thus, it rates for marketability risk. (Page 344)

32. **D.** Moody's MIG rating applies to short-term municipal notes; it indicates that the security is of investment grade. BANs and TANs are chosen here rather than PNs; PNs are backed by the full faith and credit of the U.S. government and are presumably default free. (Page 344)

33. **A.** The dated date has no effect on marketability; the date is used only to determine the amount of the first interest payment. A close call date or low call premium can make an issue less marketable because the chance of a call is greater. The maturity date can also influence the marketability of an issue, depending on which maturities are currently in demand. In general, close maturities are more marketable than far maturities. The higher the quality, the more liquid and marketable the security. The size of the block relative to the normal trading volume will also affect how readily the block can be acquired or disposed of. (Page 343)

34. **D.** Bonds backed by the full faith and credit of a municipal issuer are serviced from the general revenues of the municipality. Property taxes (ad valorem taxes) are the principal component of general revenues for municipal issuers below the state level. Fines provide additional revenues. (Page 341)

35. **B.** Double-barreled bonds are backed not only by a specified source of revenues, but also by the full faith and credit of a municipal issuer with authority to levy taxes. Double-barreled bonds are sometimes classified in the broader category of general obligation bonds. The additional backing of PHAs is the full faith and credit of the U.S. government. The additional backing of moral obligation bonds are legislative appropriations that are not mandatory. (Page 317)

36. **D.** An increase in the tax rates is potentially a problem because higher taxes can discourage new business investment and result in a flight of existing businesses or citizens that find the taxes

excessive. An increase in assessed valuation of property will increase the real estate tax receipts to the issuer without raising tax rates. The increase of the assessed value is not as burdensome as an increase in tax rates. The higher assessed value recognizes the increased economic value of the property.   (Page 343)

37.   **D.**   General obligation bonds are backed by the full faith and credit (taxing power) of the issuer for payment of principal and interest. Their main source of revenue is ad valorem (real estate) taxes. Revenue bonds are payable only from specified revenue sources: tolls and fees from the operation of airports and bridges; special taxes on luxury items like tobacco and alcohol; rental payments under leaseback arrangements between the issuing authority and the political subdivision; license taxes, or other identified sources.   (Page 343)

38.   **A.**   Special tax bonds are sometimes included in the larger and more general category of revenue bonds. Ad valorem taxes, on the other hand, support general obligation bonds. Bonds payable only from the proceeds of specified income generators, such as gasoline, cigarettes, liquor and business licenses, are special tax bonds.
                                              (Page 317)

39.   **A.**   The *additional bonds test* is an earnings test that must be met under the provisions of a revenue bond indenture before additional bonds having an equal lien on project revenues (parity bonds) can be issued.   (Page 313)

40.   **A.**   Protective covenants of a municipal revenue bond indenture (the agreement between the issuing municipality and the trustee for the benefit of the bondholders) usually contain a rate covenant specifying a minimum margin of safety of revenue coverage. This means that the issuer promises to charge rates that are sufficient to generate revenues from the facility that exceed the amounts required for operation and maintenance, debt service, debt service reserve and repairs (renewal and replacement fund). Any excess revenue coverage provides additional protection to the bondholder.   (Page 313)

41.   **A.**   If revenues from the project were attributed to other sources, the project's revenues would be understated. This would cause the debt service coverage ratio to be lower. The lower coverage ratio would create the appearance of increased risk of default, which would lead to a lower price in the open market. Lower prices equal higher yields.
                                              (Page 344)

42.   **C.**   The issuer of industrial revenue bonds is a municipality or an authority established by a municipality. However, no municipal assets or general revenues are pledged to secure the issue. The net lease payments by the corporate user of the facility are the source of revenue for debt service. Therefore, the ultimate responsibility for the payment of principal and interest on an industrial revenue bond rests with the corporate lessee.
                                              (Page 316)

43.   **D.**   Legislation authorizing the issuance of moral obligation securities usually grants the state legislature the authority to apportion money to support debt service payments on such securities, but does not legally require the legislature to do so.
                                              (Page 317)

44.   **D.**   An issuer will refund an outstanding bond issue when interest rates drop, in order to lower the issuer's interest cost. The bond most likely to be called and refunded is the one with the highest interest rate and lowest call premium. The issuer can retire the higher rate debt without paying excessive call premiums and then refund by selling new lower rate bonds.   (Page 312)

45.   **A.**   If the bond is trading at a premium and is called prior to maturity, the loss of the premium is compressed into a shorter period of time. This reduces the effective yield on the bond. The effective yield if the bond is called is the *yield to call*. Yield to call is calculated as follows:

$$\frac{\text{Annual interest} +/- \dfrac{\text{Gain/loss on call price}}{\text{Number of years to call date}}}{\dfrac{\text{Market price} + \text{Call price}}{2}}$$

                                              (Page 27)

46.   **A.**   Interpolation must be used to find the price of the third bond. We know that the 4% bond has a 102 price and the 5% bond has a 105 price. The difference in price from 4% to 5% is three points. The 4.3% bond is 30% of the way from 4% to 5% yields. 30% of three points is .9 point. Therefore, the price of a 4.3% bond is 102 plus .9, which equals 102.9.   (Page 33)

47.   **C.**   Investors are primarily interested in their return after taxes—in other words, what they really get to keep. To compare the two bonds in a meaningful fashion, you can use the tax-equivalent yield formula.

$$\text{Tax-equivalent yield} = \frac{\text{Tax-exempt yield}}{100\% - \text{Tax bracket}}$$

$$= \frac{8\%}{100 - 28\%} = 11.11\%$$

(Page 339)

48.   **B.**   Call features affect the appreciation of premium bonds. When interest rates decline and the prices of the two bonds increase, the bond with the more call protection (later call date) will be worth more in the market.   (Page 27)

49.   **A.**   A municipal dealer wishing to dispose of a block of bonds will seek a workable indication from another municipal dealer. The workable indication from another municipal dealer is not a firm bid but the price at which the dealer is likely to buy.   (Page 334)

50.   **B.**   Underwriting and acting as a principal in the secondary market and providing quotations on secondary bonds are all typical activities of a municipal bond dealer. Short selling municipal bonds is not illegal but is extremely risky because of the thin market in most municipal issues; therefore, dealers normally do not sell short.
(Page 319)

51.   **B.**   A broker's broker helps sell any bonds the syndicate has left and, as a rule, does not disclose the identity of the firm on whose behalf it is acting. Brokers' brokers do not charge fees for quoting a security. They will sometimes attempt to sell for clients, but may not effect the sale if a buyer cannot be found at an acceptable price.
(Page 336)

52.   **D.**   MSRB rules require that when a call date has been fixed by a prerefunding, the resulting yield to call must be reflected on the confirmation statement. Because of the prerefunding, this bond issue will be called at the call date. There is no uncertainty surrounding this event; therefore, it is appropriate to price the bond to the call date. The old maturity on the bond has no further significance.   (Page 338)

53.   **D.**   A municipal bond issue that has a puttable feature gives the holder of the bond the right to put the bond to the issuer. This feature is included in the indenture or bond resolution and thus does not require the issuer's approval. An investor would take advantage of rising interest rates and put the bond to the issuer. This would give the investor the opportunity to buy a new issue at the current higher rates.   (Page 312)

54.   **D.**   When a customer buys a municipal bond, the customer must pay the accrued interest that has built up between the last interest payment date and the settlement date. In this case, the bonds were bought on December 15th, and therefore, they will settle five business days later on December 22nd. So, on December 22nd, Ms. Sundberg must pay the price of the bond, plus the accrued interest that has built up from July 15th to December 22nd. Remember, when a municipal bond is purchased, the purchaser pays the accrued interest. The purchaser is not reimbursed for that interest until the next interest payment date which, in this case, is January 15th.   (Page 30)

55.   **D.**   On new issue municipal bonds, purchasers must pay accrued interest to the underwriter for interest earned by the underwriter during the period the bonds are held before being reoffered to the public. Interest accrues from the bond's dated date until the settlement date of the purchase by the customer.   (Page 30)

56. **A.** Accrued interest is part of the total dollar amount of a bond transaction. Bond trades occur at a specific price plus accrued interest. In order to calculate accrued interest, you must know the settlement date. The coupon also affects the price—for obvious reasons. The dated date is relevant only with newly issued bonds, and the scale is relevant to the underwriting syndicate when the bonds are first offered to the public. These are not factors in pricing a bond that is trading in the secondary market. (Page 324)

57. **B.** The Municipal Bond Insurance Association (MBIA) and AMBAC Indemnity Corporation (AMBAC) insure municipal bonds' principal and interest. Currently insured issues are AAA rated. The Federal Reserve Board (FRB) sets reserve requirements, establishes the discount rate and controls credit extended in the margining of securities. The Federal Deposit Insurance Corporation (FDIC) protects customer accounts against bank financial failure. (Page 344)

58. **D.** An issuer's bond counsel is concerned with the legality of the issuer's right to issue bonds. The bond counsel makes no judgment concerning the investment quality of the bonds themselves. (Page 314)

59. **D.** Answers A, B and C are all important factors in evaluating a municipal revenue bond. The main characteristic of revenue bonds is that they are payable only from the specific earnings of a revenue-producing enterprise, such as a toll bridge, airport or college dormitory. Such bonds are not payable from general taxes and the full faith and credit of the issuer is not pledged. Therefore, the municipality's operating budget does not apply. (Page 343)

60. **D.** Municipalities publish their official notices of sale soliciting bids from interested parties in *The Bond Buyer*. The notice gives the details of the bonds put up for bid and how to bid on the issue. *The Blue List* contains secondary market municipal bond quotes; the *S&P Bond Guide* gives details of outstanding issues and their ratings. *The Wall Street Journal* offers general background information primarily about issues that have already come to market. (Page 312)

61. **C.** Disclosure on new issue municipal bonds is given in the official statement, which is similar to a prospectus. The official statement details background information on the issuer and gives all pertinent information on the issue. (Page 313)

62. **D.** The priority of filling municipal orders is established by the managing underwriter in the release terms letter sent to the syndicate once the bid is won. This letter is an amendment to the agreement among underwriters. (Page 323)

63. **D.** The agreement among underwriters is signed by all members of the syndicate including the managing underwriter. It is not signed by the issuer, bond counsel or trustee. (Page 323)

64. **B.** Official notices of sale announcing the offering of municipal issues to competitive bidders are published in *The Bond Buyer*, which offers a service to subscribers that essentially summarizes these notices and is called the *New Issue Worksheet and Record Service*. It provides information about new issues put up for bid and worksheets for underwriters to determine yields and prices when bidding on the issues. (Page 319)

65. **C.** The official statement is an offering document disclosing material information on a new issue of municipal securities. It commonly includes information about the purpose of the issue, how securities will be repaid, and the financial, economic and social characteristics of the issuer, and is an appropriate place to review the creditworthiness of an issue. (Page 313)

66. **D.** The agreement among underwriters describes the rights, duties and commitments of the syndicate members with respect to the securities being underwritten. It appoints the syndicate manager to act on behalf of the syndicate, and includes provisions dealing with underwriting compensation (takedown and concession). The legal opinion is a separate document prepared by the bond counsel. And the appointment of the bond counsel is the responsibility of the issuer, prior to offering the bonds. (Page 323)

67. **B.** Because municipal bonds are exempt from registration with the SEC, a bond counsel's opinion is vital to assure investors of the legality of the issue. Bond counsel is retained by the issuer to provide an opinion that the issuer is authorized to issue the securities and that all legal requirements have been met by the issuer, and to comment on the exemption of the interest from federal taxation. Bond counsel typically aids in the preparation of required documents and validates their authenticity, including the signatures on the bonds. Notes or minutes concerning informal proceedings, like meetings between the issuer and the underwriters and the agreement among underwriters, are not the subject of review of bond counsel.   (Page 314)

68. **D.** Negotiated municipal underwritings can be performed on a firm-commitment, best-efforts or all-or-none basis. Standby underwritings are used only for corporate underwritings. *Preliminary prospectus* (or *red herring*) refers to a corporate underwriting. In a municipal underwriting, the issue is described in the official statement.   (Page 324)

69. **C.** The scale (or reoffering scale) is the yield(s) to maturity at which the syndicate will reoffer the bonds to the public. Syndicate participants consider the market for bonds of similar quality in deciding at what yields to market the issue on which they are bidding. Once the reoffering scale has been established, a coupon rate structure is determined.   (Page 324)

70. **C.** A syndicate member receives the bonds net of the total takedown (which consists of the concession plus the additional takedown). There-fore, the bonds are taken by the syndicate net of 2 1/2 points (2.5% × $100,000 = $2,500).   (Page 326)

71. **A.** Prerefunding an issue is accomplished by selling new bonds and dedicating the funds raised to retiring an older bond issue at its first call date. The new bonds normally have a lower coupon than the old bonds, effectively lowering the company's fixed interest costs. The funds raised are typically invested in Treasury issues, ensuring their availability to pay off the older issue at the call date.   (Page 312)

72. **B.** Most bonds, including municipal bonds, trade with accrued interest. There is no accrued interest on T bills, zero-coupon bonds and defaulted bonds; therefore, these are said to trade flat.   (Page 355)

73. **D.** Treasury bills and most commercial paper are sold on a discounted basis and mature for a par amount. The dollar difference between the discounted amount and par is the earned interest. GNMA pass-through certificates pay investors interest and a return of principal on a monthly basis. Municipal bonds pay interest on a semiannual basis.   (Page 70)

74. **A.** MSRB rules state that the nature of any control relationship or conflict of interest be disclosed to the client in writing prior to the transaction. This includes both primary and secondary transactions.   (Page 336)

75. **B.** Because one bond point equals $10, a 1/2-point takedown per bond represents a profit of $5 per $1,000 bond.   (Page 25)

1. What is the breakeven point if you buy 100 ABC at 53 and sell 1 call for 7 1/2?

   _____

2. What is the breakeven point if you buy 100 Big Tractor at 58 1/4 and sell 1 call at 6 1/2?

   _____

Use the following information to answer questions 3 through 7.

You buy 100 Big Tractor at 58 1/4 and sell 1 Big Tractor call exercisable at 55 at the current market price of 7.

3. What is the maximum sale proceeds received when selling the stock at the exercise price?

   _____

4. What are the dollar proceeds from the call?

   _____

5. What are the maximum proceeds?

   _____

6. How much did you pay for the stock?

   _____

7. What is the maximum profit potential?

   _____

Identify the six positions described in questions 8 through 13 by writing one of the following terms in the space provided.

A. Price spread
B. Time spread
C. Diagonal spread
D. Long straddle
E. Short straddle
F. Combination

8. _____ Buy 1 XYZ May 40 call; sell 1 XYZ May 50 call.

9. _____ Buy 1 XYZ May 40 call; buy 1 XYZ May 40 put.

10. _____ Buy 1 XYZ Aug 40 call; sell 1 XYZ Dec 40 call.

11. _____ Buy 1 ABC May 30 call; buy 1 ABC Jul 40 put.

12. _____ Write 1 ABC Jan 30 call; write 1 ABC Jan 40 put.

13. _____ Buy 1 ABC Mar 35 call; write 1 ABC Jun 45 call.

14. Which two of the following are spreads?

 I. Long 1 ABC May 40 call; short 1 ABC May 50 call
 II. Long 1 ABC May 40 call; long 1 ABC May 50 call
 III. Long 1 ABC Aug 40 call; short 1 ABC May 40 call
 IV. Long 1 ABC Aug 40 call; short 1 ABC Aug 50 put

 A. I and II
 B. I and III
 C. II and III
 D. II and IV

15. George Jetson sells an XYZ Mar 35 call. To establish a straddle he would

 A. sell an XYZ Mar 35 call
 B. buy an XYZ Mar 35 put
 C. sell an XYZ Mar 35 put
 D. buy an XYZ Mar 40 call

16. Which of the following positions violate the rules governing position limits? (Assume BVD is a less actively traded stock subject to 3,000 options positions limits.)

 I. Long 2,200 BVD Aug 40 calls; short 1,500 BVD Aug 40 puts
 II. Long 2,200 BVD Aug 40 calls; short 1,500 BVD Jan 40 puts
 III. Long 2,200 BVD Aug 40 calls; short 1,500 BVD Aug 40 calls

 A. I and II only
 B. I and III only
 C. II and III only
 D. I, II and III

17. Which of the following individuals must observe position and exercise limits on trading in concert?

 I. An investment advisor placing exercise orders for his discretionary accounts
 II. Two or more individuals who have an agreement to act together
 III. A registered rep accepting unsolicited orders to exercise options
 IV. An individual dealing with several brokerage firms

 A. I only
 B. I, II and IV only
 C. II and IV only
 D. I, II, III and IV

18. Trading in expiring options series stops on the business day before the expiration date at

 A. 12:00 pm EST
 B. 3:10 pm EST
 C. 4:00 pm EST
 D. 5:00 pm EST

19. Listed options expire at

 A. 3:00 pm EST on the third Friday of the expiration month
 B. 4:30 pm EST on the third Friday of the expiration month
 C. 4:30 pm EST on the Saturday immediately following the third Friday of the expiration month
 D. 11:59 pm EST on the Saturday immediately following the third Friday of the expiration month

20. A firm may assign option exercises by which of the following methods?

 I. FIFO
 II. Random assignation
 III. LIFO

 A. I only
 B. I and II only
 C. II only
 D. I, II and III

21. When an investor exercises a call or a put, how does the OCC assign the exercise to a clearing member firm?

    A. Randomly
    B. On a first-in, first-out basis
    C. By finding out who wrote the option
    D. By any of the above methods

22. Which of the following securities do NOT have loan value in a margin account?

    A. Stocks and bonds listed on national stock exchanges
    B. U.S. Treasury bills
    C. Listed options
    D. Municipal bonds

23. Bank letters of guarantee are used for

    A. covering short naked calls
    B. covering short naked puts
    C. both A and B
    D. neither A nor B

24. Bob Bullock wants to write a put and provides a letter of guarantee from a bank approved by an exchange. Which of the following statements is true?

    A. The put would not be covered.
    B. No margin would be required.
    C. The bank approved by the exchange would deliver the money to the OCC if the put is exercised.
    D. The client must deposit a minimum of $2,000.

25. A client can use which of the following to cover a written call?

    I.   Escrow receipt
    II. Security convertible into the underlying shares
    III. Shares of the underlying stock

    A. I and II only
    B. I and III only
    C. III only
    D. I, II and III

26. When a client purchases a $1,000 listed call option in a margin account, Reg T requires the client to

    A. have $1,000 in the account before the order is entered
    B. deposit $500 by the settlement date
    C. deposit $1,000 by the seventh business day
    D. transfer the amount required to a cash account because options are not marginable

27. Your client purchases a straddle in his margin account. He pays 4 for the call and 6 for the put. What is the margin requirement for the straddle?

    A. $200
    B. $400
    C. $600
    D. $1,000

28. Mary Bullock opens a margin account and purchases 100 shares of CowTec at $48 and 1 CowTec 50 put at 6. Reg T is 50%. How much cash must she deposit?

    A. $1,800
    B. $2,000
    C. $3,000
    D. $5,400

29. Your customer, George Flint, purchases 100 shares of Lighter Inc. at $55 in a margin account and writes a Lighter 50 call at 7. Reg T is 50%. If the call is exercised, what percentage return on investment will the client earn? (Do not annualize or include margin interest.)

    A. 3.64%
    B. 4.17%
    C. 7.27%
    D. 9.76%

30. If Mary Bullock buys one out-of-the-money call and sells one in-the-money call (resulting in a credit spread) with the same expiration date, what is her initial margin requirement?

A. Premium on the buy side in full
B. Difference between the strike prices
C. Difference between the premiums
D. Premium plus 20% of the current market value of the stock

31. Cyclops stock is currently selling at $35 per share. Your client, Ivan Orb, buys 5 Oct 40 calls at 2 and sells 5 Oct 30 calls at 7. What is Ivan's margin requirement?

A. $2,500
B. $3,625
C. $5,000
D. $6,125

32. Cyclops stock is currently selling at $35 per share. Your client, Ivan Orb, buys 5 Oct 40 calls at 2 and sells 5 Oct 30 calls at 7. How much cash must the investor deposit?

A. $2,000
B. $2,500
C. $4,000
D. $5,000

33. Assume that a customer writes a straddle with a strike price of 40, receiving 3 for the put and 2 for the call. The current market value of the stock is 39. What is the margin required?

A. $450
B. $780
C. $980
D. $1,280

34. An investor who has a large option account writes 1 XYZ Apr 35 call and 1 XYZ Apr 40 put. The investor receives 5 for the call and 3 for the put. The stock is trading at 38. How much margin is required?

A. $879
B. $1,070
C. $1,560
D. $2,000

35. An active options trader establishes the following position: long 10 Apr 40 calls at 6, short 10 Apr 50 calls at 2. What is the break-even point?

A. 4
B. 40
C. 44
D. 46

36. An options trader establishes the following position: long 10 Apr 40 calls at 6, short 10 Apr 50 calls at 2. What will be the client's maximum gain and loss?

A. Gain 2, loss 6
B. Gain 4, loss 2
C. Gain 6, loss 4
D. Gain unlimited, loss 6

37. Your client writes a combination that consists of a 45 call and a 50 put. The premiums total $650. Your client will break even when the price of the underlying stock is

I. $43.50
II. $50.50
III. $51.50
IV. $56.50

A. I and III
B. I and IV
C. II and IV
D. IV

38. John Pierce bought 5 ARO Sep 50 calls at 5 and also bought 5 ARO Sep 50 puts at 3. This position is called a

    A. spread
    B. ratio write
    C. straddle
    D. combination

39. A customer is long 100 shares of stock and has written 5 calls against that stock. This option strategy is called a

    A. triple-covered write
    B. reverse spread
    C. ratio (variable) write
    D. combination

40. Your client, Mrs. Solong, has sold her business to Goodbuy, Inc. for $100,000 cash and a large block of Goodbuy's stock. This stock is not restricted. Mrs. Solong has told you that she needs additional cash but does not want to take additional capital gains this year. Which of the following strategies should you recommend to Mrs. Solong?

    A. Sell some of her stock.
    B. Deposit her stock with your firm and write out-of-the-money calls that do not expire until next year.
    C. Deposit her stock in her margin account and borrow against it.
    D. None of the above

41. Which of the following positions subject an investor to unlimited risk?

    I. Short naked call
    II. Short naked put
    III. Long put
    IV. Short sale of stock

    A. I and II only
    B. I, II and IV only
    C. I and IV only
    D. I, II, III and IV

42. A call is in-the-money when the

    A. strike price is above the market price of the underlying stock
    B. strike price is equal to the market price of the underlying stock
    C. strike price is below the market price of the underlying stock
    D. intrinsic value plus the premium is above the market price of the underlying stock

43. Mr. Bullock bought a Jan 30 CowTec call for 4 1/2 and sold a Jan 35 call for 2 1/2. If he is to profit from this position, the spread between the prices of the two options will have to

    A. widen
    B. narrow
    C. remain the same
    D. fluctuate

44. Ms. Shyester has a short position in TwitCo that she has held for almost 11 months. If she bought a call on TwitCo, what effect would this purchase have on the holding period of the stock for tax purposes?

    A. It would eliminate the holding period.
    B. It would freeze the holding period for the interval that she owned the call.
    C. It would automatically reduce the holding period by the number of months remaining until the expiration of the call.
    D. It would have no effect.

45. Mr. Shyester has several accounts with your firm: an individual account, a joint account with his wife and a custodial account for his son. On Tuesday, he instructs you to exercise 3,900 XYZ Oct 30 calls in his own account. On Wednesday, his wife calls and tells you to exercise 3,900 XYZ Oct 30 calls in the couple's joint account. Assume XYZ is a heavily traded security. Which of the following statements is true?

    A. Because these are separate accounts, the couple could not act in concert.
    B. Exercising these calls would violate exercise limits.
    C. More information is needed to determine whether there has been a violation.
    D. No violation has occurred.

46. Which of the following option positions in a heavily traded issue are in violation of the rules governing position limits?

    I.   Long 7,350 MOT Jan 25 calls; short 750 MOT Jan 25 puts
    II. Long 7,350 MOT Jan 25 calls; short 750 MOT Apr 25 puts
    III. Long 7,350 MOT Jan 25 calls; short 750 MOT Jan 25 calls

    A. I and II only
    B. I and III only
    C. II and III only
    D. I, II and III

47. Mr. Schnott is short 100 shares of XYZ at 35. The market price is 35 1/4. He believes there will be a near-term rally. Which of the following strategies would best hedge his position?

    A. Buy an XYZ call with an exercise price of 35.
    B. Buy an XYZ call with an exercise price of 40.
    C. Write an XYZ put with an exercise price of 40.
    D. Write an XYZ call with an exercise price of 40.

48. In September, an investor writes 2 ABC Jan 60 puts at 3. If the investor buys back the 2 puts at 4 1/2, the result for tax purposes is a

    A. $150 capital gain
    B. $150 capital loss
    C. $300 capital gain
    D. $300 capital loss

49. In September, an investor writes 2 ABC Jan 60 puts at 3. If the puts expire in January, what is the tax consequence for the writer?

    A. $600 gain realized in September
    B. $600 loss realized in September
    C. $600 gain realized in January
    D. $600 loss realized in January

50. On January 1st, an investor buys an XYZ Apr 50 call at 4 and an XYZ Apr 50 put at 2 1/2. Both options expire unexercised. What is the result of the call transaction for tax purposes?

51. On January 1st, an investor buys an XYZ Apr 50 call at 4 and an XYZ Apr 50 put at 2 1/2. Both options expire unexercised. What is the result of the put transaction for tax purposes?

52. If a customer buys 1 ABC Nov 70 put and sells 1 ABC Nov 60 put when ABC is selling for 65, this position is a

    A. bull spread
    B. bear spread
    C. combination
    D. straddle

53. Tippecanoe Boats, Inc. issues a news release that your customer believes will greatly affect the market price of its stock, but he is not sure whether the effect will be positive or negative. In this situation, which of the following strategies would be best?

    A. Buy a call
    B. Write a call
    C. Write a straddle
    D. Buy a straddle

54. All of the following are credit spreads EXCEPT

    A. write 1 Nov 35 put; buy 1 Nov 30 put
    B. buy 1 Apr 40 call; write 1 Apr 30 call
    C. buy 1 Jul 50 call; write 1 Jul 60 call
    D. buy 1 Jan 50 put; write 1 Jan 60 put

Identify the spreads described in questions 55 through 61 by writing "bull spread" or "bear spread" below each one.

55. Write 1 Nov 35 put; buy 1 Nov 30 put.

    _____

56. Buy 1 Jan 70 call; write 1 Jan 75 call.

    _____

57. Write 1 Apr 30 call; buy 1 Apr 40 call.

    _____

58. Buy 1 Jul 50 call; write 1 Jul 60 call.

    _____

59. Buy 1 Dec 45 put; write 1 Dec 40 put.

    _____

60. Write 1 Jan 60 put; buy 1 Jan 50 put.

    _____

61. Buy 1 May 25 put; write 1 May 20 put.

    _____

62. In which of the following strategies would the investor want the spread to widen?

    I.   Buy 1 May 30 put; write 1 May 25 put
    II. Write 1 Apr 45 put; buy 1 Apr 55 put
    III. Buy 1 Nov 65 put; write 1 Nov 75 put
    IV. Buy 1 Jan 40 call; write 1 Jan 30 call

    A. I and II
    B. I and IV
    C. II and III
    D. III and IV

63. In an initial transaction, an investor buys 100 shares of stock on a margin account at 38 and sells a call on the same stock for 1 1/2. The member firm will call for a cash deposit of

    A. $1,750
    B. $1,850
    C. $1,900
    D. $2,000

64. An investor buys 300 shares of XYZ and subsequently buys 1 XYZ Jul 50 put. How does this affect the holding period on his stock?

    A. It does not interrupt the holding period on his long stock.
    B. It ends the holding period on 100 shares.
    C. It ends the holding period on 300 shares.
    D. It ends the holding period on the put.

65. In which of the following circumstances would an investor risk an unlimited loss?

    I.   Short 1 XYZ Jul 50 put
    II. Short 100 shares of XYZ stock
    III. Short 1 XYZ Jul 50 uncovered call
    IV. Short 1 XYZ Jul 50 covered call

    A. II only
    B. II and III only
    C. II, III and IV only
    D. I, II, III and IV

66. Which of the following statements regarding straddles is(are) true?

  I.   An investor who wishes to generate income and who does not anticipate that the price of a stock will change will sell a straddle.
  II. An investor who anticipates a substantial advance in the price of a stock will buy a straddle.
  III. An investor who anticipates a substantial decline in the price of a stock will sell a straddle.
  IV. An investor who anticipates substantial fluctuations in the price of a stock will buy a straddle.

  A. I only
  B. I and IV only
  C. II and III only
  D. I, II, III and IV

67. ABC is currently trading at 62. An investor anticipates a substantial decline in the price of the stock and wishes to obtain maximum leverage. He would be MOST likely to

  A. buy an ABC Jul 60 put
  B. buy an ABC Jul 70 put
  C. buy an ABC straddle
  D. sell an ABC straddle

68. An investor buys XYZ stock at 60. He subsequently writes 1 XYZ 60 call at 4 and 1 XYZ 70 put at 5. If XYZ stock is trading at $74 on the expiration date, the investor will realize a profit of

  A. $100
  B. $400
  C. $500
  D. $900

69. If a 50% stock dividend is declared, the owner of 1 XYZ Jul 30 call will now own

  A. two contracts for 100 shares with an exercise price of 20
  B. two contracts for 150 shares with an exercise price of 20
  C. one contract for 150 shares with an exercise price of 20
  D. one contract for 100 shares with an exercise price of 20

70. Which of the following statements regarding the adjustment of a listed option are true?

  I.   Adjustments are made for all distributions except cash dividends.
  II. Cash distributions that are considered to be a return of capital do not cause an adjustment in the terms of the contract.
  III. Stock splits that are an uneven multiple (such as 3-for-2) result in an increase in the number of shares and a decrease in the exercise price.
  IV. Adjustments are always made to the next lowest 1/8 point.

  A. I and III only
  B. I, III and IV only
  C. II and IV only
  D. I, II, III and IV

71. In determining whether a particular type of options trading is suitable for a customer, the member firm should consider the customer's

  I.   understanding of strategies being employed
  II. ability to calculate maximum profit or loss
  III. ability to assume risk
  IV. ability to meet the margin call

  A. II, III and IV only
  B. III only
  C. III and IV only
  D. I, II, III and IV

72. A person who buys a put will lose most of his investment if just before expiration the price of the underlying stock is

   I.   the same as the exercise price
   II. considerably greater than the exercise price
   III. considerably less than the exercise price

   A. I and II
   B. I and III
   C. II
   D. III

73. Compared to selling short, buying a put option

   A. requires a smaller capital commitment
   B. has a lower loss potential
   C. does not require waiting for an uptick in the stock
   D. has all the characteristics listed in A, B and C

74. A customer would incur an unlimited financial risk if he were

   A. long 1 ABC Jan 50 put
   B. short 1 ABC Jan 50 put
   C. short 1 ABC Jan 50 put and short 100 shares of ABC stock
   D. short 1 ABC Jan 50 put and long 100 shares of ABC stock

75. In April, a customer sold short 100 shares of XYZ stock at $50 and simultaneously wrote 1 XYZ Jan 50 put for a premium of $7. At what price will he break even?

   A. $43
   B. $50
   C. $57
   D. $64

76. In April, a customer sold short 100 shares of XYZ stock at $50 and simultaneously wrote 1 XYZ Jan 50 put for a premium of $7. If the January put is exercised when the market value of XYZ is 43 and the stock acquired is used to cover the short stock position, what would be the customer's profit or loss per share?

   A. $0
   B. $7 loss
   C. $7 gain
   D. $14 loss

77. An investor purchases 1,000 shares of ABC stock and sells 1 ABC put and 1 ABC call with the same terms. He subsequently sells the stock. His position now would be which of the following?

   A. Spread
   B. Straddle
   C. Covered writer
   D. Combination

78. If an investor primarily interested in speculation does not expect the price of XYZ stock to change, he would

   A. write an uncovered straddle
   B. write a straddle and buy stock
   C. write a straddle and short the stock
   D. buy a straddle

79. An investor purchased ABC stock at 50. The stock is now 60 and he fears that the price will decline to 55. He should

   A. sell a straddle at 60
   B. buy a straddle at 60
   C. buy a 60 put and write a 60 call
   D. write a 60 put and buy a 60 call

80. An investor is interested in purchasing 1 XYZ Jul 50 call representing 115 shares of stock selling at a premium of 14 1/2. His cost will be

   A. $1,450
   B. $1,667.50
   C. $1,750
   D. $3,550

81. An investor writes 1 XYZ 320 put for 21 3/8. XYZ stock closes at 304 1/2 and he makes a closing transaction at the intrinsic value. The resulting profit or loss is

    A. $155 profit
    B. $155 loss
    C. $587.50 profit
    D. $587.50 loss

82. Your client purchased XYZ stock at 60. The stock is now 70. Your client believes the price will decline to 65. He should

    A. write a 70 call and buy a 70 put
    B. sell a straddle at 70
    C. buy a 70 call and write a 70 put
    D. buy a straddle at 70

83. An investor wants to purchase ABC stock, currently trading at 38. He expects that the price of ABC stock is going to rise slowly in the near future. If he would like to purchase the stock below its current market value, he should

    A. write a call at 35
    B. buy a put and exercise the option
    C. write a put at 35
    D. buy a call and exercise the option

84. Which of the following customer accounts is(are) in violation of the exchange's position limits?

    I. Long 7,500 XYZ Mar calls and long 600 XYZ Jul calls
    II. Long 7,500 XYZ Mar calls and long 600 XYZ Mar puts
    III. Long 7,500 XYZ Mar calls and short 600 XYZ Jul calls
    IV. Long 7,500 XYZ Mar calls and short 600 XYZ Mar puts

    A. I only
    B. I and IV only
    C. II and IV only
    D. I, II, III and IV

85. An investor has written 1 XYZ Apr 60 put. According to exchange definitions, this option would be covered if the investor is also

    A. short 1 XYZ Apr 60 call
    B. long 1 XYZ Apr 50 put
    C. short 100 shares of XYZ stock
    D. long 1 XYZ Apr 70 put

86. In April, a customer purchases 1 ABC Jul 85 call for 5 and purchases 1 ABC Jul 90 put for 8. ABC stock is trading at 87. If ABC stays at 87 and both options are sold for the intrinsic value, the customer would realize a(n)

    A. $500 profit
    B. $800 loss
    C. $1,000 profit
    D. $1,100 profit

87. An investor bought 1 Apr XYZ 40 call for 6 and 1 XYZ Apr 50 put for 8 when XYZ was 45. If the stock goes to 44 and both the call and the put are sold close to expiration (no time value), the result would be a

    A. $100 loss
    B. $100 profit
    C. $400 loss
    D. $400 profit

◆ Answers & Rationale

1. **45 1/2.** Breakeven on the underlying stock is the stock price minus the premium received (53 − 7 1/2 = 45 1/2). (Page 388)

2. **51 3/4.** 58 1/4 − 6 1/2 = 51 3/4 (Page 388)

3. **$5,500.** Remember, the call is exercisable at 55. (Page 358)

4. **$700.** A quote of 7 means $7 times the 100 shares in a standardized contract. (Page 358)

5. **$6,200.** The strike price of 55 plus the premium of 7 times 100 shares. (Page 388)

6. **$5,825.** This is $58.25 per share. (Page 4)

7. **$375.** The stock was purchased at 58 1/4. If the market goes up, the call will be exercised. The stock will be delivered at the exercise price of $55. Also, the premium received will increase the sale proceeds to $62 per share. The net profit, therefore, will be 3 3/4 per share ($62 − 58 1/4). (Page 388)

8. **A.** Price spread. The most common spread is the price spread, in which the two options (one long and one short) have the same expiration date but different exercise prices. (Page 379)

9. **D.** Long straddle. The investor is long a call and a put, both having the same strike price and expiration date. (Page 379)

10. **B.** Time spread, also called a *horizontal* or *calendar* spread. A time spread entails one long and one short option of the same class (put or call) at the same strike price but with different expiration months. (Page 379)

11. **F.** Combination. A combination is similar to a straddle in that the position includes a put and call on the same stock. With a combination, though, the strike prices or expiration dates are different. (Page 380)

12. **F.** Combination. A combination is similar to a straddle in that the position includes a put and call on the same stock. With a combination, though, the strike prices or expiration dates are different. (Page 380)

13. **C.** Diagonal spread. This spread entails one long and one short option of the same class (put or call) at different strike prices and different expiration months. (Page 379)

14. **B.** Choices I and III fit the definition of a call spread because each includes one long and one short option of the same type with different strike prices (I, a price spread) or different expiration dates (III, a time spread). Choice II involves options of the same type, but both are long. Choice IV involves options of different types. (Page 379)

15. **C.** Straddles involve options of different types, but both options must be long or both must be short. They must have the same expiration date and strike price. (Page 379)

16. **A.** The expiration dates and strike prices may be different or the same. However, the total number of puts and calls that may be owned on a less actively traded stock is limited to 3,000. The Options Clearing Corporation (OCC) considers long calls and short puts to be on the same side of the market. (Page 367)

17. **B.** An individual investor, or a group of investors acting in concert, can exercise no more than 8,000 options on a heavily traded security or 3,000 options on a less active stock on the same side of the market within any five consecutive business days. These limits apply to an individual advisor acting for a group of discretionary accounts and to an individual who has accounts with several firms. (Page 368)

18. **C.** Expiring options stop trading at 4:00 pm EST on the business day before the expiration

date. These expiring options may be exercised until 3:30 pm EST on the business day before the expiration date. The last business day before expiration is usually the third Friday of the month. Before April 1984, trading stopped at 3:00 pm EST.   (Page 368)

19. **D.** Options expire on the Saturday immediately following the third Friday of the expiration month at 11:59 pm EST. Options trading stops on Friday, so this expiration time gives member firms all day Saturday to balance their books and correct errors.   (Page 368)

20. **B.** A firm may assign an exercise by either the random or the FIFO method. LIFO is not acceptable.   (Page 368)

21. **A.** Formerly, the OCC assigned puts and calls on a first-in, first-out basis, but this practice has been changed. Now, puts and calls are assigned at random on the business day following receipt. The member firm, in turn, may assign the exercise on a FIFO basis or at random.   (Page 368)

22. **C.** Options have no loan value. Clients must pay for options in full, whether those options are purchased in a cash or margin account.   (Page 180)

23. **C.** Banks issue letters of guarantee for customers who would prefer giving letters to their brokers rather than depositing cash or other equity in margin accounts.   (Page 402)

24. **B.** The put would be covered. No margin would be required because the bank is guaranteeing sufficient cash to purchase the stock if the put is exercised. The client would be buying the shares, not selling them.   (Page 402)

25. **D.** An escrow receipt is certification, issued by an OCC-approved bank, that the covering shares are on deposit and will be delivered upon demand. An approved bank depository reserves shares for the benefit of the OCC in case the call is exercised.   (Page 401)

26. **C.** A client may purchase options on a margin account if full payment is made within seven business days (Reg T).   (Page 401)

27. **D.** Buying a straddle is simply purchasing two options. The margin required is 100% of the purchase prices.   (Page 404)

28. **C.** Ms. Bullock must deposit 50% of the cost of the stock ($2,400) plus 100% of the cost of the option ($600). Because of its limited life, the put does not reduce the margin required.   (Page 403)

29. **D.** Step 1: Compute the actual profit on the transaction.

	Debit	Credit
Cost of stock	$5,500	
Stock sale proceeds		$5,000
Call sale proceeds		700
Net debit/credit	$5,500	$5,700
Net profit/loss		$ 200

Step 2: Determine the investment capital commitment.

Margin requirement on stock ($5,500 × 50)	$2,750
Call sale proceeds	− 700
Net invested capital	$2,050

Step 3: Compute the return on invested capital.

$$\frac{\$200 \text{ net profit}}{\$2,050 \text{ net capital commitment}} = 9.76\% \text{ ROI}$$

(Page 9)

30. **B.** Ms. Bullock has opened a limited risk credit spread. The risk on her position is the difference between the strike prices, which is the margin requirement on the position. Her initial deposit must equal the amount she is at risk minus the net premium received.   (Page 404)

31. **C.** In a limited risk credit spread, the difference in exercise prices is the risk to the spreader. For margin purposes, the short call is uncovered. The initial margin will be the lesser of the regular calculation or the amount at risk. To calculate the margin the regular way, first the investor will have to pay for the calls purchased in full, a $1,000 debit

(5 calls × $200). Next, the margin on the short naked calls is 100% of the option's premium (5 calls × $700 = $3,500) plus 20% of the current market value of the underlying security ($3,500 × 5 options = $17,500; $17,500×20% = $3,500). The total margin requirement figured this way is $8,000 ($1,000 + $3,500 + $3,500). If the short call is exercised, the investor could acquire the stock by exercising the long calls ($4,000 − $3,000 = $1,000; $1,000 × 5 = $5,000).   (Page 404)

32. **B.** Mr. Orb's actual deposit will be $2,500 because it will be reduced by the net premiums received for the calls sold ($3,500 received in premiums received minus $1,000 in premiums for the purchase).   (Page 404)

33. **D.** To determine the margin required for a straddle, calculate both positions, then take the larger margin requirement and add the premium of the other option. To calculate the margin, take 100% of the option's premium ($300 for the in-the-money put, $200 for the out-of-the-money call) plus 20% of the current market value of the underlying security ($3,900 × 20% = $780). The option with the larger margin requirement would be the put ($300 + $780 = $1,080). Then add the call premium ($200) to determine the margin requirement of $1,280. Subtract the $300 put premium received to obtain the net deposit required of $980.   (Page 405)

34. **C.** To determine the margin required for a combination, calculate both positions and then take the larger margin requirement and add the premium of the other option. To calculate the margin, take 100% of the option's premium ($300 for the in-the-money put, $500 for the in-the-money call) plus 20% of the current market value of the underlying security ($3,800 × 20% = $760). The option with the larger margin requirement would be the call ($500 + $760 = $1,260), so add to that the premium of the call ($1,260 + $300 = $1,560). Subtract the premiums received to obtain the net deposit required of $780.   (Page 405)

35. **C.** Add the difference in premiums (6 − 2 = 4) to the lower strike price.   (Page 383)

36. **C.** The area of gain is between 44 and 50 for a gain of 6. Should the stock decline, both options will expire for a loss of 4 (6 − 2).   (Page 383)

37. **A.** Your client will break even when one of the options is worth $650 and the other is worthless. When the price of the stock is $43.50, the put is $650 in-the-money. When the price of the stock is $51.50, the call is $650 in-the-money.   (Page 387)

38. **C.** An investor establishes a straddle by buying or writing a call and a put, both of which have the same strike price and expiration date.   (Page 379)

39. **C.** A stockholder establishes a ratio write by writing a call that covers more shares than he owns. This strategy is also called a *variable hedge*.   (Page 390)

40. **B.** Mrs. Solong will receive premiums for the calls she sells. If the calls she will write are out-of-the-money, the stock will probably not be called away and, therefore, will not produce capital gains until next year.   (Page 370)

41. **C.** Short stock and short naked calls subject an investor to unlimited risk because no one knows how high the price of a stock might rise. Risk can be defined for the other positions.   (Page 374)

42. **C.** An option is in-the-money when it has intrinsic value. A call option is in-the-money when the price of the underlying security is higher than the exercise price of the option.   (Page 370)

43. **A.** Mr. Bullock bought the more expensive option. This option created the debit and must increase in value in order for him to profit. As an example of a profitable closing transaction, assume that he bought back the Jan 35 call for 1 1/2 and sold the Jan 30 call for 5 1/2: the spread has widened.   (Page 385)

44. **D.** A profit or loss resulting from a short position is always taxed as a short-term capital gain or loss, so a short position has no holding period.   (Page 408)

45. **D.** The combined number of options that both people exercised was under the 8,000 limit, so these transactions do not violate the prohibition against acting in concert. However, the accounts should be watched in the future.   (Page 368)

46. **A.** The expiration dates and striking prices may be different or the same. It is the total number of puts and calls that may be owned on a heavily traded stock that is limited to 8,000.   (Page 367)

47. **A.** Answer B would create a no man's land; the investor would be at risk 5 points if the price of the stock reached 40. Answer C would be of no help if the price of the stock went above 40. Answer D would provide additional cash, but the investor could be called if the price of the stock went above 40.   (Page 389)

48. **D.** $900 closing cost minus $600 opening proceeds equals a $300 loss.   (Page 407)

49. **C.** Expiration of a short option generates a gain at the time the option expires.   (Page 407)

50. $400 capital loss. In a straddle, the options are treated separately for tax purposes.   (Page 407)

51. $250. A $250 capital loss.   (Page 407)

52. **B.** This put spread is established at a debit because the customer pays more for the 70 put than he receives for the 60 put. Bears buy puts and write put spreads having debit balances.   (Page 383)

53. **D.** If the stock goes either up or down sharply, the customer will profit from owning a straddle.   (Page 385)

54. **C.** The lower the strike price, the more expensive the call option. The investor has pur-chased the more expensive option with the lower strike price; therefore, this is a debit spread.   (Page 384)

55. Bull spread. This is a put credit spread. The investor receives more for the Nov 35 put than she pays for the Nov 30 put. Bulls sell put spreads. The put with the higher strike price is more likely to be in-the-money as the market falls.   (Page 381)

56. Bull spread. This is a call debit spread. Bulls buy calls. A lower strike price call is more likely to be in-the-money as the market goes up.   (Page 381)

57. Bear spread. This is a call credit spread. Bears sell calls.   (Page 381)

58. Bull spread. This is a call debit spread. Bulls buy calls.   (Page 381)

59. Bear spread. This is a put debit spread. Bears buy puts.   (Page 381)

60. Bull spread. This is a put credit spread. Bulls sell puts.   (Page 381)

61. Bear spread. This is a put debit spread. Bears buy puts.   (Page 381)

62. **A.** Choices I and II are debit spreads. An investor wants a debit spread to widen. As the distance between premiums increases, the investor's potential profit also increases. This is because the investor intends to sell the option with the higher premium and buy back the option with the lower premium.   (Page 385)

63. **B.** Because the ownership of the stock covers the short call, no margin is required to write the call. However, margin is required to buy the stock. Reg T for the purchase of stock is 50%. 50% times 3,800 equals $1,900. Because the writer earns $150 in premiums, the call would be for $1,750. If this were a transaction in an existing account, it would be assumed that the account meets the NASD minimum equity requirement of $2,000 and the call would be for only $1,750. Because the question

states that this is an initial transaction, the account must meet the $2,000 equity minimum. Thus, the call would be for $2,000 net of the $150 in premiums received, or for $1,850. (Page 401)

64. **B.** The purchase of the put wipes out the holding period on the number of shares owned that the put allows the holder to sell. Because the holder owns 1 put, this wipes out the holding period on 100 shares owned. The other 200 shares are unaffected. (Page 408)

65. **B.** A short stock position gives an investor unlimited risk potential if the stock should rise because the investor eventually must buy back the stock at the higher price. Because stock can rise an unlimited amount, there is unlimited risk. The sale of a naked call requires that, if exercised, the writer must buy the stock in the market and deliver it at the strike price. Because the stock can rise an unlimited amount, the writer assumes unlimited risk. The sale of a covered call does not pose this risk because the writer already owns the stock at an established price. When selling a naked put, if exercised, the writer is required to buy stock at a fixed price. Because the price of the stock can only drop to zero, the writer's maximum loss is fixed; the worst that can happen is that he is forced to buy worthless stock. (Page 377)

66. **B.** A long straddle is the purchase of a put and a call on the same stock with both options having the same terms. The long call is profitable if the market moves upward, while the long put is profitable if the market moves downward. In this manner, both sides of the market are *straddled*. (Page 385)

67. **A.** To profit from a decline in the market price, the investor could either sell short the stock (requiring 50% margin) or sell a naked call (requiring 15% margin plus any in-the-money or minus and out-of-the-money), or buy a put (requiring the payment of the premiums in full). To obtain the greatest leverage (use the least cash), the purchase of a put is best. The lowest premium would be on a put that is currently at- or out-of-the-money. Because the market price of the stock is 62, a Jul

60 put is 2 points out-of-the-money, while a Jul 70 put is 8 points in-the-money. The Jul 60 put, therefore, would require a lower premium. (Page 377)

68. **D.** With XYZ trading at 74 on the expiration date, the XYZ 60 call will be exercised while the XYZ 70 put will expire. The investor originally bought the stock in the market at 60, and will deliver the stock at 60 to satisfy the exercised call. (Page 379)

69. **C.** When a company pays a stock dividend or effects a fractional stock split, the underlying option is adjusted by increasing the number of shares covered by the contract and reducing the strike price proportionately. (Page 367)

70. **A.** Options are adjusted for stock dividends and splits but not for cash dividends. Cash dividends that are a return of capital are not a true dividend and would cause the option to be adjusted. Adjustments are made to the nearest 1/8th, not the next highest or lowest 1/8th. (Page 367)

71. **D.** All factors would be considered when determining suitability: understanding of strategies; ability to calculate maximum profit or loss; ability to assume risk; and ability to meet a margin call. (Page 247)

72. **A.** A long put is profitable if the price falls; if the price rises or stays the same, the put will expire worthless. (Page 374)

73. **D.** Buying a put requires a smaller capital commitment than shorting the stock and has a lower loss potential (the premiums only) because selling short involves unlimited risk. The purchase of a put on an exchange does not require an uptick, which is needed when selling short stock on an exchange. (Page 375)

74. **C.** A short stock position gives unlimited loss potential as the stock rises in price. A short put, on the other hand, is profitable if the stock price falls. With a short put, the writer's loss is limited to the purchase of worthless stock at the strike price of the option (if exercised). (Page 375)

75. **C.** If the stock price falls, the loss on the short put is exactly offset by the gain on the short stock position. The customer then keeps the premiums of $700. On the other hand, if the price rises above 50, the short put will expire. The short stock position is then losing money. Because $700 was collected in premiums, the short stock position can lose 7 points and still break even (50 + 7 = 57 breakeven point).   (Page 390)

76. **C.** Because the stock is purchased upon exercise of the short put for $50 and is then used to cover the $50 short sale, there is no gain or loss on the stock. The writer of the put still keeps the $700 collected in premiums, for a profit of $7 per share.   (Page 390)

77. **B.** The investor's position after the sale of the stock is: short 1 ABC call/short 1 ABC put (both at the same terms). This is a short straddle.   (Page 379)

78. **A.** An investor who expects prices to remain stable would write an uncovered straddle (short straddle). In selling the put and call at the same terms, the writer collects double premiums. Both expire if the price remains stable; however, if the price moves, then one side or the other will lose money.   (Page 386)

79. **C.** The investor bought the stock at $50 and the stock has risen to $60. To protect against a decline in the price of the stock, he could buy a 60 put, which locks in a $60 sale price. By writing the $60 call, he collects premiums that offset the premium paid to buy the $60 put. If the price falls, he is protected; but if the price rises, the short call will be exercised and he will lose the stock.   (Page 377)

80. **B.** This option has been adjusted for a stock dividend. Because the contract now covers 115 shares, at a premium of 14 1/2 per share, the cost is $1,667.50 (115 × 14 1/2).   (Page 358)

81. **C.** The strike price on the put is 320. The stock price is 304 1/2; therefore, the put is in-the-money by 15 1/2.   (Page 371)

82. **A.** To protect against a price decline, the client can buy a 70 put, locking in the 10-point gain on the stock (because he has the right to sell at 70). The client can then write a 70 call, using the premiums received to offset those paid to buy the put. If the price drops, the client is fully protected. If the price rises, the short call will be exercised and the stock will be taken away at the strike price.   (Page 374)

83. **C.** If the investor writes a put, he collects premiums. As the stock price rises, the put will be out-of-the-money and will expire. The investor keeps the premiums, which help offset his purchase cost of $38 per share. He will not write a call at 35 because, as the stock price slowly rises, the call will be in-the-money. It would then either be exercised (and the stock taken away) or be bought back at a higher premium for a loss.   (Page 375)

84. **B.** The maximum limit is 8,000 contracts on either side of the market. The *up side* is long calls and short puts. The *down side* is long puts and short calls. Choice I is a violation, being a total of 8,100 long calls. Choice II is not a violation, being a total of 7,500 long calls and 600 long puts. Choice III is not a violation, being a total of 7,500 long calls and 600 short calls. Choice IV is a violation, being a total of 7,500 long calls and 600 short puts.   (Page 367)

85. **D.** Under OCC rules, a short put is covered if the investor is long a put on the same stock at the same strike price or higher.   (Page 402)

86. **B.** The opening purchase of the ABC Jul 85 call was made at 5, and the closing sale of that call was made at 2; the difference of 3 represents a $300 loss. The opening purchase of the ABC Jul 90 put was made at 8, and the closing sale of that put was made at 3; the difference of 5 represents a $500 loss. The total loss for the account was $800.   (Page 385)

87. **C.** The opening purchase of the XYZ Apr 40 call was made at 6, and the closing sale of that call was made at 4; the difference of 2 represents a $200 loss. The opening purchase of the XYZ Apr 50 put was made at 8, and the closing sale of that put was made at 6; the difference of 2 represents a $200 loss. The total loss for the account was $400.   (Page 385)

17 Investment Company Products

1. Mr. Sorensen buys the ABC Growth Fund and enjoys a substantial paper capital gain. When Mr. Sorensen believes the market has reached its peak, he switches into the ABC Income Fund within the ABC Family of Funds. He incurs a small service fee, but he is not charged an additional sales charge. What is the tax effect?

   A. Any gain or loss is deferred until he liquidates the ABC Income Fund.
   B. The tax basis of the ABC Income Fund is adjusted to reflect the gain in the ABC Growth Fund.
   C. It is a tax-free exchange.
   D. Any gain in the ABC Growth Fund is taxable because the switch is treated as a sale and a purchase.

2. A registered representative is seeking to sell shares in an investment company to a client. Which of the following statements would be accurate and permissible for the registered representative to say regarding his recommendation?

   I. "When you redeem your shares, you will not know immediately the dollar value of your redeemed shares."
   II. "If you purchase the shares of two or more funds in the same family of funds, you may be entitled to a reduced sales charge."
   III. "If you invest just before the dividend distribution, you can benefit by receiving the added value of that dividend."

   A. I and II only
   B. I and III only
   C. II and III only
   D. I, II and III

3. What services must a mutual fund sponsor offer in order to be permitted to charge the maximum allowable sales charge for the fund shares?

   A. Rights of accumulation
   B. The privilege to reinvest dividend distributions at no sales charge
   C. Price breakpoints offering reduced commissions for larger purchases
   D. All of the above

4. A senior security is one issued under the

   A. Investment Company Act of 1940
   B. Investment Advisers Act of 1940
   C. Maloney Act
   D. Trust Indenture Act of 1939

5. The Steady Fund is a mutual fund that has as its primary objective the payment of dividends, regardless of the current state of the market; preservation of capital and capital growth are secondary objectives. Which of the following industry groups would be appropriate for the Steady Fund's portfolio?

   A. Aerospace
   B. Public utilities
   C. Computer technology
   D. Consumer appliances

6. A customer wishes to redeem 1,000 shares of a mutual fund. The bid and ask quote is 11–11.58. A 1/2% redemption fee will be administered. How much will the customer receive?

   A. $10,945
   B. $11,000
   C. $11,522
   D. $11,580

7. Lotta Leveridge signed a letter of intent stating that she would purchase $25,000 worth of Pennywise Mutual Fund over the next 9 months. After 13 months, she had only invested $12,000. What will be the effect of her actions?

   A. Her entire investment will be charged an 8 1/2% sales charge.
   B. She qualifies for the second breakpoint only, and will be charged 8%.
   C. The entire amount is still due because she signed a binding contract when she signed the letter of intent.
   D. Nothing; she will be charged whatever sales charge she is entitled to for the actual amount she invested.

8. You have advised your client to use dollar cost averaging as a strategy over the next few months. An advantage of this strategy during a bull market is that it will result in an average cost per share that is *less* than the price of the stock on any given day, assuming that

   I.   the price of the underlying shares fluctuates
   II. a set number of shares is purchased regularly
   III. a set dollar amount is invested regularly
   IV. a set dollar amount is maintained invested

   A. I and II
   B. I and III
   C. II and III
   D. III and IV

9. All of the following would be considered typical of a money-market fund EXCEPT that

   A. the underlying portfolio is normally made up of short-term debt instruments
   B. most or all money-market funds are offered as no-load investments
   C. money-market funds have a high beta and are safest in periods of low market volatility
   D. the net asset value of a money-market fund normally remains unchanged

10. Which of the following is(are) characteristics of REITs?

    I.   They offer limited liability.
    II. They offer the opportunity for capital gains.
    III. They offer a pass-through of losses.

    A. I
    B. I and II
    C. I and III
    D. II and III

11. Which of the following statements is(are) true about REITs?

    I.   Operating losses flow through directly to REIT owners.
    II. Profits from operations usually flow through directly to REIT owners.
    III. They are a type of direct participation program.
    IV. They provide long-term financing to real estate projects.

    A. I, II and III only
    B. II and IV only
    C. IV only
    D. I, II, III and IV

12. In order to avoid taxation at the corporate level, REITs must derive at least 75% of their income from real property and must distribute what percentage of the net income to shareholders?

A. 75%
B. 90%
C. 95%
D. 98%

13. REITs provide which of the following features to investors?

A. Flow-through of income and deductions
B. Diversification with limited capital investment
C. Switching privileges between REITs in a family
D. Management fees that are lower overall than those of mutual funds

14. All of the following statements are true of money-market funds EXCEPT that

A. investors pay a management fee
B. interest is computed daily and credited to the investor's account monthly
C. investors can buy and sell shares quickly and easily
D. high interest rates are guaranteed

15. All of the following statements are true of a closed-end investment company EXCEPT that it

A. can redeem its own shares
B. is a type of management company
C. sells at the market price plus a commission
D. may be referred to as a mutual fund

16. Which of the following statement(s) is(are) true regarding money-market funds?

I. The rate of return is generally two points over the prime rate.
II. The owners are shareholders.
III. A prospectus must precede or accompany the original purchase.
IV. The client is subject to a substantial penalty for early withdrawal.

A. I
B. I and II
C. II and III
D. II and IV

17. Lotta and Tiny Leveridge are in a high tax bracket and are interested in maximizing their aftertax income while diversifying their portfolio. You should recommend that they buy

A. TANs
B. GNMAs
C. tax-exempt convertible bonds
D. tax-exempt unit trusts

◆ Answers & Rationale

1. D. The exchange is treated as a sale, regardless of the holding period and the fact that it does not involve a new sales charge. The gain (or loss) on the ABC Growth Fund is determined by comparing the cost basis with the net asset value of the shares at the time of the exchange. Any difference is a capital gain or loss. (Page 424)

2. A. Purchase of two funds in the same family of funds may qualify an investor for combination privileges. At redemption, he will receive the next price calculated (forward pricing), which is not yet known. Purchase of a mutual fund just prior to a dividend is a detriment. The distribution about to be paid is included in the purchase price and, when received by the investor, will be treated as ordinary income, even though he is essentially being returned a portion of his investment. (Page 422)

3. D. NASD rules prohibit sales charges in excess of 8 1/2% on mutual fund purchases by public customers. Unless a mutual fund grants its shareholders certain privileges, the amount charged must be lower than 8 1/2%. To qualify for the maximum sales charge (8 1/2%), the following privileges must *all* be extended to the fund's shareholders:

- rights of accumulation
- dividend reinvestment at net asset value
- quantity discounts (breakpoints)

(Page 421)

4. D. The term *senior security* generally indicates a corporate security that has certain rights and preferences over other securities in the event of a liquidation or dissolution of a corporation (corporate debt would be considered senior to common stock). All nonexempt corporate debt security issues of $1,000,000 or more must be issued under the Trust Indenture Act of 1939. Investment company securities are required to be registered under the act of 1940. Persons who give investment advice for a fee must register under the Investment Advisers Act of 1940. The Maloney Act allows for the registration of self-regulatory organizations (such as the NASD and the NYSE). (Page 38)

5. B. Utilities belong to the group known as *defensive industries*, as compared to the other types mentioned. They more consistently produce dividends, although their relative growth potential is limited. (Page 254)

6. A. Always redeem at NAV (bid): 1,000 shares × $11 = $11,000. Then determine the redemption fee: $11,000 × .005 (a 1/2% redemption fee) = $55 (the dollar amount of the redemption fee). Then subtract the fee from the gross redemption proceeds: $11,000 − $55 = $10,945. A shortcut alternative to the last two steps is to multiply the gross redemption proceeds by the complement of the redemption fee: $11,000 × .995 = $10,945. (Page 420)

7. D. An LOI is not a binding contract, so Ms. Leveridge is not required to deposit the rest of the money. She will be entitled to whatever breakpoint her $12,000 investment qualifies for. (Page 421)

8. B. Dollar cost averaging will result in a lower average cost per share as long as the price of the shares fluctuate, the general trend of the stock price is up, and the same number of dollars is invested during each interval. (Page 423)

9. C. Money-market funds have no price volatility; the rate of interest on money-market funds fluctuates in conjunction with that of the instruments underlying the original money-market certificates. (Page 418)

10. B. Operating losses do not flow through REITs, which offer limited liability. The investor cannot lose more than he has invested. Also, the REIT can appreciate in value, thus offering capital gains opportunities to the investor. (Page 426)

11. B. Real estate investment trusts (REITs) are companies, usually traded publicly, that manage equity and debt investments in real estate in order to earn profits for shareholders. Although

REITs must by law pass through 95% or more of their earnings to retain their status as REITs, they do not pass losses through directly to investors and, therefore, are not direct participation programs.
(Page 426)

12. **C.** REITs must distribute at least 95% of their net income to the shareholders in order to avoid corporate taxation. (Page 426)

13. **B.** REITs consist of diversified portfolios of real estate and real estate mortgages. Because REITs are bought and sold on exchanges and over the counter as shares of beneficial interest, investors can purchase as few or as many shares as they choose, and can vary their investment size accordingly. (Page 426)

14. **D.** Money-market instruments earn high interest rates but the rates are not guaranteed. Money-market funds are typically no-load funds with no redemption fee, but investors do pay a

management fee. The interest earned on an investor's shares is computed every day and credited to the account at month end. An advantage of money-market funds is the ease with which shares can be purchased and sold. (Page 418)

15. **A.** A closed-end investment company does not redeem its own shares. The terms *mutual fund* and *open-end investment company* are often used interchangeably. (Page 415)

16. **C.** All mutual funds, as new issues, require delivery of a prospectus; there is no penalty for early withdrawal. Investors are shareholders in the fund and have voting rights. The interest rate depends on the performance of the fund's portfolio, and is not pegged to the prime rate. (Page 418)

17. **D.** Each of the other answers is a debt instrument that finances a single project or item. Unit trusts are typically composed of several underlying securities. (Page 283)

18 ⬦ Retirement Planning and Annuities

1. What was the primary purpose for establishing ERISA?

   A. To establish a retirement fund for government employees
   B. To establish a means for self-employed persons to provide for their own retirement
   C. To protect employees from the mishandling of retirement funds by corporations and unions
   D. To provide all employees, both government and nongovernment, with an additional source of retirement income in the event that the Social Security system defaults

2. In a defined-benefit plan

   A. all employees receive the same benefits at retirement
   B. all participating employees are immediately vested
   C. high-income employees who are near retirement will benefit the most
   D. the same amount must be contributed for each eligible employee

3. A registered representative who is recommending investments for an ERISA account would give primary consideration to

   A. maximum current income
   B. tax status of the beneficiary
   C. liquidity
   D. risk

4. The requirements of the Employee Retirement Income Security Act apply to pension plans established by which of the following?

   A. Self-employed individuals with no employees
   B. Only public entities, such as the city of New York
   C. Only private organizations, such as Exxon
   D. Both public and private organizations

5. Which of the following statements is(are) true about a qualified, noncontributory defined-benefit plan?

   I. Contributions are taxable.
   II. Distributions are taxable.
   III. Contributions may vary.

   A. I and II
   B. II
   C. II and III
   D. III

6. Lotta Leveridge makes $65,000 a year as an advertising executive, and her husband, Tiny, makes $40,000 a year as Lotta's assistant. How much can the Leveridges contribute to IRAs?

   A. They cannot make a contribution because their combined income is too high.
   B. They can contribute up to $2,250 split over both accounts, with no more than $2,000 in either account.
   C. They can each contribute $2,000 to an IRA.
   D. They can each contribute $2,500 to an IRA.

7. Max Leveridge has been reading the financial news and thinks that interest rates will decline soon. He wants to protect the principal he has accumulated in his IRA, and plans to begin making withdrawals in seven years. Under the circumstances, you would recommend

   A. purchasing seven-year zero-coupon Treasury STRIPS
   B. leaving all of his cash in money-market funds
   C. withdrawing now and investing in corporate debentures
   D. a unit investment trust that begins to mature in seven years

8. Mr. Jones invests in a tax-qualified variable annuity. What is the tax treatment of the distributions he receives?

   A. Partially tax-free; partially ordinary income
   B. Partially tax-free; partially capital gains
   C. All ordinary income
   D. All capital gains

9. Ms. Charolais invests in a variable annuity. At age 65, she chooses to annuitize. Which of the following statements are true?

   I. She will receive the entire value of the annuity in a lump-sum payment.
   II. She will receive monthly payments for the rest of her life.
   III. The value of the accumulation unit is used to calculate the total number of annuity units.
   IV. The accumulation unit value is used to calculate the annuity unit value.

   A. I and III
   B. I and IV
   C. II and III
   D. II and IV

10. For a retiring investor, which of the following is the most important factor in determining the suitability of a variable annuity investment?

   A. The fact that the annuity payment may go up or down
   B. Whether the investor is married
   C. Whether the investor has concerns about taxes
   D. The fact that the periodic payments into the contract may go up or down

11. Ms. Smith purchases a nonqualified annuity at age 60. Before the contract is annuitized, she withdraws some of her funds. What are the consequences?

   A. 10% penalty plus payment of ordinary income on all funds withdrawn
   B. 10% penalty plus payment of ordinary income on all funds withdrawn in excess of basis
   C. Payment of capital gains in excess of basis
   D. Payment of ordinary income in excess of basis

12. Once a variable annuity has been annuitized, which of the following statements is true?

   A. The value of each annuity unit varies but the number of annuity units is fixed.
   B. The value of each annuity unit is fixed but the number of annuity units varies.
   C. The number of accumulation units is fixed but the value per unit varies.
   D. The value of each annuity unit and the number of annuity units vary.

13. Which of the following statements are true regarding both variable annuities and mutual funds?

    I.   They contain managed portfolios.
    II. The property of the owner must pass to his estate at the time of his death.
    III. They are regulated by the Investment Company Act of 1940.
    IV. All income realized by the portfolio through investment income and capital gains is taxable to the owner in the year in which it is generated.

    A. I and III
    B. I and IV
    C. II and III
    D. II and IV

14. Your 65-year-old client owns a nonqualified variable annuity. $29,000 was originally invested in 1984; it now has a value of $39,000. The client makes a lump-sum withdrawal of $15,000. He is in the 28% tax bracket. What tax liability results from the withdrawal?

    A. $0
    B. $2,800
    C. $3,800
    D. $4,200

15. Your client, who is 50 years of age, wants to withdraw funds from her IRA. She asks you about the tax implications of early withdrawal. You should tell her that the withdrawal will be taxed as

    A. ordinary income
    B. ordinary income plus a 10% penalty
    C. capital gains
    D. capital gains plus a 10% penalty

16. Your client, who is 40 years of age, wants to withdraw funds from her Keogh. She asks you about the tax implications of early withdrawal. You should tell her the withdrawal will be taxed as

    A. ordinary income
    B. ordinary income plus a 10% penalty
    C. capital gains
    D. capital gains plus a 10% penalty

17. Guido Vitro has a salaried, full-time position but his employer does not offer a company retirement plan. Guido also has his own clock repair business, which earns less than his salaried position. He wants to invest for his retirement. Which of the following investments are options for him?

    A. An IRA if he does not have a Keogh plan
    B. A Keogh plan if he does not have an IRA
    C. Both an IRA and a Keogh plan
    D. An IRA, but not a Keogh plan because his self-employment is not his main source of income

18. Which of the following are characteristics of a Keogh plan?

    I.   Dividends, interest and capital gains are tax-deferred.
    II. Distributions after age 70 1/2 are tax-free.
    III. Contributions are allowed for a non-working spouse.
    IV. Lump-sum distributions are allowed.

    A. I and II
    B. I and III
    C. I and IV
    D. II and III

19. All of the following factors influence the amount of money that can be contributed to a Keogh plan in one year EXCEPT

    A. the rules regarding maximum contributions
    B. whether the plan is qualified or non-qualified
    C. the amount of self-employment income
    D. whether the plan is defined-benefit or defined-contribution

20. Which of the following would disqualify a person from participation in a Keogh plan?

    A. She turned 70 eight months ago.
    B. She has a salaried position in addition to her self-employment.
    C. Her spouse has company-sponsored retirement benefits.
    D. She has an IRA.

21. Which of the following statements regarding individual retirement accounts is NOT true?

    A. IRA rollovers must be complete within 60 days of receiving the distribution.
    B. Cash-value life insurance is a permissible IRA investment but term insurance is not.
    C. The investor must be under 70 1/2 years of age to open an IRA.
    D. Distributions may begin at age 59 1/2 and must begin by age 70 1/2.

22. One of your customers and his wife are going to make their annual contribution to their IRA. He earned $40,000 this year and his wife earned $45,000. How much may they contribute?

    A. $2,000
    B. $2,250
    C. $4,000
    D. $5,000

23. Under the Tax Reform Act of 1986, all of the following investments offer either full or partially tax-deductible contributions to individuals who meet eligibility requirements EXCEPT

    A. IRAs
    B. Keogh plans
    C. unit trusts
    D. defined-contribution plans

24. Which of the following individuals will NOT be penalized on an IRA withdrawal?

    A. Man who has just become disabled
    B. Woman who turned 59 one month before the withdrawal
    C. Person, age 50, who decides on early retirement
    D. Man in his early 40s who uses the money to buy a house

◆ Answers & Rationale

1. **C.** ERISA was created originally to protect the retirement funds of members of unions and employees of large corporations. ERISA has set guidelines stating that all qualified retirement plans must: be in writing; not be discriminatory; segregate funds from corporate or union assets; invest in prudent investments; and report to the participants annually. All these activities are audited by ERISA. (Page 430)

2. **C.** The rules regarding the maximum amount of contributions are different for defined-contribution plans and defined-benefit plans. Defined-contribution plans set the amount that can be contributed, according to the employee's salary level. Defined-benefit plans set the amount of retirement benefits that a retiree will receive as a percentage of the previous several years' salaries, to a maximum of $90,000 per year. For the highly paid individual who is nearing retirement, the defined-benefit plan allows a larger contribution in a shorter period of time. (Page 442)

3. **D.** ERISA places various requirements on trustees handling the investment of pension fund assets. Trustees are charged with preserving the value of the pension fund's capital and seeking reasonable rates of return. This is a *prudent man* type of investment guideline. If such a strategy is pursued with reasonable diligence, the trustees will not be held liable for losses or below-normal rates of return. Seeking high-income investment (such as junk bonds) without regard to its riskiness is imprudent. The tax status is not particularly relevant because investments that are fully taxable (such as corporate bonds) are treated as tax-free investments as long as they are in an ERISA account. Liquidity is less important in retirement accounts because they are presumed to be long-term investments. Risk is the key consideration in an ERISA account. (Page 430)

4. **C.** ERISA was established to protect the pension retirement funds of employees working in the private sector only. It does not apply to self-employed persons or public organizations. (Page 430)

5. **C.** Contributions to a qualified, noncontributory plan are made by the employer, not the employee. All contributions are then taxed upon receipt by the participant. Because the benefits provided by this type of qualified plan may vary (depending upon the participant's age, sex, income, etc.), the contributions made on his behalf will vary. All distributions from the plan are taxed upon receipt by the participant. (Page 443)

6. **C.** No matter how much an individual or a couple make, IRA contributions can still be made. Each spouse is entitled to contribute 100% of earned income up to $2,000. (Page 434)

7. **A.** Max will be able to lock in an interest rate and be assured of safety of his principal with zero-coupon Treasury STRIPS. By purchasing bonds that mature in seven years, he will be able to match his withdrawal plans with their maturity. (Page 435)

8. **C.** In a tax-qualified annuity, the annuitant has no basis unless voluntary aftertax contributions were made. Such aftertax contributions are the exception and are not mentioned in this question. Because the annuitant has no basis, all payments are considered ordinary income. In a nonqualified annuity, contributions are made with aftertax dollars, which establish the annuitant's basis. Annuity payments from these nonqualified annuities are treated as ordinary income to the extent that they exceed the basis. (Page 450)

9. **C.** When a variable contract is annuitized, the number of accumulation units is multiplied by the unit value to arrive at the total contract investment value. An annuity factor is taken from the annuity table, which considers the investor's sex, age, etc. This factor, called the *annuity payment rate*, is used to establish the dollar amount of the first annuity payment. The first annuity payment value is then divided by the value of an annuity unit to determine the number of annuity units to be paid each month thereafter. (Page 448)

10.   **A.**   The most important consideration in purchasing a variable annuity is that benefit payments will fluctuate with the investment performance of the separate account. Answer D is not a consideration because normally the payments into an annuity are level or in a lump sum.

(Page 445)

11.   **D.**   Contributions to a nonqualified variable annuity are made with aftertax dollars. This is in contrast to tax-qualified retirement vehicles (such as an IRA or a Keogh), in which contributions are made with pretax dollars. Distributions from a tax-qualified plan are considered to be 100% taxable ordinary income because the original contributions were never subject to tax. Distributions from a nonqualified plan represent both a return of the original investment made in the plan with aftertax dollars (a nontaxable return of capital) and the income from that investment. Because the income was deferred from tax over the plan's life, it is taxable as ordinary income once it is distributed.

(Page 450)

12.   **A.**   The annuity period of a variable annuity is the payout period that occurs after the contract has been annuitized. Payments are based on a fixed number of annuity units established when the contract was annuitized. This number of annuity units is multiplied by the value of an annuity unit (which can vary) to arrive at the payment for the period. Accumulation units relate to the accumulation phase of a variable annuity when payments by owners are made to the contract.   (Page 448)

13.   **A.**   Both mutual funds and variable annuities are regulated by the act of 1940. Mutual funds owned in a single name pass to the estate of the owner at death. Variable annuity proceeds, however, typically pass directly to the owner's designated beneficiary at death, like a typical insurance policy. Investment income and capital gains realized generate current income to the owner of mutual funds, but in variable annuities current income is deferred until withdrawal begins.   (Page 446)

14.   **B.**   This annuity is nonqualified, which means the client has paid for it with aftertax dollars and, therefore, has a basis equal to the original $29,000 investment. Consequently, the client will

pay taxes only on the growth portion of the withdrawal ($10,000). The tax on this is $2,800 ($10,000 × 28%). Because the client is over age 59 1/2, there will be no 10% premature distribution penalty tax. However, had the client been *under* age 59 1/2, a $1,000 penalty tax ($10,000 × 10%) would be payable in addition to the $2,800 income tax.   (Page 430)

15.   **B.**   An early withdrawal from an IRA is taxed as ordinary income plus a 10% penalty.

(Page 437)

16.   **B.**   An early withdrawal from a Keogh is taxed in the same way as an early withdrawal from an IRA—as ordinary income plus a 10% penalty.

(Page 441)

17.   **C.**   Guido can start an IRA, assuming that he is under age 70 1/2. How much of his IRA contributions are deductible depends on his income level. He is also eligible to invest in a Keogh plan because he is self-employed, regardless of how much or how little he earns from his self-employment or how those earnings compare to his salary. Investment in an IRA does not affect his eligibility for a Keogh plan.   (Page 434)

18.   **C.**   Keogh plan earnings from dividends, interest and capital gains are tax-deferred. Lump-sum distributions are allowed, as well as regular payment distributions. Distributions are taxable, regardless of age. Contributions for a nonworking spouse are not allowed in a Keogh plan.

(Page 441)

19.   **B.**   The size of the contribution to a Keogh plan in a year is dependent upon the factors listed in answers A, C and D. By definition, Keogh plans are qualified plans.   (Page 438)

20.   **A.**   A person can participate in a Keogh plan if she is self-employed. The fact that she is a salaried employee and also has an IRA does not affect her eligibility. However, because withdrawals from a Keogh must begin by age 70 1/2, she is no longer eligible to contribute because of her age.

(Page 438)

21. **B.** Cash-value life insurance is not a permissible IRA investment, nor are term insurance or collectibles. Answers A, C and D accurately describe IRAs.   (Page 435)

22. **C.** Individuals may contribute 100% of earned income up to $2,000. Because both the husband and his wife work, together they may contribute a maximum of $4,000. If the wife did not work, the husband could contribute a maximum of $2,250. However, their combined income is over the cut-off for deductibility of contributions.
(Page 434)

23. **C.** Contributions to a unit trust that is not in a retirement plan are not tax-deductible. Contributions to an IRA or a Keogh may be tax-deductible, depending on the individual's earnings and his access to company-sponsored retirement plans.
(Page 443)

24. **A.** Disability is a legitimate reason for distributions before age 59 1/2. The other individuals described will be taxed on the withdrawal because they are under 59 1/2 years of age.   (Page 436)

19 ◈ Direct Participation Programs

1. All of the following are characteristics of both oil and gas and real estate partnerships EXCEPT

   A. limited liability
   B. depreciation
   C. deferral benefits
   D. depletion

2. All of the following statements are true with respect to a limited partnership subscription agreement EXCEPT

   A. the investor's registered representative must verify that the investor has provided accurate information
   B. the general partner endorses the subscription agreement, signifying that a limited partner is suitable
   C. the investor's signature indicates that he has read the prospectus
   D. the general partner's signature grants the limited partners power of attorney to conduct the partnership's affairs

3. Which of the following would MOST likely be considered a potential conflict of interest in a limited partnership?

   A. The general partner owns leases adjacent to the limited partnership's leases.
   B. The general partner has a substantial amount of funds at risk in the limited partnership.
   C. There is a disproportionate sharing arrangement.
   D. The limited partner is in competition with the partnership.

4. An investor has $25,000 in partnership losses for the year. During the year he received $10,000 of cash distributions. At the beginning of the year, he had a tax basis in the partnership of $30,000. What is the maximum loss he can write off for the year?

   A. $15,000
   B. $20,000
   C. $25,000
   D. $30,000

5. An investor purchases a limited partnership in the business of buying airplanes and then leases the equipment to an airline. The potential benefits to the investor may be all of the following EXCEPT

   A. income from lease payments
   B. tax benefits from investment tax credits
   C. deferral of income taxes
   D. equipment depreciation benefits

6. A general partner may be allowed to do all of the following EXCEPT

   A. make general management decisions regarding the partnership
   B. sell property to the limited partnership
   C. act as an agent for the partnership in managing partnership assets
   D. borrow money from the partnership

7. An investor expects to have a large amount of passive income over the next two years. Which type of partnership is likely to provide the largest amount of shelter?

   A. Equipment leasing program
   B. Undeveloped land purchasing program
   C. Oil and gas drilling program
   D. Real estate income program

8. Ms. Smith invested $150,000 in a limited partnership. Because of economic problems, the partnership had to liquidate and $1,200,000 of $4,500,000 nonrecourse debt was left unpaid. Her percentage of the partnership was 10%. How much will she lose as a result of this liquidation?

   A. $120,000
   B. $150,000
   C. $270,000
   D. $450,000

9. Limited partners have all of the following rights EXCEPT the right to

   A. monitor the partnership
   B. sue the general partner for violations of the partnership agreement
   C. justified returns
   D. decide which properties will be purchased by the partnership

10. Which of the following best describes the point at which taxable income exceeds deductions in a limited partnership?

   A. Alternative minimum tax
   B. Crossover point
   C. Conversion point
   D. Recapture point

11. The managing partner of a limited partnership has responsibility for all of the following EXCEPT

   A. organizing the business
   B. managing the operations
   C. providing unlimited capital for the partnership business
   D. paying the debts of the partnership

12. A maximum underwriting spread of 10% may be charged for which of the following investments?

   A. Mutual fund
   B. Unit investment trust
   C. Variable annuity
   D. Direct participation program

13. Programs that allow for the direct pass-through of losses and income to investors include all of the following EXCEPT

   A. REITs
   B. Subchapter S corporations
   C. oil and gas drilling direct participation programs
   D. new construction real estate direct participation programs

14. Ten investors each buy a 10% interest in a limited partnership for $100,000 cash. Each investor also signs a note for his share of $1,000,000 in recourse financing, which the partnership is borrowing to buy an apartment complex. In the event of default by the partnership, what is each investor's maximum potential loss?

   A. $100,000
   B. $200,000
   C. $1,000,000
   D. $10,000,000

15. Ten investors each buy a 10% interest in a limited partnership for $100,000 cash. Each investor also signs a note for his share of $1,000,000 in recourse financing, which the partnership is borrowing to buy an apartment complex. As defined by the IRS, the cost basis of the investors is

   A. $100,000
   B. $200,000
   C. $1,000,000
   D. unknown

16. Which of the following handles registration of the securities and packages the program for a limited partnership?

   A. Syndicator
   B. Property manager
   C. General partner
   D. Underwriter

17. What type of arrangement exists in an oil and gas program when the general partner bears the nonexpensed cost and the limited partners bear the expensed costs?

   A. Net operating profits interest arrangement
   B. Functional allocation arrangement
   C. Proportionate sharing arrangement
   D. Disproportionate sharing arrangement

18. A general partner in an oil and gas partnership pays 25% of all costs in exchange for 40% of all revenues. What type of sharing arrangement is this?

   A. Functional allocation
   B. Overriding royalties
   C. Reversionary interests
   D. Disproportionate sharing

19. Which of the following would decrease an investor's basis in a limited partnership?

   I. Cash distributions
   II. Partnership income
   III. Depletion
   IV. Recourse debt

   A. I
   B. I and III
   C. II and III
   D. II and IV

20. Your client's real estate limited partnership goes bankrupt. Who will be paid before your client?

   I. Fellow limited partners
   II. Bank that holds the mortgage on the property
   III. Bank that holds the unsecured note
   IV. General partner

   A. I and II
   B. II and III
   C. II, III and IV
   D. III and IV

21. An investor's basis in both oil and gas and real estate limited partnerships is affected the same way by all of the following EXCEPT

   A. cash distribution
   B. recourse debt
   C. nonrecourse debt
   D. partnership losses

22. Centralization of management in a direct participation program is characterized as

   A. limited liability
   B. the most difficult corporate characteristic to avoid
   C. the easiest corporate characteristic to avoid
   D. equal participation among the partners in management of the program

Use the following information to answer questions 23 and 24.

A direct participation program shows the following operations results for the year:

Revenues	$3,000,000
Operating expenses	$1,000,000
Interest expense	$200,000
Management fees	$200,000
Depreciation	$3,000,000

23. Profit or loss for the year is

   A. $3,000,000 loss
   B. $1,400,000 loss
   C. $1,600,000 income
   D. $2,700,000 income

24. Cash flow from program operation is

   A. negative
   B. $1,400,000
   C. $1,600,000
   D. $3,000,000

25. What might be the effect of a limited partner's making business decisions for the partnership?

   A. He might be removed from the partnership.
   B. His limited liability status would be maintained.
   C. His limited liability status might be jeopardized.
   D. There would be no effect, because of partnership democracy.

26. In an oil and gas limited partnership program, what is the allowable percentage depletion on the oil sold?

   A. 15%
   B. 16%
   C. 18%
   D. 20%

27. A method of analyzing limited partnerships by identifying the sources of revenues and expenses is known as

   A. capital analysis
   B. cash flow analysis
   C. technical analysis
   D. liquidity analysis

28. Kozy Condo reports the following operation information for 1990:

Revenues	$200,000
Operating expenses	$50,000
Principal	$10,000
Debt service	$100,000
Depreciation	$40,000

An investor purchased Kozy Condo for $100,000 and assumed a $300,000 mortgage. He would report what amount of taxable income?

   A. $10,000
   B. $20,000
   C. $30,000
   D. $40,000

29. The crossover point in a DPP is the point at which

   A. taxable income is greater than the cash distributed, and phantom income is generated
   B. revenue exceeds expenses, and a profit is shown
   C. accelerated depreciation crosses straight-line depreciation
   D. ownership is transferred in the sale of an interest

30. Which two of the following could be used by an analyst to establish the rate of return on a direct participation program?

   I. Present value
   II. Internal rate of return
   III. Yield to maturity
   IV. First in, first out

   A. I and II
   B. I and III
   C. II and III
   D. II and IV

◆ Answers & Rationale

1. D. Depreciation applies to buildings in real estate and to tangible property in oil and gas, as does deductions for interest expense. Depletion applies only to nonreplenishable natural resources, such as minerals or standing timber, and is a deduction to reflect the using up (depleting) of the primary assets of a natural resource investment program. (Page 468)

2. D. The limited partner's signature on the subscription agreement grants the general partner power of attorney to conduct the partnership's affairs. The subscription agreement for a limited partnership is deemed accepted when the general partner signs the subscription agreement. (Page 460)

3. A. General partners have a fiduciary responsibility to the partnership. This means that they are not allowed to engage in self-dealing or other potential conflicts of interest, such as owning leases adjacent to partnership leases or accepting compensation not to compete unless it is fully disclosed. (Page 464)

4. B. A partner's basis in a partnership is reduced for the share of partnership losses and cash distributions, but not below $0. A partner's share of losses must be factored into the basis only after all other adjustments for the tax year. After the cash distribution, the partner's basis is only $20,000, which is then the amount of loss the partner could take that year. The other $5,000 loss ($25,000 minus $20,000) will be carried forward. (Page 471)

5. B. Leased equipment will generate revenue during the period of the lease. Depreciation expenses can be used to offset passive income, thus deferring income. The Tax Reform Act of 1986 did away with investment tax credit. (Page 470)

6. D. In all these situations, there is the potential for conflicts of interest; however, the general partner is not forbidden by law to engage in any of these acts, except for borrowing money—the general partner may never borrow money from the partnership. (Page 463)

7. C. Oil and gas drilling programs allocate the majority of investment dollars to drilling. These costs are intangible drilling costs (IDCs), which are 100% deductible when drilling occurs. In equipment leasing programs, the investment dollars are recovered through depreciation over the life of the leased assets. (Page 467)

8. B. In a limited partnership, the limited partner's maximum liability is any amount of money contributed to the partnership plus any debt for which the partner has agreed to be liable (i.e., recourse debt). No one is personally liable for nonrecourse debt. (Page 480)

9. D. The limited partners have the right to inspect partnership records and to sue a general partner who acts outside the partnership agreement. The compensation of the general partner is normally set by the general partner in the original agreement. The general partner makes all management decisions relative to the partnership's interests. (Page 465)

10. B. The crossover point is when the partnership investment is generating taxable income for the partners. This occurs when revenues earned by the partnership exceed accrued expenses, which are deductible for tax purposes. Ideally, the partnership can have cash flow while showing a loss for tax purposes because of noncash expenses (e.g., depreciation). This could allow cash distributions, which themselves do not affect the taxable income. If deductions exceed income, the investment can still shelter income from other sources so long as the crossover point has not yet been reached. The number of units sold has no direct effect on the crossover point. (Page 481)

11. C. The general partner organizes and manages the partnership. He assumes unlimited liability, including paying all partnership debts. However, it is the limited partner who usually provides the bulk of the capital. (Page 463)

12.   **D.**   Regarding DPPs, under Appendix F of the NASD Rules of Fair Practice, the maximum sales compensation, including wholesaling costs, is limited to 10%.   (Page 459)

13.   **A.**   REITs allow for the direct pass-through of income but not of losses. The other programs are all forms of business that allow for pass-through of income and losses.   (Page 426)

14.   **B.**   A recourse loan gives the limited partner liability beyond the initial investment. The limited partner is at risk for the total amount, which consists of his initial investment ($100,000) plus his share of the recourse loan ($100,000).
                    (Page 480)

15.   **B.**   The amount of the recourse loan is added to the investor's original contribution, giving a cost basis in this example of $200,000.
                    (Page 480)

16.   **A.**   In putting the deal together by organizing the administrative apparatus and handling registration of the securities, the person is acting as a syndicator. The general partner is responsible for buying the partnership assets. The property manager handles the day-to-day activities. The underwriter is responsible for distributing the partnership's interest.   (Page 459)

17.   **B.**   In a functional allocation agreement, the sponsor bears all the nonexpensible (i.e., nondeductible) drilling costs, which must be capitalized. The investors bear the expensible (i.e., deductible) costs, including intangible drilling costs, which are immediately deductible. This is a popular arrangement in drilling programs because the investors see tax benefits at the onset of the program.   (Page 469)

18.   **D.**   The general partner receives a percentage of all revenues and bears a different percentage of all expenses. In a functional allocation, the general partner incurs all nondeductible costs and receives a percentage of all revenues. In an overriding royalties arrangement, he receives a percentage of all gross revenues without sharing in expenses. In a reversionary interest, he receives a percentage of all revenues after the limited partners receive their specifically agreed upon return.
                    (Page 469)

19.   **B.**   Cash distributions and depletion decrease an investor's tax basis. Undistributed partnership income (distributive share of profit) increases tax basis in a partnership. Recourse debt increases tax basis.   (Page 481)

20.   **B.**   Creditors, both secured and unsecured, have priority over partners. Your client's fellow limited partners will be paid at the same time as your client. The general partner will receive his money last.   (Page 462)

21.   **C.**   As a general rule, nonrecourse debt is not part of an investor's basis. However, real estate nonrecourse is the exception; it is part of an investor's basis and results in an increase in basis.
                    (Page 480)

22.   **B.**   If a direct participation program has too many of the characteristics of a corporation, it could be judged a taxable corporation and its participants would lose the advantage of participating directly in the tax benefits of the program's operations. Most programs are successful in avoiding free transferability of ownership and continuity of life. Most do not try to avoid limited liability for their participants. Centralized management, however, is nearly impossible to avoid: somebody has to run the business, and the limited partners cannot actively participate in management without jeopardizing their limited liability.   (Page 459)

23.   **B.**   Taxable income for a partnership is determined as follows:

    $ 3,000,000 Gross revenue
    - 1,200,000 Operating expenses
                 (including management fees)
    _____
    $ 1,800,000 Net revenue
    -   200,000 Interest
    - 3,000,000 Noncash expenses
                 (depreciation)
    _____
    - $ 1,400,000 Taxable loss

                    (Page 479)

24. **C.** Cash flow for a partnership is calculated as follows:

$3,000,000 Gross revenue
– 1,200,000 Operating expenses
(including management fees)
$1,800,000 Net revenue
– 200,000 Debt interest
$1,600,000 Cash flow

(Page 479)

25. **C.** If a limited partner has control over the partnership operation (i.e., he makes partnership decisions), he could be judged a general partner and thus have unlimited liability. This should not jeopardize the status of other limited partners. Partnership democracy refers to what the limited partners can do as a group without putting their status in jeopardy (e.g., sell assets, remove the general partner and so on). (Page 465)

26. **A.** Depletion is to natural resources what depreciation is to manufactured assets. A limited partnership investing in natural resources holds property that dwindles away as it is used (i.e., a wasting asset). Depletion deductions compensate for the wasting away of resources. For oil and gas, the statutory percentage depletion allowance is 15%. This means that an investor can deduct from other passive income 15% of his share of yearly gross income from an oil and gas partnership. (Page 468)

27. **B.** Cash flow analysis compares income (revenues) to expenses. (Page 482)

28. **B.** Payment of principal is never deducted from revenue in determining taxable income. (Page 481)

29. **A.** The point at which a partnership begins to show negative cash flow with taxable income rather than positive cash flow with deductions is known as the *crossover point*. Negative cash flow with taxable income is known as *phantom income*. (Page 481)

30. **A.** The present value (of the dollars the investor will receive as principal at the maturity of the partnership) and the internal rate of return (the present values of the future cash flow) are both used by analysts to establish a rate of return for a DPP. (Page 253)

Final Exam One

1. All of the following lend money EXCEPT the

   A. GNMA
   B. FRB
   C. FHLB
   D. FICB

2. The Federal Farm Credit Bank system consists of all of the following EXCEPT the

   A. FICB
   B. banks for cooperatives
   C. Federal Land Bank
   D. Federal Home Loan Bank

3. Income from which of the following qualifies for the 70% corporate dividend exclusion?

   I. Common stock
   II. Preferred stock
   III. Convertible bonds
   IV. Municipal bonds

   A. I and II
   B. II, III and IV
   C. II and IV
   D. III and IV

4. Bond trust indentures are required for which of the following?

   A. Corporate debt securities
   B. Municipal general obligation bonds
   C. Municipal revenue bonds
   D. Treasury securities

5. What is the advantage of a Treasury receipt over a Treasury bill?

   A. The investor does not have to pay taxes on accrued interest.
   B. All interest is paid at maturity.
   C. The capital requirement is less.
   D. Interest is taxed as it accrues yearly, regardless of whether it has been received.

6. Using Table 20.1, what was ABCorporation's close on September 12th?

   A. 68
   B. 71 1/2
   C. 74 1/2
   D. 78

7. Using Table 20.1, what was ABCorporation's approximate earnings per share?

   A. $.75
   B. $3.00
   C. $6.00
   D. $33.29

Table 20.1

NEW YORK STOCK EXCHANGE COMPOSITE TRANSACTIONS Tuesday, September 13, 1998										
52 Weeks					Yld	P-E	Sales				Net
High	Low	Stock	Div	%	Ratio	100s	High	Low	Close	Chg.
80	40	ABCorp	.75	.1	12	3329	78	68	73	-1 1/2

8. Which of the following investments would produce the LEAST market risk?

   A. Stocks
   B. Fixed-income debentures
   C. Treasury bills
   D. Zero-coupon bonds

9. Which is the earliest date a customer can sell a stock and still receive a previously declared dividend?

   A. Ex-date
   B. Payable date
   C. Record date
   D. Next day

10. In order to be paid a dividend, an owner's name should be recorded on the stock record book of the issuer's transfer agent by the

    A. ex-date
    B. payable date
    C. record date
    D. next day

11. An investor purchasing 1,000 shares of a mutual fund that has a maximum sales charge of 8 1/2% and an NAV of $10.30 at the time of purchase will pay a total sales charge (rounded to the nearest dollar) of

    A. $88
    B. $96
    C. $875
    D. $957

12. Government securities settle on the

    A. ex-date
    B. payable date
    C. record date
    D. next business day

13. Using Table 20.2, how much would an investor have received and reported as taxable income per share in 1987?

    A. $1.00
    B. $1.40
    C. $1.50
    D. $1.60

14. A customer owns 100 shares of ABC at a cost basis of $25 per share. ABC distributes a 5% stock dividend. Under the Internal Revenue Code, what is the customer's basis in this stock?

    A. 100 shares at a cost of $25 and 5 shares at a cost of $0
    B. 105 shares at an average cost of $23.81 per share
    C. 105 shares at an average cost of $25 per share
    D. 100 shares at a cost of $25 and 5 shares at a cost of $21 3/4

15. If a broker-dealer executes a registered bond trade between two customers, which of the following must be notified?

    A. National Clearing Corporation
    B. National Association of Securities Dealers, Inc.
    C. Issuer's transfer agent
    D. Issuer's registrar

16. Which of the following are actively traded?

    I. Rights
    II. Nondetachable warrants
    III. Common stocks
    IV. Options on stock

    A. I, III and IV only
    B. II only
    C. II and IV only
    D. I, II, III and IV

Table 20.2   General Jennurel, Inc. $1.00

Rate –.40Q Pd '87–$1.40

Dividend Amount	Declared	Ex-date	Record Date	Payable
0.50	Nov 16	Nov 30	Dec 6	Jan 15
0.40	Feb 15	Feb 28	Mar 6	Apr 15
0.40	May 16	Jun 15	Jun 9	Jul 15
0.20	Sep 16	Oct 17	Oct 23	Nov 15
0.40	Nov 22	Dec 3	Dec 9	Jan 15 '88

17. Which of the following statements is(are) true regarding rights and warrants?

    I.   Warrants are issued with an exercise price higher than the underlying stock.
    II. Rights are issued with an exercise price lower than the underlying stock.
    III. Warrants are long-lived, may even be perpetual, and may be issued to anyone.
    IV. Rights are short-lived and are issued only to present stockholders.

    A. I only
    B. I and II only
    C. I, II and III only
    D. I, II, III and IV

18. Which of the following is issued with a maturity of 12 months or less?

    A. Treasury bill
    B. Treasury note
    C. Treasury bond
    D. Treasury stock

19. Which of the following is considered to have intermediate maturity?

    A. Treasury bill
    B. Treasury note
    C. Treasury bond
    D. Treasury stock

20. Which of the following is considered to have long-term maturity?

    A. Treasury bill
    B. Treasury note
    C. Treasury bond
    D. Treasury stock

21. Using Table 20.3, the bid price of the 8 1/2 of Nov 1987 is

    A. $1,000
    B. $1,001.25
    C. $1,001.875
    D. $1,005

22. Which of the following is the issuer of government securities?

    A. Federal Reserve Banks
    B. Federal Reserve Board
    C. Treasury Department
    D. Commerce Department

23. All of the following are true of a negotiable CD EXCEPT that

    A. yields are quoted for no shorter than a 14-day time period
    B. interest is paid at maturity
    C. it is guaranteed by the issuing bank
    D. it is registered

24. Which of the following do NOT trade in the secondary market?

    A. Bankers' acceptances
    B. Certificates of deposit
    C. Repurchase agreements
    D. Treasury bills

25. If enough stop orders are entered in the market, which two of the following statements would be true?

    I.   Buy stops will accelerate a bull market.
    II. Sell stops will accelerate a bull market.
    III. Buy stops will accelerate a bear market.
    IV. Sell stops will accelerate a bear market.

    A. I and II
    B. I and IV
    C. II and III
    D. III and IV

Table 20.3

TREASURY BONDS AND NOTES					
Rate	Mat. Date	Bid	Asked	Chg.	Yld.
7 5/8	1987 Nov n	99.30	100.1	−.1	3.65
8 1/2	1987 Nov p	100.4	100.6	+.1	4.51

26. Which of the following best describe the information displayed on Level 3 of the NASDAQ system?

    I.   Highest bid
    II. Highest ask
    III. Lowest bid
    IV. Lowest ask

    A. I and II only
    B. I and IV only
    C. II and III only
    D. I, II, III and IV

27. The *broker* part of the term "broker-dealer" indicates which of the following?

    A. Acting for others in both purchase and sale
    B. Acting for others in both purchase and sale, and selling from inventory
    C. Acting for the firm and for others in both purchase and sale
    D. None of the above

28. Which of the following is true of a GTC order on the specialist's book?

    A. It is automatically canceled after six months.
    B. If properly renewed, it doesn't lose its priority.
    C. It must be reentered after one year.
    D. It never has to be reviewed or renewed.

29. If a customer designates an order as *not-held*, which of the following statements is true?

    A. The floor broker has been given discretion as to time and price.
    B. The registered representative has been given discretion as to time and price.
    C. The order will not be held up; it will be executed immediately.
    D. The order will be given to the specialist for execution.

30. A customer is long 2,000 shares of DDD and sells 2,000 shares of DDD short against the box for $30,000. Under NYSE rules, how much money may he withdraw from his margin account on completion of this transaction? (Reg T is 50%.)

    A. $15,000
    B. $26,000
    C. $28,500
    D. $30,000

31. A customer opens a new cash account. The signature(s) of which of the following is(are) required before orders can be executed?

    I.   Customer
    II. Registered representative
    III. Registered principal

    A. I only
    B. I and II only
    C. II and III only
    D. I, II and III

32. A new customer deposits $32,000 cash in his margin account. How much can he buy in marginable securities? (Reg T is 50%.)

    A. $16,000
    B. $32,000
    C. $48,000
    D. $64,000

33. A change in which of the following should be indicated in a customer's file?

    I.   Name or address
    II. Marital status
    III. Objectives

    A. I only
    B. I and II only
    C. I and III only
    D. I, II and III

34. George has $300,000 worth of securities with ABC Brokerage, his spouse has $300,000 in securities, and they have a joint account with $400,000 in securities. ABC files for bankruptcy. What is the couple's SIPC coverage?

    A. $300,000
    B. $600,000
    C. $700,000
    D. $1,000,000

35. All of the following are characteristics of an investment in a REIT EXCEPT

    A. ownership of real property without management responsibilities
    B. diversification of real estate investment capital
    C. pass-through tax treatment of income
    D. pass-through tax treatment of operating losses

36. An investor is in a low tax bracket and wishes to invest a moderate sum in an investment that will provide him with some protection from inflation. Which of the following would you recommend?

    A. Municipal unit investment trust
    B. Growth stock mutual fund
    C. Money-market mutual fund
    D. Ginnie Mae fund

37. Which of the following investment funds would provide high appreciation potential together with high risk?

    A. Balanced
    B. Bond
    C. Income
    D. Specialized

38. Two customers who combine their capital would NOT qualify for which of the following?

    A. Avoiding the odd-lot differential
    B. Opening a joint tenants in common account
    C. Breakpoints on a mutual fund purchase
    D. Joint registration on stock certificates

39. Which of the following statements about the NASD 5% markup policy are true?

    I. The type of security is a consideration.
    II. A transaction in common stock customarily has a higher percentage markup than a bond transaction of the same size.
    III. A riskless transaction is not generally covered by the 5% markup policy.
    IV. The markup policy does not apply to securities sold at a specific price and with a prospectus.

    A. II and III only
    B. I, II and IV only
    C. I, III and IV only
    D. I, II, III and IV

40. A doctor has compensation of $160,000. What is the maximum he may contribute to his Keogh plan?

    A. $5,000
    B. $22,000
    C. $28,000
    D. $30,000

41. An investment in a REIT unit differs from an investment in a real estate limited partnership interest in that the REIT investment

    A. does not pass through losses
    B. has limited liability
    C. is managed similarly to the way in which an investment company is managed
    D. passes through income

42. If the Federal Reserve Board changes the reserve requirement, the effect of the change to the economy will MOST likely be

    A. regressive
    B. nonregressive
    C. multiplied
    D. deflationary

43. An economic downturn that lasts for six months is called

    A. a recession
    B. a depression
    C. progressive
    D. regressive

44. Orders for durable goods are considered what type of indicator?

 A. Leading
 B. Lagging
 C. Coincident
 D. Coterminous

45. Which of the following is a coincident indicator?

 A. GNP
 B. Durable goods
 C. S&P 500
 D. Personal income

46. A company with cumulative nonparticipating voting preferred stock would

 A. pay preferred dividends prior to paying the coupons due on their outstanding bonds
 B. pay past due and current preferred dividends before paying dividends to their common stockholders
 C. pay the current dividends on the preferred but not the past dividends on the preferred before paying a dividend on the common
 D. force conversion of the preferred that is trading at a discount to par and thereby eliminate the necessity of paying past due dividends

47. Which of the following situations might fall into the category of hot issues?

 A. A new issue is offered at $30 and immediately appreciates to $35.
 B. A new issue is offered at $30 and immediately decreases to $25.
 C. A market maker buys at $17 and immediately sells with a spread of $2.
 D. A broker-dealer sells inventory at $60 three weeks after buying at $30.

48. To open a margin account with a securities broker-dealer, which of the following persons would require special procedures under NYSE rules?

 I. Secretary in an insurance company
 II. Officer of an insurance company
 III. Executive vice-president of a bank
 IV. Secretary of a bank

 A. I and II only
 B. I and IV only
 C. II and III only
 D. I, II, III and IV

49. Which of the following debt instruments pays no interest?

 A. Treasury STRIP
 B. Treasury note
 C. Treasury bond
 D. Treasury stock

50. Which of the following statements is(are) true of a Treasury STRIP bond?

 I. The rate of return is locked in.
 II. There is no reinvestment risk.
 III. The interest is taxed as a capital gain.
 IV. The interest is realized at maturity.

 A. I
 B. I, II and III
 C. I, II and IV
 D. I and IV

51. The Federal Farm Credit Bank issues all of the following types of securities EXCEPT

 A. equity
 B. mortgage-backed
 C. agricultural
 D. debentures

52. Securities issued by which of the following are backed by the federal government?

 A. Federal National Mortgage Association
 B. Federal Home Loan Mortgage Corporation
 C. Government National Mortgage Association
 D. Federal Intermediate Credit Bank

53. Which of the following statements is true of GNMA mortgage-backed securities?

    A. They are backed by the Federal National Mortgage Association, which may borrow from the Treasury to pay principal and interest.
    B. They are backed by a pool of mortgages.
    C. Interest payments are exempt from federal income taxes.
    D. The minimum purchase is $25,000.

54. Federal Farm Credit System Consolidated Systemwide Issues are characterized by which of the following statements?

    A. They are issued only in the form of discount notes.
    B. The interest on them is not subject to federal income tax.
    C. They have the same degree of safety as Treasury issues.
    D. They are backed only by the full faith and credit of the issuer.

55. All of the following pay semiannual interest EXCEPT

    A. GNMAs
    B. Treasury bonds
    C. Treasury notes
    D. public utility bonds

56. T bills are issued with all of the following maturities EXCEPT

    A. 1 month
    B. 3 months
    C. 6 months
    D. 12 months

57. Which of the following have authority to enforce MSRB rules?

    I. SEC
    II. NASD
    III. Comptroller of the Currency
    IV. Federal Reserve Board

    A. I and II only
    B. III and IV only
    C. I, II and IV only
    D. I, II, III and IV

58. All of the following statements are true of a Treasury receipt EXCEPT that

    A. it may be issued by a securities broker-dealer
    B. it is backed by the full faith and credit of the federal government
    C. the interest coupons are sold separately
    D. it may be purchased at a discount

59. Which of the following best describes the federal funds rate?

    A. Average rate for short-term bank loans of the previous week
    B. Rate charged by major New York City banks
    C. Rate that changes daily and that banks charge each other
    D. Rate that major New York City banks charge broker-dealers

60. Which of the following are characteristics of the interbank system?

    I. Unregulated
    II. Regulated by the Federal Reserve Board
    III. Centralized
    IV. Decentralized

    A. I and III
    B. I and IV
    C. II and III
    D. II and IV

61. Which of the following do NOT issue commercial paper?

    A. Commercial banks
    B. Finance companies
    C. Service companies
    D. Broker-dealers

62. Which of the following is(are) characteristics of a money-market fund?

    I.   Portfolio of short-term debt instruments
    II. High beta
    III. Offered without a sales load
    IV. The NAV does not appreciate

    A. I only
    B. I, II and IV only
    C. I, III and IV only
    D. I, II, III and IV

63. A newly issued bond has call protection for the first five years after it is issued. This feature would be most valuable if, during this five-year period, interest rates are generally

    A. fluctuating
    B. stable
    C. falling
    D. rising

64. The capitalization of a corporation includes $1,000,000 of 7% preferred stock and $1,000,000 of 7% convertible debentures. If all the convertible debentures were converted into common stock, what would happen to the company's earnings?

    A. They would increase.
    B. They would decrease.
    C. There would be no change.
    D. The change in earnings cannot be forecast.

65. Except under limited circumstances, NASD rules on freeriding and withholding prohibit the purchase of a hot issue by which of the following people?

    I.   Finder
    II. Bank officer who has a significant relationship with the issuer
    III. Officer of a broker-dealer firm that is a member of the NASD
    IV. Registered representative

    A. I and II only
    B. I, III and IV only
    C. III and IV only
    D. I, II, III and IV

66. The newspaper indicates that T bill yields have gone down. This means that T bill prices

    A. are up
    B. are mixed
    C. are down
    D. cannot be determined

67. Each of the following terms would be associated with an underwriting of corporate securities EXCEPT

    A. stabilization
    B. matched orders
    C. blue-sky
    D. due diligence

68. Which of the following securities are exempt from the 1933 act?

    I.   Federal and state issues
    II. Small business investment companies
    III. Nonprofit organizations
    IV. State-chartered commercial banks

    A. I only
    B. I and II only
    C. I, II and III only
    D. I, II, III and IV

69. An insider can sell securities under Rule 144 without being required to file notice with the SEC if the

    I. number of shares is 500 or less
    II. value of the shares is $10,000 or less
    III. value of the shares is greater than $1 million
    IV. number of shares is greater than 100,000

    A. I and II
    B. I and III
    C. II and IV
    D. III and IV

70. A 5% bond is purchased with an 8% yield to maturity. After the capital gains tax is paid, the effective yield is

    A. less than 5%
    B. 5%
    C. between 5% and 8%
    D. 8%

71. Each of the following four bonds has a 6.1% coupon rate. A 5-basis-point change in each bond would have the greatest effect on the dollar price of which bond?

    A. 1 year to maturity, 6.10 basis
    B. 2 years to maturity, 6.50 basis
    C. 2 1/2 years to maturity, 7.25 basis
    D. 2 3/4 years to maturity, 7.35 basis

72. The doctrine of tax-free reciprocity for municipal bonds originated in

    A. U.S. Supreme Court decisions
    B. state laws
    C. federal laws
    D. IRS interpretations

73. All of the following trade flat or without accrued interest EXCEPT a

    A. bond in default of interest
    B. zero-coupon bond
    C. bond for which the settlement date and the interest payment dates are the same
    D. registered industrial revenue bond

74. The settlement for a government bond trade in a cash account is

    A. the same day
    B. the next business day
    C. five business days after the trade date
    D. seven business days after the trade date

75. Which two of the following statements are true regarding an NASD Form DK?

    I. It is sent to the contra broker.
    II. It is sent to the customer.
    III. It is sent to the NASD or NYSE.
    IV. It is used to report unmatched trades.

    A. I and III
    B. I and IV
    C. II and III
    D. II and IV

76. What is typically NOT a reason for a fail to deliver of a certificate?

    A. Rapidly changing market
    B. Incorrect delivery instructions
    C. Mutilated certificate
    D. Partially called issue

77. Monarch Printing Co. intends to acquire King Printing Inc. The terms are one share of Monarch for three shares of King. Monarch is trading at 30 and King at 10 1/2. The acquisition is being reviewed for possible problems with antitrust laws. A trader has bought 4,000 shares of Monarch at 30 and has sold short 12,000 shares of King at 10 1/2. This trader's transaction would be considered a

    A. bona fide arbitrage
    B. risk arbitrage
    C. straddle
    D. reverse hedge

78. Under the SEC customer protection rule, broker-dealers must deliver to other broker-dealers no later than

    A. 5 business days after trade date
    B. 10 business days after settlement date
    C. 30 calendar days after settlement date
    D. 30 business days after settlement date

79. A customer is buying 800 shares of DWQ stock. The trader responds to the firm's request for an 800-share quote with Bid–15, Ask–15 1/2. The trader must sell

    A. 100 shares at 15
    B. 100 shares at 15 1/2
    C. 800 shares at 15
    D. 800 shares at 15 1/2

80. A customer enters a day order to sell 400 shares of XYZ at 34 1/2. During the day XYZ trades between 33 and 33 3/4. If prior to the close the customer wishes to change the order to a good-till-canceled order, you should suggest that the customer

    A. cancels the day order promptly and immediately re-enters it as a GTC order
    B. cancels the day order, and enters a new GTC order the next day at the opening
    C. enters a new GTC order promptly and allows the day order to remain on the books until expiration
    D. allows the day order to remain on the books and, if it is not executed, re-enters it the next day as a GTC order

81. Which of the following limited partnership programs would be LEAST appropriate for an investor seeking to shelter current passive income?

    A. Oil and gas income program
    B. Oil and gas exploratory program
    C. Sale-leaseback arrangement
    D. Program investing in existing apartment buildings

82. In general, a registered representative could have power of attorney for accounts of each of the following EXCEPT a(n)

    A. corporation
    B. individual
    C. partnership
    D. custodian

83. A registered representative of an NYSE member firm who wishes to work outside the firm after hours would require permission from the

    A. member firm
    B. NASD
    C. NYSE
    D. SEC

84. Which of the following orders would have to be marked "short"?

    A. You have exercised warrants and sold the underlying stock.
    B. You have sold part of a long position when you are short against the box.
    C. You have sold stock owned long.
    D. You have exercised a call and then sold the underlying stock.

85. Which of the following statements is true of a limited power of attorney that a customer gives his rep?

    A. The rep needs written permission from the customer for each trade.
    B. The customer must renew the power of attorney every year.
    C. The customer can still enter independent orders.
    D. The branch manager must initial each order before it is entered.

86. A mutual fund has an NAV of $13.37. An investor was charged a 4% sales charge on a lump-sum purchase of $50,000. How many shares were purchased?

    A. 3,422
    B. 3,564
    C. 3,589
    D. 3,595

87. All of the following are true of taxable zero-coupon bonds EXCEPT that

    A. the discount is accreted
    B. tax is paid annually
    C. interest is paid semiannually
    D. they are purchased at a discount

88. In a margin account, marking to the market may result in a request for an additional deposit equal to the difference between

  A. Regulation T and the maintenance margin
  B. Regulation T and the current market value
  C. the settlement and the contract price
  D. the maintenance margin and the current equity

89. Which of the following statements about a bond quoted as "GMA Zr 12" would be true?

  A. The bond pays $12 interest annually.
  B. The bond pays $120 interest annually.
  C. The bond pays no interest until maturity.
  D. None of the above

90. After short selling a stock at 60, an investor holds the position as the stock declines to 42. The investor could use which of the following strategies to lock in the gain?

  A. Buy stop limit at 44
  B. Write calls
  C. Write puts
  D. Buy calls

91. Where does a customer get the information needed to determine the amount of accretion on an original issue discount bond?

  A. Investor
  B. Underwriter
  C. IRS
  D. Issuer

92. The federal funds rate has been increasing for a long time. Which of the following is likely to occur?

  A. The FRB will increase bank reserve requirements.
  B. Member banks' deposits at Federal Reserve Banks will decrease.
  C. Money-market interest rates will decrease.
  D. The prime rate will decrease.

93. General communications by a broker-dealer firm, such as advertising or research reports, could NOT be approved by which of the following?

  A. Member
  B. Principal of a member
  C. Supervisory analyst
  D. Certified financial analyst

94. The yield on a bond with 20 years to maturity decreases by 10 basis points. The price of the bond will

  A. decrease by approximately $1
  B. increase by approximately $1
  C. decrease by approximately $10
  D. increase by approximately $10

95. An investor in ABC stock has a margin account that is restricted by $800. ABC pays a dividend of $1,000. The investor can withdraw

  A. $0
  B. $200
  C. $500
  D. $1,000

96. A customer bought a T bill on margin. What is the required margin? (Reg T 50%)

  A. $0
  B. 30%
  C. 50%
  D. NYSE minimum margin

97. An improvement in the business cycle is indicated by an increase in all of the following EXCEPT

  A. industrial production
  B. inventory
  C. S&P index
  D. consumer orders

Use the following information to answer questions 98 and 99.

A corporation has the following capitalization:

$100,000 of 5% debentures convertible at $20
$100,000 of 5% preferred stock cumulative
$100,000 of common stock, par $20

98. With operating income of $50,000 and a 34% tax bracket, EPS is

A. $3.50
B. $4.94
C. $5.60
D. $5.94

99. With operating income of $50,000, the corporation has fully diluted EPS of

A. $2.00
B. $2.47
C. $2.80
D. $5.60

100. An investor's portfolio includes ten bonds and 200 shares of common stock. If both positions increase by 1/2 point, what is the gain?

A. $50
B. $105
C. $110
D. $150

101. A U.S. company that sells stereo equipment places a 600,000,000 yen order in August for Japanese stereo components for its Christmas inventory. Payment must be made in Japanese yen in three months. At the time the order is placed, the yen is worth 50 hundredths of a cent. However, the U.S. company thinks that the dollar may weaken against the yen. Which of the following foreign currency option transactions would best protect the U.S. company from a possible weakening of the dollar against the yen?

A. Buy calls on Japanese yen.
B. Buy puts on Japanese yen.
C. Sell calls on Japanese yen.
D. Sell puts on Japanese yen.

102. Which of the following statements is(are) correct if an investor is long stock and long a put?

I. If both the put and the security used to exercise the put were acquired on the same day and the put is identified as a hedge, the holding period of the stock will determine whether a gain or loss is long term or short term.
II. If the stock used to exercise the put was purchased after the put, the gain or loss is short term.
III. If the stock used to exercise the put was held long term when the put was acquired, the gain or loss is long term.

A. I only
B. I and II only
C. II and III only
D. I, II and III

103. An investor purchases 1 ABC Oct 40 call for 2 3/8 and at the same time writes 1 ABC Oct 45 call for 1/2 when ABC is at $38 1/2. He must deposit

A. $97.50
B. $187.50
C. $287.50
D. $387.50

104. An investor has written a put and furnished an exchange-approved option guarantee letter from a bank for an amount equal to the total exercise price of the put position. What margin would be required?

A. $0
B. $250
C. 20% of the market value of the stock
D. 20% of the strike price of the option

105. An investor sells 1 ABC Oct 25 call at 7 and buys 1 ABC Oct 35 call at 1. The price of ABC is currently $30 per share. What is the deposit to the account?

A. $400
B. $600
C. $1,000
D. $1,150

106. Puts may be sold in a cash account if

    A. the underlying security is short in the account
    B. the underlying security is long in the account
    C. an escrow receipt is promptly deposited
    D. funds equal to the aggregate exercise price are on deposit

107. An investor has a margin account with no cash or securities position. He purchases 100 shares of XYZ at 68 and 1 XYZ Jan 75 put at 10. With Reg T at 50%, what is the required deposit?

    A. $3,900
    B. $4,250
    C. $4,400
    D. $4,750

108. What is the normal priority for filling orders in a municipal underwriting?

    A. Group orders, presale orders, designated orders, member takedown orders
    B. Designated orders, presale orders, member takedown orders, group orders
    C. Presale orders, group orders, designated orders, member takedown orders
    D. Presale orders, designated orders, group orders, member takedown orders

109. Your firm is a member of the underwriting syndicate of a municipal bond issue. Why would your firm be willing to enter a net designated order on behalf of a customer to purchase $50,000 of the bonds held by the syndicate?

    A. To earn a larger takedown credit on those bonds
    B. To comply with MSRB syndicate sharing regulations
    C. To give the order priority ahead of the member takedown orders
    D. For all of the above reasons

110. Your firm is the managing underwriter for a syndicate underwriting a new issue of general obligation municipal bonds. The director of your municipal bond department decides to allocate the bonds in a different priority than that specified in the agreement among underwriters. Which of the following is true?

    A. As long as the bonds affected total less than 25% of the entire underwriting, this is within the discretionary authority of the manager and no further action is required.
    B. He must justify his action to show that it was in the best interests of the syndicate as a whole.
    C. He must file the appropriate papers with the MSRB and amend the agreement among underwriters.
    D. This is not permitted under any circumstances.

111. Which of the following statements are true when a brokerage firm holds its customers' fully paid securities?

    I. The firm is regulated by the Customer Protection Rule.
    II. The firm must segregate the firm's securities from securities owned by customers.
    III. The securities must be placed on deposit in the closest bank.
    IV. The brokerage firm votes all proxies for the securities it holds.
    A. I and II only
    B. I and IV only
    C. II, III and IV only
    D. I, II, III and IV

112. An issuer would go to which of the following parties to purchase insurance on its new issue?

    A. FDIC
    B. SIPC
    C. FNMA
    D. Investor-owned insurance companies

113. When explaining aftertax yields on a security to a customer, you might use which alternative term?

   A. Current yield
   B. Gross yield
   C. Yield to maturity
   D. Tax-equivalent yield

114. The placement ratio listed in *The Bond Buyer* is arrived at by dividing

   A. bonds placed by visible supply
   B. bonds placed by new issues offered
   C. new issues offered by visible supply
   D. bonds traded by issues offered

115. One of your clients has heard that Mount Horeb Wisconsin bonds are currently being offered by your firm, and would like to know when the new issue will be delivered. You can find the answer by looking in

   A. *The Blue List*
   B. the official statement
   C. *Munifacts*
   D. *The Wall Street Journal*

116. An analyst for a rating service reviewing the financial health of a general obligation bond would be MOST likely to look over the

   A. feasibility study
   B. municipal budget
   C. competitive facilities
   D. bond counsel's opinion

117. Your customer is interested in up-to-the-minute information on municipal bonds. To obtain the most accurate, current information available, you would go to

   A. *The Blue List*
   B. *The Bond Buyer*
   C. *The Yellow List*
   D. *Munifacts*

118. An order designated FOK means the order must be executed

   A. immediately and in its entirety
   B. in its entirety, but not immediately
   C. immediately, but a partial execution is acceptable
   D. at the opening of trading

119. The Mineral Point Opossum Control Authority has issued new bonds and committed the money to paying off the old bonds as soon as they become callable. The municipality can be said to have

   A. retired the issue
   B. advance refunded the issue
   C. refunded the issue
   D. double-barreled the issue

120. In order for a municipality considering a new offering of bonds to meet the additional bonds test, it must know that

   A. additional bonds can be issued only as junior lien bonds if these are backed by the same collateral and revenues
   B. applicable revenues must cover the debt service on the outstanding bonds plus the amortization of principal and interest on the new bonds, times a preset multiple
   C. additional general obligation bonds cannot be issued
   D. an analysis of the existing bonds outstanding must be performed by a qualified analyst before the sale of additional bonds

121. The Platteville Water Works would probably choose to issue a general obligation bond rather than a revenue bond if

   I.   the overall interest costs of a general obligation issue would be appreciably less
   II. the costs for the planned expansion are assessed only to current and future users
   III. the facility is used by the municipality
   IV. it wishes to avoid the formalities of obtaining voter approval

   A. I, II and III only
   B. I and III only
   C. II and IV only
   D. I, II, III and IV

122. The Mt. Vernon Illinois Port Authority wants to issue bonds to pay for a new yacht club, and wants to make the offering as attractive as possible. Which of the following would be of LEAST concern to potential investors?

   A. Size of the offering
   B. Dated date
   C. Insurance on the bond
   D. Maturity and call dates

123. Brothers Inc. wants to refinance by calling in $1 million of 6% preferred stock and issuing $1 million of 6% debentures. The company is in the 34% tax bracket. How will this refinancing affect the EPS of Brothers Inc.?

   A. It will have no effect on the EPS.
   B. The EPS will increase.
   C. The EPS will decrease.
   D. The EPS will remain unchanged but the stock price should increase.

124. Which of the following would have an inflationary effect?

   A. The discount rate increases from 4.4% to 6%.
   B. Government spending has increased and there is a tax rebate.
   C. Last year there was a high level of defense spending and wages and taxes rose.
   D. The rate for federal funds moves up, taxes are decreased and government spending is reduced.

125. Which of the following would probably lead to an increase in the money supply?

   I.   Increase in time and savings deposits at commercial banks
   II. Sale of securities in the open market by the Federal Reserve
   III. Increase in bank loans and investments
   IV. Lowering the reserve requirements

   A. I and II only
   B. I, III and IV only
   C. II, III and IV only
   D. I, II, III and IV

◆ Answers & Rationale

1. **A.** GNMAs sell pass-through certificates, which represent ownership interests in a pool of mortgages. (Page 70)

2. **D.** The Federal Farm Credit Bank system consists of: the Federal Land Banks, which make low-interest mortgages to farmers; the Federal Intermediate Credit Banks, which make short-term loans to financial institutions serving farmers; and the Banks for Cooperatives, which make agricultural loans to cooperatives owned by farmers. The Federal Home Loan Bank works with the savings and loan industry. (Page 69)

3. **A.** The dividend exclusion rule for 1988 has changed. It currently states that the exclusion is 70%, unless the holder has 20% or more of the company's stock. If the holder qualifies by owning 20% or more, the exclusion is still 80%. Because it is a dividend exclusion, only securities that issue dividends (common and preferred stocks) would be included. (Page 267)

4. **A.** Nonexempt issuers of debt securities (such as corporations) are required by the Trust Indenture Act of 1939 to include a bond contract. Exempt issuers (such as municipalities and the U.S. government) are not required to enter into a trust indenture, although most municipalities do anyway. (Page 41)

5. **C.** The Treasury receipt is a creation of a broker-dealer. The broker-dealer buys Treasury bonds and "strips" them of their coupons. They sell the coupons separately and create a pool with the bonds. The investor will purchase a piece of the pool and receive a receipt for his purchase (called a *Treasury receipt*). Because the investor can purchase a unit of the pool, instead of an actual stripped bond, the capital requirement could be less. (Page 64)

6. **C.** The September 13th close was at 73, down (or net change of) 1 1/2 from the previous day's close of 74 1/2. (Page 142)

7. **C.** Earnings per share is not given in the display. It can be calculated by using the PE (or price-earnings) ratio. The PE is the market price per share divided by earnings per share (EPS). To find the EPS, divide the market price by the PE. $73 \div 12 = 6.083$. (Page 241)

8. **C.** Market risk is a measure of how much the price of a given security will change when general interest rates change. The longer the security's maturity, the greater the change in its price for a given change in interest rates. Of the securities listed, Treasury bills have the shortest maturity. (Stocks, although they do not have an actual maturity date, are highly responsive to interest rate fluctuations.) (Page 251)

9. **A.** If the customer is holding the stock and wishes to sell the stock yet still receive the dividend, he must wait until the ex-date to sell. Remember that the ex-date is four business days prior to the record date. The regular way settlement is five business days. If he sells on the ex-date, the transaction will settle the day after the record date. The record date is set by the corporation and is used to determine who qualifies for the dividend (usually the holder of record on that day). (Page 171)

10. **C.** To receive a dividend, the buyer must be the bona fide owner (in other words, he must be on the books of the issuer as the owner) on or by the record date. (Page 171)

11. **D.** The 1,000 shares have a net asset value of $10,300. Divide that amount by the complement of 8 1/2% (91 1/2%). The result is $11,257, which is the amount of the current offering price. The difference is $957. (Page 421)

12. **D.** Regular way settlement of government securities occurs on the next business day. (Page 168)

13. **C.** Investors pay tax on what they have actually received in that calendar year; therefore, you must look at the payable date instead of the record date. The total dividends received, based on the payable dates, are $1.50. (Page 261)

14. **B.** The customer has 100 shares of stock that he purchased for a total of $2,500. After the 5% dividend he has 105 shares of stock with the same total cost basis of $2,500. Each share is now worth $2,500 divided by 105, for a basis of $23.81 per share. The Internal Revenue Code (IRC) requires that with stock splits or dividends, the basis (or cost) of the stock must be adjusted to reflect the new value of the shares.   (Page 263)

15. **C.** The transfer agent must be notified so that it can change the registration of the bonds from the seller to the buyer. The issuer must be notified as to the change because the ownership of principal and interest is listed on the books of the corporation.   (Page 16)

16. **A.** Detachable rights, detachable warrants, common stock and options all have an active secondary market. Nondetachable rights and warrants do not trade separately.   (Page 56)

17. **D.** Warrants are usually issued as a sweetener to a deal. For example, if a company wants to issue bonds at an interest rate lower than general market rates, the company could add warrants to make the bonds more attractive. Warrants are usually issued with a very long life, and give the holder the right to purchase stock above the current market price. When a corporation has common stock outstanding and wishes to issue more common stock, it must offer the shares to the current stockholders first (preemptive rights).   (Page 56)

18. **A.** T bills have maturities of 3, 6 and 12 months.   (Page 62)

19. **B.** T notes are intermediate-term securities issued with 1- to 10-year maturities.
(Page 62)

20. **C.** Treasury bonds are long-term securities, having maturities of 10 to 30 years.
(Page 63)

21. **B.** U.S. government securities are quoted in 1/32nds of a point. (Remember that a point is $10.) Therefore, the bid price for the Novembers is

100 4/32. 4/32nds of a point ($10) is .3125 times 4, or $1.25; so the bid price of the bond is $1,001.25.
(Page 65)

22. **C.** The Treasury Department is the issuer of government securities.   (Page 61)

23. **D.** Because certificates of deposit are issued by banks, they are exempt from registration under the act of 1933.   (Page 80)

24. **C.** Repurchase agreements are not as much a security as they are a contract between two parties. Although one party may transfer its obligations or rights to a third party, there really is no active secondary market for repos.   (Page 77)

25. **B.** Buy stops are placed above the current market and, when activated, become market buy orders. This will bring more buy orders into a rising (or bull) market. Sell stops are placed below the current market and are used to protect profits. They become market sell orders as the market reaches the stop price. These can accelerate bear markets.
(Page 124)

26. **D.** The Level 3 terminal is used by the trader to enter bids and askeds. The trader needs to see all of the quotes of the various market makers, which would include lowest ask, highest ask, lowest bid, highest bid and everything in between. Level 2 also shows all of these quotes, but a subscriber with Level 2 service is not able to enter and change quotations through it.   (Page 136)

27. **A.** When the term "broker" is used, it means that the firm is acting as an agent and is bringing a buyer and a seller together. Answers B and C describe a dealer.   (Page 110)

28. **B.** Good-till-canceled (open) orders must be reconfirmed the last day of April and October in order to remain on the specialist's book. If the order is not verified, it will be canceled and lose its position.   (Page 126)

29. **A.** When a customer wants to buy or sell certain shares of stock but does not know at what price or when, the customer can say, "Sell my 200

shares of XYZ at the time you think best and the price you think best, and you will not be held responsible." (Page 127)

30. **C.** The customer has sold his securities short against the box to defer a tax liability while freeing up some cash. Because the customer holds long shares of the same security he sold short, the NYSE requires him to maintain only 5% of the CMV of the underlying security in his account. Because the customer sold the securities short for $30,000 (the CMV), he can withdraw everything in excess of 5% of that amount, or $30,000 less $1,500, which equals $28,500. (Page 196)

31. **C.** When a customer opens a new account, the card is signed by the RR introducing the client to the firm and the principal who is accepting the client for the firm. The customer is not required to sign the new account card. The customer's signature is required only on a margin account. (Page 148)

32. **D.** If the customer deposits $32,000 in cash, he has $32,000 in SMA. With $32,000 of cash, the customer can purchase twice the amount in securities at 50% margin. (Page 190)

33. **D.** All of the information that affects your recommendations or the financial situation of a customer must be noted immediately in the file. (Page 149)

34. **D.** SIPC insurance is figured by account ownership. George is covered for his $300,000 in securities. His wife is covered for her $300,000 in securities. The joint account will be treated separately, and would be covered for the $400,000 in securities. The total securities coverage for the two of them and their three accounts is $1,000,000. Insurance coverage per account is $500,000, no more than $100,000 of which can be in cash. (Page 285)

35. **D.** REITs serve as *conduits* for the income received from their underlying investments in real estate, and pass through that income to their investors. The Internal Revenue Code requires 95% of all income received by a REIT to be distributed to investors in order for that REIT to be exempt from taxation on that income. But a REIT is not a direct participation program: REIT operating losses do not flow through to investors. (Page 426)

36. **B.** A growth stock fund will give the investor some protection from inflation. Historically, common stock is a better inflation hedge than fixed-income instruments. The other three answers are income-oriented funds. (Page 248)

37. **D.** A sector fund has a higher appreciation potential (coupled with higher risk) than an income-oriented fund. (Page 417)

38. **C.** In order to qualify for a breakpoint, the investor must be a *separate legal individual*. Two customers pooling their money solely to qualify for the benefits of breakpoints do not constitute a *separate* individual. (Page 421)

39. **B.** Riskless transactions are covered by the 5% markup policy. (Page 138)

40. **D.** Keogh contributions are limited to 25% of aftertax income (the equivalent of 20% of pretax income) to a maximum of $30,000. The doctor's $160,000 income times 20% equals $32,000, $2,000 more than the maximum contribution. (Page 438)

41. **A.** Although REITs pass through 95% or more of their income directly to their investors, they do not pass through any of the losses they incur. (Page 426)

42. **C.** Whenever the Federal Reserve changes a national policy or requirement (such as reserve requirements, margin requirements or the discount rate), the effect tends to be multiplied throughout the economy. If the reserve requirement is raised, money will be tightened because banks have to hold more in reserve, thus causing interest rates to rise; in turn, those companies that borrow will have to raise prices, and so on. (Page 214)

43.   **A.**   When the economy is bad for six months (or two consecutive quarters) we are in a recession; if it continues, we are in a depression.
(Page 205)

44.   **A.**   The production of durable goods, housing starts and the stock market are all considered leading indicators: the movement up or down of these indicators predicts the economy of the future. The production of nonessential items (nondurable goods) such as clothing, small appliances, etc., are called lagging indicators because they lag behind the economy.   (Page 208)

45.   **A.**   The gross national product is the total of all goods and services produced in the United States and is considered a coincident indicator. Orders for durable goods and the S&P 500 are leading indicators. A rise in personal income is an inflation indicator.   (Page 208)

46.   **B.**   Current and unpaid past dividends on cumulative preferred stock must be paid before common stockholders can receive a dividend.
(Page 12)

47.   **A.**   When a stock rises in price dramatically upon issue, it is said to be *hot*. Although there is no mathematical formula, a rise in price of 1/8th to 1/4th point or more upon issue is generally considered an example of a hot issue.   (Page 103)

48.   **B.**   The NYSE rule requires that employees of banks or insurance companies receive employer permission when opening a margin account (although not when opening a cash account). Officers of these organizations are not considered employees.
(Page 152)

49.   **A.**   The rate of return is locked in and the *face value* is realized at maturity. There is no reinvestment risk because you are not receiving anything over the life of the bond to reinvest. The gain is taxed as ordinary income and must be accreted annually. Treasury stock is not a debt instrument and pays neither interest nor dividends. (Page 64)

50.   **C.**   A STRIP has no reinvestment risk because the investor receives no interest payments that have to be reinvested. Because there is no reinvestment risk, the total rate of return is locked in, or set at issuance. The interest on the bond is paid at maturity but it is taxed as interest income over the life of the bond.   (Page 64)

51.   **A.**   The Federal Farm Credit Bank issues, through its agents, mortgage-backed securities (Federal Land Bank), agriculture-backed securities (Bank of Cooperatives), debentures and short-term notes (FICB). The FFCB does not issue equity.
(Page 68)

52.   **C.**   GNMAs are guaranteed by the government. These are the only agency issues that are backed directly by the government. The other answers are indirect federal debt.   (Page 70)

53.   **D.**   GNMAs are issued in minimum denominations of $25,000.   (Page 70)

54.   **D.**   Federal Farm Credit System Consolidated Systemwide Banks issue short-term discount notes, as well as short- and long-term bonds that are agency-backed.   (Page 68)

55.   **A.**   GNMA issues monthly payments that include both principal and interest portions.
(Page 70)

56.   **A.**   T bills are issued with 3-, 6- and 12-month maturities.   (Page 62)

57.   **D.**   The Comptroller of the Currency, the FRB and the FDIC regulate banks. The NASD enforces MSRB rules with NASD members that trade municipals.   (Page 348)

58.   **B.**   Although the Treasury securities underlying Treasury receipts are backed by the full faith and credit of the federal government, the stripped securities are not.   (Page 64)

59.   **C.**   The federal funds rate is what banks charge each other for overnight loans. It can fluctuate hourly.   (Page 215)

60. **B.** The interbank system is a market that trades in foreign currencies and government debt obligations. It is international, decentralized and unregulated. (Page 84)

61. **A.** Commercial paper is not issued by commercial banks. The CP market was developed to circumvent banks so that corporations could lend to and borrow from each other more economically. CPs are unsecured corporate IOUs. (Page 79)

62. **C.** Money-market mutual funds invest in a portfolio of short-term debt instruments such as T bills, commercial paper and repos. They are offered without a sales load or charge. The principal objective of the fund is to generate current interest income, and generally the NAV does not appreciate. (Page 418)

63. **C.** In this case, call protection means that the bonds cannot be called by the issuer for at least five years. If interest rates are falling, the issuer would have reason to want to call the bonds in and, perhaps, issue new bonds at a lower interest rate. Therefore, the call feature protects the investor for a specific period of time. (Page 36)

64. **A.** Bond interest is an expense of the firm and, when it is paid, it reduces the earnings of the firm. If the bonds were to convert, there would be no more interest payments; therefore, the company would have higher earnings. There will be more shares of common stock outstanding and this will normally translate to a lower earnings per share for the common. Interest costs would be reduced, earnings would increase and the number of shares would increase. (Page 48)

65. **D.** Officers and directors of a broker-dealer can never buy a hot issue, nor can the firm for its own inventory. A registered rep can never buy a hot issue. Choices I and II, as well as relatives, cannot buy a hot issue unless the amount they are purchasing is insignificant and they have an underwriter to assist in the solicitation of public interest during the 20-day cooling-off period. (Page 103)

66. **A.** If the yields have gone down, it means that the discount has been reduced; therefore, the dollar cost of the bills has gone up. (Page 62)

67. **B.** Matched orders refer to orders of the same size being executed on the floor of the exchange (instead of a partial fill). The underwriter must exercise diligence in ensuring that the information in the prospectus is correct. The issue must be blue-skyed in order to be sold within a state. Stabilization is the process of supporting the price of a new issue in the secondary market to ensure a normal and systematic issue of the securities in the primary market. (Page 100)

68. **D.** Each of the securities listed is exempt from registration under the act of 1933. Others would include commercial paper, Rule 147, Regulation A and Regulation D issues. (Page 105)

69. **A.** Because Rule 144 was designed to allow the SEC to monitor insider trading, the intent is to monitor insiders selling large positions that might affect the price of the stock. This rule also might indicate the trading on insider or nonpublic information. The SEC does not require that the trade be reported if the number of shares sold is 500 or less and the total sale price is $10,000 or less. (Page 274)

70. **C.** Because the yield is above the coupon, this bond is trading at a discount. Therefore, if it is held to maturity the customer will realize a return on the bond of 8% and incur a capital gains tax. Because the tax paid will reduce the return on his investment, the effective yield will be less than 8%. (Page 27)

71. **D.** The change in yields must be made up over a longer period, so that the yield change results in a greater change in price for a longer term bond. (Page 33)

72. **A.** The doctrine of reciprocal immunity or mutual exclusion was determined in the Supreme Court Case of McCulloch vs. Maryland. (Page 310)

73. **D.** Like most bonds, industrial revenue bonds trade with accrued interest. If a bond is in default it means the bond is not paying interest payments; therefore, interest would not accrue. If the settlement day is the first day of the new interest period, then the seller would be entitled to receive the entire six months' payment and the bond will trade without accrued interest. Zeros are stripped bonds; therefore, there is no interest.

(Page 316)

74. **B.** Be careful to distinguish between a cash account and a cash transaction. Regular way settlement for a government bond is next business day. Most other securities settle regular way on the fifth business day.

(Page 168)

75. **B.** A DK (Don't Know) notice is sent broker-to-broker if the comparisons do not match up. When a trade occurs, a confirmation is sent to the customer and a comparison is sent to the contra broker no later than the next business day. If the two brokers do not agree on what is to happen on the settlement day, a DK must be sent and received no later than the fourth business day.

(Page 297)

76. **A.** A fail does not occur when the value of the securities has changed. A fail occurs when one broker-dealer fails to comply with the terms of a trade.

(Page 168)

77. **B.** Because the outcome of the merger is still in question and the trader has already established positions, he is in a risk situation. He is attempting to make money on the disparity of prices; therefore, this is an arbitrage situation. If the merger goes through, the speculator will deliver the Monarch shares to cover the short position.

(Page 115)

78. **C.** The SEC says that broker-dealers must reconcile any dispute that relates to settlements within 30 calendar days. This is part of SEC Rule 15c3-3 of the Securities Exchange Act of 1934.

(Page 282)

79. **D.** The trader has responded to a quote for a specific size.   (Page 117)

80. **D.** Orders are filled in the order in which they are received. The customer will lose his position by canceling the order.   (Page 126)

81. **A.** An oil and gas income program provides few tax benefits.   (Page 467)

82. **D.** A custodian for an UGMA account cannot grant trading authority to a third party.

(Page 155)

83. **A.** A rep always needs to get permission from her own firm before working for another firm.

(Page 299)

84. **B.** The SEC considers a short against the box as a net position of zero. All later sales must be marked "short" because the investor does not have a net long position.   (Page 128)

85. **C.** The registered rep must have prior written authority from the customer and must have received approval from a supervisory person before accepting discretionary authority. While a designated principal must frequently review the account, the branch manager need not initial each order before it is entered.   (Page 157)

86. **C.** The first step is to determine the complement of the sales charge percentage (100 − 4% = 96%); then divide the NAV by the complement ($13.37 ÷ 96% = $13.93). The final step is to divide the invested amount by the purchase price ($50,000 ÷ $13.93 = 3,589), and this is the number of shares purchased.   (Page 421)

87. **C.** A portion of the original issue discount on taxable zero-coupon bonds must be declared as income and taxed annually until the bonds mature. This is known as *accreting the discount.*

(Page 339)

88. **D.** As the market price of a security changes, the broker-dealer may mark to the market and require a deposit of additional funds from an investor.   (Page 181)

89. **C.** The GMA is a zero-coupon bond maturing in the year 2012. Zero-coupon bonds are

bought at a discount and mature at face value. If the bonds are held to maturity, the difference between the purchase price and the maturity price is considered interest.   (Page 40)

90.   **D.**   Only the purchase of a call could guarantee the investor a purchase price for the stock. A buy stop limit may never be executed if the limit is missed (answer A). Writing a call would obligate the investor to sell more stock (answer B). Writing a put would not protect him if the market went up, except by the amount of the premium.
(Page 372)

91.   **D.**   The issuer determines the amount of accretion and will be entitled to an interest deduction for that year.   (Page 339)

92.   **B.**   If the cost of borrowing funds is increasing, members will need to keep more of their own funds available.   (Page 215)

93.   **D.**   A CFA is a securities analyst. Research reports are approved by a supervisory analyst.
(Page 292)

94.   **D.**   Remember the inverse relationship of bond yields to price. As bond yields decline, prices increase. Therefore, the choice is between increasing by $1 or $10. Because the bonds mature in 20 years, it is reasonable to assume that the bonds will increase by $10 because, for a given change in yield, prices on long-term bonds change more than prices on short-term bonds.   (Page 33)

95.   **D.**   A customer may withdraw 100% of the interest and dividends even if the account is restricted (within 30 days).   (Page 189)

96.   **D.**   U.S. government obligations and political subdivisions are exempt from Reg T, though not from the NYSE margin requirements.
(Page 180)

97.   **B.**   If inventories are going up, it is generally taken as an indication that sales are going down.   (Page 208)

98.   **B.**

$ 50,000	Operating income
− 5,000	Interest ($100,000 × 5%)
$ 45,000	Income before taxes
− 15,300	Taxes
$ 29,700	Aftertax income
− 5,000	Preferred dividends
	($100,000 × 5%)
$ 24,700	Earnings available
	to common
÷ 5,000	Shares of common
	($100,000 × $20 par)
$ 4.94	

(Page 240)

99.   **C.**

$ 50,000	Operating income
− 17,000	Taxes
$ 33,000	Aftertax income
− 5,000	Preferred dividends
$ 28,000	Earnings available
÷ 10,000	Shares outstanding
$ 2.80	

$100,000 convertible debentures divided by $20 conversion price results in 5,000 shares more after conversion.   (Page 241)

100.   **D.**   The gain would be $50 for the ten bonds (1/2 point for one bond is $5) and $100 for the common stock (1/2 point is $.50; $.50 × 200 shares = $100).   (Page 33)

101.   **A.**   If the dollar weakens against the yen, the purchase of 600,000,000 yen will cost more in dollars. To guard against this possibility, the U.S. company could purchase calls on Japanese yen, which would guarantee that the firm could purchase yen at no more than the strike price.
(Page 397)

102.   **D.**   If an investor has held stock short term when the put is acquired, the holding period is wiped out. If the stock is held long term when the put is acquired, the holding period is unaffected. If both the put and the stock are acquired on the same day and the put is identified as a hedge, the holding period is not wiped out. These rules are used to stop

stock owners from using puts to attempt to stretch short-term gains into long-term gains.

(Page 389)

103. **B.** The short ABC Oct 45 call is covered by the long ABC Oct 40 call. Only the net premiums need be deposited. 2 3/8 paid for the long call net of 1/2 received for writing the short call equals 1 7/8 per share. 1 7/8 times 100 shares equals $187.50. (Page 402)

104. **A.** For margin purposes short puts are covered by an exchange-approved letter of guarantee from a bank. (Page 402)

105. **A.** This is a credit spread in which the short side is not covered by the long side (because the long strike price is higher). The required deposit for a credit spread is the total dollar risk (the difference in the strike prices) less the net premium received. The risk in this transaction is $1,000 (the strike price of $35 less the strike price of $25, times 100 shares). The net premium received is $600 ($700 credit less the $100 debit),

$1,000	Actual risk
− 600	Net premiums received
$ 400	Cash deposit required

The maintenance requirement is $1,000 (the actual risk) and is reduced by the net premium received ($600) to come up with the required cash deposit of $400. (Page 404)

106. **D.** Puts may be sold in a cash account if funds equal to the aggregate exercise price are on deposit; this covers the put. Shorting the stock (which covers for margin purposes) can be performed only in a margin account. (Page 402)

107. **C.** The investor must put up 50% of the stock purchase ($6,800 × 50% = $3,400). He must also pay for the put in full ($1,000). The total deposit, therefore, is $4,400. (Page 401)

108. **C.** The typical priority for filling municipal orders is: presale orders, group orders, designated orders, member takedown orders.

(Page 327)

109. **C.** Even though on designated orders syndicate members share the takedown credit with other designated members (and thus earn less money on those particular bonds), they are willing to accept them because designated orders have a higher priority than an individual member's order. In an oversubscribed issue, this difference in priority can make the difference between the order being filled and not being filled. Remember the order priority for a municipal bond underwriting: presale orders, group orders, designated orders and, finally, member takedown orders. (Page 328)

110. **B.** MSRB rules require a manager to establish a priority for the acceptance of orders placed for a new issue. However, the manager is allowed to deviate from the established priority if such action benefits the syndicate as a whole. The manager must be prepared to justify that any deviation satisfies this condition. (Page 327)

111. **A.** Fully paid securities owned by a customer but held by the brokerage firm are regulated by the Customer Protection Rule. These securities must be segregated from the securities of the firm and clearly marked as customers' securities.

(Page 282)

112. **D.** AMBAC, FGIC and MBIA are all investor-owned corporations. (Page 344)

113. **D.** The aftertax yield of a corporate or U.S. government bond (that is, the amount of income left for the investor after all federal income taxes have been paid) is also known as that bond's *tax-equivalent yield*. Tax-equivalent yield is the yield an investor would have to receive from a municipal bond in order to have the same amount of cash in pocket after taxes. (Page 339)

114. **B.** The placement ratio serves to show the relationship between the number of bonds actually placed (sold) out of the total number available in the market that week. (Page 321)

115. **A.** *The Blue List* contains information regarding the delivery date of a new issue, as well as

other important information about municipal offerings, including par value, maturity dates, prices and yields.   (Page 321)

116. **B.** A general obligation bond is backed by the strength of the municipality, its financial health and its budget, but not by any specific revenues or revenue-generating facility.   (Page 341)

117. **D.** *Munifacts* supplies its subscribers with up-to-the-minute information via computer terminals. *Munifacts* is a service offered by *The Bond Buyer*.   (Page 321)

118. **A.** The initials FOK on an order mean "fill or kill." This phrase signifies that an order is to be executed immediately and in its entirety, or else the entire order must be canceled. An immediate-or-cancel order (IOC) can be partially filled.   (Page 126)

119. **B.** Municipalities occasionally pay off an outstanding issue of securities early if they can refinance those securities by issuing new securities at a substantially lower overall interest cost.   (Page 312)

120. **B.** Before a municipality can issue additional revenue bonds backed by the same facility as the previously issued bonds, it must first be able to show that the debt service of both issues will be adequately covered by the projected revenues of the facility (including a multiplier that serves as a safety factor).   (Page 316)

121. **B.** If the cost of raising money is lower for a GO bond, a municipality will generally issue a GO bond rather than a revenue bond, especially if the facility serves the entire municipal community.   (Page 314)

122. **B.** The actual dated date (the date from which interest will begin to accrue, regardless of the actual delivery date) is rarely a factor in a bond's marketability.   (Page 338)

123. **B.** Interest is paid with before-tax dollars and is tax deductible. Preferred dividends, on the other hand, are paid with aftertax dollars and are not deductible. On an aftertax basis, the net interest cost is 3.96% (34% of the 6% interest is tax deductible). The preferred dividend rate is 6% on an aftertax basis. Because the debt financing is "cheaper" than the preferred stock financing, reported earnings per share will increase.
(Page 231)

124. **B.** During inflationary periods, people buy more than can be produced. Increased government spending tends to aggravate inflation by increasing demand. Decreasing taxes also contributes to inflation by making more funds available for spending. A decrease in government spending accompanied by an increase in taxes tends to have a deflationary effect.   (Page 217)

125. **B.** An increase in time and savings deposits at commercial banks results in an increase in the money supply; then such deposits are by definition part of M2. An increase in bank loans and investments results in an increase in funds available to businesses and consumers, thereby increasing the money supply. Lowering reserve requirements creates excess reserves that banks can use for loans; this also increases the money supply. The sale of securities in the open market by the Federal Reserve decreases the money supply because banks use their reserves to purchase these securities.
(Page 213)

21 Final Exam Two

1. A Mar 60 put will be expiring in two weeks. The current market value is 45. What is the MOST likely premium?

   A. 3/4
   B. 1 1/2
   C. 15 1/4
   D. 20

2. Riskless and simultaneous transactions by a broker-dealer are

   A. not permissible under any circumstances
   B. permissible as long as they comply with a 5% markup policy
   C. permissible only if there's profit for a customer
   D. permissible only in new issue underwritings

3. All of the following statements are true of revenue bonds EXCEPT that

   A. they are not backed by ad valorem taxes
   B. they generally have sinking funds
   C. they are usually double-barreled
   D. users pay expenses

4. Who insures municipal issues?

   I. FGIC
   II. BIGI
   III. AMBAC
   IV. FDIC

   A. I
   B. I, II and III
   C. II and III
   D. III and IV

5. The excess revenues received by the issuers of a revenue bond placed are

   A. placed in a surplus fund
   B. deposited in a sinking fund
   C. invested by the issuer's treasurer
   D. used to call the bonds

6. The formula used to compare corporate return with municipal return is

   A. $\dfrac{\text{Yield to maturity}}{100\% - \text{Investor's tax bracket}}$

   B. $\dfrac{\text{Current yield}}{100\% - \text{Investor's tax bracket}}$

   C. $\dfrac{\text{Nominal yield}}{100\% - \text{Investor's tax bracket}}$

   D. $\dfrac{\text{Coterminous yield}}{100\% - \text{Investor's tax bracket}}$

7. All of the following are characteristics of an order book official on the CBOE EXCEPT that he

   A. is an employee of the exchange
   B. cannot trade for himself above the public price
   C. cannot accept a limit order
   D. is responsible for the inside price on his book

8. The premium of an option is also referred to as the

   A. cost of the option
   B. profit on the option
   C. cost to exercise the option
   D. exercise price

9. Which of the following guarantees a listed option?

   A. OCC
   B. NASD
   C. NYSE
   D. SEC

10. A manufacturing company sold goods to a London firm and agreed to accept payment of 1 million British pounds in two months. In which of the following ways could the company protect the payment?

    A. Buy pound puts or sell pound calls.
    B. Buy pound calls or sell pound puts.
    C. Buy U.S. dollar puts or sell U.S. dollar calls.
    D. Buy U.S. dollar calls or sell U.S. dollar puts.

11. If interest rates are rising, which interest rate option strategies would be profitable?

    I.   Buy T bond calls.
    II.   Buy T bond puts.
    III. Sell T bond calls.
    IV.   Sell T bond puts.

    A. I and II
    B. I and IV
    C. II and III
    D. II and IV

12. Which of the following types of options would be used to protect against systematic risk?

    A. Stock
    B. Index
    C. Currency
    D. Interest rate

13. The CBOE uses which of the following criteria to determine which stocks are optionable?

    I.   Number of shares outstanding
    II.   Number of shareholders
    III. Trading volume
    IV.   Market price

    A. I only
    B. I and II only
    C. I, II and III only
    D. I, II, III and IV

14. Foreign currency option premiums are quoted in which of the following?

    A. U.S. cents
    B. Units of foreign currency
    C. Percentage of the value of the foreign currency
    D. Both B and C

15. In order for someone to trade in a corporate cash account, the brokerage firm will need a

    A. corporate agreement
    B. hypothecation agreement
    C. corporate charter
    D. legal opinion

Use the following information to answer questions 16 and 17.

ABC Real Estate Limited Partnership

Limited partner's share of operations:	
Revenues	$300,000
Operating expense	$200,000
Interest expense	$95,000
Depreciation expense	$55,000

16. A limited partner would realize which of the following on his tax return for the year?

    A. $5,000 loss
    B. $5,000 gain
    C. $50,000 loss
    D. $50,000 gain

17. The cash flow for a limited partner would be

    A. positive $5,000
    B. negative $5,000
    C. $50,000 loss
    D. $50,000 gain

18. The advantages of owning a real estate DPP include all of the following EXCEPT

    A. cash flow
    B. depreciation
    C. depletion
    D. appreciation

19. A participant in an oil and gas DPP has invested $20,000. At the end of the first year, his results are capital distribution of $12,000 and depletion allowance of $6,000. What is his cost basis at the end of the year?

    A. $0
    B. $2,000
    C. $8,000
    D. $14,000

20. A customer owns $565,000 worth of securities and also has $150,000 in a cash account. If the firm were to go bankrupt, the customer could recover up to

    A. a maximum value of $500,000
    B. either $500,000 in securities or $100,000 in cash
    C. the total amount
    D. $500,000 in securities and $100,000 in cash

21. A customer writes a ZZZ 80 uncovered call for 2 1/2 in an existing account when the common has a market value of 78 1/2. How much deposit is required for the transaction?

    A. $1,420.00
    B. $1,427.50
    C. $1,450.50
    D. $1,477.50

22. Which of the following activities would be the most appropriate in a pension fund portfolio?

    A. Buying government securities and writing uncovered calls
    B. Buying government securities and writing uncovered puts
    C. Buying government securities and writing covered calls
    D. Shorting government securities and writing covered calls

23. All of the following may be called at par. Which confirmation must show yield to call?

    A. 6% municipal, basis 10%, due 2018
    B. 9% municipal, par, due 2018
    C. 6% municipal, basis 9.5%, due 1998
    D. 9% municipal, basis 6.5%, due 1998

24. Which of the following is the LEAST important source of income to support a state's general obligation bonds?

    A. Income taxes
    B. Ad valorem taxes
    C. License fees
    D. Sales taxes

25. A corporation buys a public purpose municipal bond at a premium with a maturity of 10 years at 110. Five years later the bond is called at 105. What are the tax consequences if the bond is delivered at the call?

    A. No gain, no loss
    B. $50 capital loss
    C. $50 capital gain
    D. $50 ordinary income

26. Geographic diversification of municipal securities investments protects against all of the following EXCEPT

    A. adverse legislation in a certain area
    B. economic decline in a certain area
    C. a change in interest rates
    D. default by a particular issuer

27. A municipal syndicate is structured with a 3/4-point concession and an additional takedown of 1 point. A syndicate member selling 100 bonds will receive

    A. $250
    B. $750
    C. $1,000
    D. $1,750

28. The syndicate manager takes which of the following actions in a divided municipal syndicate that does not sell out?

    A. Prorates the bonds according to syndicate participation
    B. Confirms the bonds to the member that did not sell its share
    C. Holds an auction
    D. Returns the bonds to the issuer

29. What secures an industrial revenue bond?

    A. State tax
    B. Municipal tax
    C. Trustee
    D. Net lease payments from the corporation

30. A municipal bond counsel uses which of the following in forming a legal opinion?

    I. State constitution
    II. Municipal bylaws charter
    III. Court cases and legal proceedings
    IV. Voter referendum

    A. I, II and III only
    B. I and III only
    C. II and IV only
    D. I, II, III and IV

31. A municipal bond rating service would consider which of the following when evaluating a general obligation issue?

    A. Public's attitude toward debt
    B. Consultant's report
    C. Debt service coverage ratio of the issuer
    D. Operating revenues of the issuer versus its long-term liabilities

32. A *flow of funds* clause would be found in the indenture of which of the following issues?

    A. General obligation bonds
    B. Project notes
    C. Bond anticipation notes
    D. Revenue bonds

33. White's Rating Service for municipal bond issues is concerned primarily with a bond's

    A. security
    B. marketability
    C. legality
    D. tax-exempt status

34. Which of the following is limited in the case of a limited tax municipal bond?

    A. Rate of tax that can be levied
    B. Number of taxpayers
    C. Number of buyers
    D. Amount of bonds issued

35. An unqualified legal opinion in a municipal bond underwriting would indicate that the

    A. bond attorney is not qualified to express the opinion
    B. opinion is without restriction or condition
    C. municipality has exceeded its debt limits on revenue bond issues
    D. legal opinion may not be printed on the bond

36. Which of the following types of covenants on a municipal revenue bond will insure adequate coverage for maintenance, debt service and debt service reserve?

    A. Maintenance
    B. Insurance
    C. Additional bond
    D. Rate

37. In a municipal securities underwriting, the term *takedown* refers to the discount at which members of the syndicate can buy municipal securities from the

    A. syndicate
    B. issuer
    C. selling group
    D. market maker

38. Which of the following would insure that the principal and interest are paid when a municipal issuer is in financial difficulty?

    I. MBIA
    II. AMBAC
    III. SIPC
    IV. FDIC

    A. I and II only
    B. III only
    C. III and IV only
    D. I, II, III and IV

39. In a gross revenue pledge, the first claim on revenues is

    A. operations and maintenance
    B. debt service
    C. debt service reserve
    D. repair and replacement

40. A customer has a restricted account and wants to sell $1,000 worth of securities. How much can be withdrawn by the customer?

    A. $500
    B. $1,000
    C. $1,500
    D. $2,000

41. A customer buys 100 XYZ at 50 and 1 XYZ 50 put for 5. The breakeven point for the customer is

    A. 30
    B. 45
    C. 50
    D. 55

42. A customer opened a new margin account with the following transactions:

    Sold short 100 shares XYZ at $40.
    Bought 500 shares ABC at $40.
    Sold 1 XYZ 40 put at $4.
    Sold 2 ABC 40 calls at $5.

    What is his margin deposit?

    A. $10,600
    B. $11,300
    C. $14,200
    D. $14,600

43. What is the margin call when a client buys 100 shares of ABC at 40 and sells 1 ABC 40 call at 4?

    A. $1,600
    B. $2,000
    C. $2,400
    D. $4,000

44. Using Table 21.1, what would be the required deposit for a customer buying 10 Amdahl May 10 calls and selling 10 Amdahl May 15 calls?

    A. $625
    B. $750
    C. $1,250
    D. $4,375

45. If a municipal firm purchases a block of municipal bonds in anticipation of a price increase, the firm is engaged in

    A. arbitraging
    B. hedging
    C. position trading
    D. in-house trading

Table 21.1

Option & NY Close	Strike Price	Calls—Last			Puts—Last		
		Jan	May	Aug	Jan	May	Aug
Amdahl	10	7/8	1 1/8	1 1/2	1/8	3/8	5/8
10 1/2	15	1/8	1/2	3/4	4 3/4	5 1/4	5 1/2

46. Which tax preference item(s) is(are) subject to the alternative minimum tax?

    I.   Capital gains
    II. Intangible oil and gas drilling costs in excess of net oil and gas income
    III. FIFO inventory valuation
    IV. Corporate depreciation

    A. I only
    B. I and II only
    C. II only
    D. I, II, III and IV

47. Which of the following is NOT an advantage of a real estate limited partnership?

    A. Shelter of ordinary income from taxes
    B. Amortization
    C. Flow-through of income and expenses
    D. Limited liability

48. Why would a trader normally NOT sell short a municipal bond?

    A. Short sales are illegal under the 1934 act.
    B. The market is limited due to interest rate fluctuation.
    C. There is an increased likelihood of default.
    D. A municipal bond shorted may not be available later in the secondary market.

49. Which of the following statements are true about recourse loans in a limited partnership program?

    I.   The general partner assumes responsibility for the loan's repayment.
    II. The limited partner assumes responsibility for the loan's repayment.
    III. The principal repayment lowers the limited partner's basis.
    IV. The principal repayment has no effect on the limited partner's basis.

    A. I and III
    B. I and IV
    C. II and III
    D. II and IV

50. A broker-dealer that is a financial advisor to a municipal issuer cannot also act as a negotiated underwriter unless the

    I.   financial advisor relationship is terminated
    II. broker-dealer discloses to the issuer the potential conflict of interest
    III. broker-dealer discloses to the issuer the amount of profit it will make on the underwriting

    A. I and II only
    B. II only
    C. III only
    D. I, II and III

51. Your customer buys a put. Prior to expiration, the put is exercised. What is your customer required to deposit?

    I.   Cash equal to the aggregate exercise price
    II. The margin that is required for a short position
    III. 100 shares of the underlying stock

    A. I
    B. I or II
    C. II
    D. II or III

52. The NYSE composite consists primarily of

    A. industrial securities
    B. financial securities
    C. utility securities
    D. transportation securities

53. Where would you find the bid worksheet on a new municipal bond issue?

    A. *The Bond Buyer* worksheet
    B. *The Blue List*
    C. *Munifacts*
    D. *Moody's*

54. Which of the following appears on the confirmation statement for a when-issued trade of municipal bonds?

    A. Settlement date
    B. Total contract price
    C. Accrued interest
    D. Principal or agency trade

55. A corporation purchases a $100,000 par value public purpose municipal bond in the secondary markets at 90, 10 years prior to maturity. For accounting purposes, the corporation uses straight-line accretion to determine the book value of this investment. After three years, the corporation sells the bond at 93. What is the reported gain or loss on this investment for tax purposes?

    A. $1,500 loss
    B. $1,500 gain
    C. $3,000 loss
    D. $3,000 gain

56. What is the spread on a U.S. government security with a bid price of 97.12 and an offering price of 97.16?

    A. $.04
    B. $1.00
    C. $1.25
    D. $12.50

57. All of the following would affect option premiums EXCEPT the

    A. volatility of the stock
    B. stock price
    C. time to expiration
    D. account position

58. An investor has purchased a municipal bond at a premium and sold the same bond before maturity. Each of the following would be needed to determine capital gain or loss EXCEPT the

    A. issue date
    B. purchase date
    C. sale date
    D. maturity date

59. A work-out quote or a workable indication is the same as a

    A. firm bid
    B. likely bid
    C. likely ask
    D. firm bid and offer

60. An investor shorts an ABC Oct 50 call in an account with a CMV of $23,000 when the market price of ABC is $52 for a premium of $4. The margin requirement is

    A. $1,080
    B. $1,300
    C. $1,440
    D. $1,580

61. All of the following would be likely conflicts of interest on the part of the general partner of an oil and gas direct participation program EXCEPT when the general partner

    A. takes a loan from the program
    B. commingles funds from several programs
    C. owns lease rights on adjacent undeveloped land
    D. manages partnership property

62. Who makes the final judgment on the tax return of a limited partnership?

    A. IRS
    B. Comptroller of the Currency
    C. SEC
    D. NYSE

63. Which of the following information is distributed via *Munifacts*?

    I. New issue information
    II. Issues still available from dealers
    III. Quantities of new issues still available
    IV. Economic indicators

    A. I and II only
    B. I and III only
    C. II and III only
    D. I, II, III and IV

64. The Municipal Securities Rulemaking Board does not permit a municipal securities firm to engage in certain business activities with an investment company. The activities NOT permitted include

A. accepting presale orders
B. hiring officers from the investment company
C. soliciting transactions in municipal securities as compensation for investment company shares sold
D. refusing to transact business with the investment company

65. An open-end mutual fund has a bid price of $16.00 and an offering price of $17.39. The sales charge for buying an investment of $50,000 - $99,000 is 5%. How many shares can an investor purchase if the investor invests $60,000?

A. 3,125
B. 3,450
C. 3,562
D. 3,700

66. A member of an undivided $5,000,000 municipal syndicate has a $500,000 participation. At the close of the offering, there are $1,000,000 of bonds remaining. The member sold $300,000 of its commitment. How many dollars' worth of bonds will it have to buy?

A. $100,000
B. $200,000
C. $300,000
D. $500,000

67. Place in the proper sequence from highest to lowest priority the following methods of allocating bond orders in a new municipal underwriting.

I.   Presale
II. Group net
III. Designated
IV. Member

A. I, II, III, IV
B. I, III, IV, II
C. I, IV, III, II
D. IV, I, III, II

68. A registered representative receives a call from a custodian wishing to buy shares of a specific new issue security. The registered representative should

A. refuse to accept an order
B. accept the order only if it is placed in a margin account
C. discuss and review suitability
D. talk the investor into buying another stock.

69. Which of the following statements would be included in an unqualified legal opinion?

A. The issue may be marketed in various states.
B. The issuer has authority to incur debt for the project.
C. The attorney has qualified the official statement.
D. The attorney has qualified the interest payments.

70. All of the following are municipal securities underwriting terms EXCEPT

A. firm
B. when-issued
C. standby
D. AON

71. A customer would like to know the approximate price of her 7.2% 20-year municipal bond. If 8% 20-year bonds are currently selling for 106 and 7% 20-year bonds are currently selling for 102, the customer's bond would probably sell for

    A. 100
    B. 100.2
    C. 102.8
    D. 103.2

72. Which of the following terms is usually used in connection with a new issue of GO bonds?

    A. Private placement
    B. Best efforts
    C. Negotiated
    D. Competitive

73. Which of the following documents would include information about the financial condition of the issuer?

    A. Notice of sale
    B. Trust indenture
    C. Official statement
    D. Bond resolution

74. In connection with the issuance of a municipal general obligation bond, the bond counsel will register an opinion on all of the following EXCEPT the

    A. statutory authority of the issuer
    B. Internal Revenue Code aspect of the annual interest
    C. fairness of the underwriting spread
    D. circumstances under which the issue can be called

75. An underwriting bid for a municipal GO issue would include which two of the following?

    I. Dollar amount bid
    II. Coupon rate
    III. Yield to maturity
    IV. Underwriting spread

    A. I and II
    B. I and III
    C. II and III
    D. II and IV

76. A municipal bond dealer that submits an order to a syndicate must disclose that the securities are being purchased for all of the following EXCEPT

    A. its dealer account
    B. a bank president
    C. the account of a related portfolio
    D. an accumulation account

77. What does the Trust Indenture Act of 1939 require trust indentures to include?

    A. Trustee's name
    B. Protective covenants
    C. Schedule of interest payments
    D. Investors' names

78. A registered representative has a new client who has just received a $25,000 inheritance and who wishes to use the money to purchase 8 1/4% Steel City industrial development bonds selling at an 8.45% yield. The $1,000,000 bond issue is due in 15 years and is rated Ba. Which of the following factors would support a recommendation of a purchase of these bonds?

    A. The client is in the 18% tax bracket.
    B. This would be the client's only investment.
    C. The client is willing to accept a moderate amount of risk.
    D. The client's job is not very secure.

79. How would the net yield of a municipal bond that would subject its owner to AMT compare to one that would not?

    A. The yield would be higher.
    B. The yield would be lower.
    C. The two yields would be the same.
    D. The yield is not affected by AMT.

80. One of your clients purchased a municipal bond at 110 that was eight years from maturity. Six years later, she sells the bond for 106. What is her cost basis at the time of sale?

    A. 100
    B. 101 1/2
    C. 102 1/2
    D. 106

81. Municipal securities are regulated by which of the following?

    A. SEC
    B. IRS
    C. NASD
    D. NYSE

82. Which of the following represents a municipal bond quote?

    A. 8.20–8.00
    B. 8.5%
    C. 85.24–85.30
    D. 85 1/2

83. Which of the following represents a serial bond quote?

    A. 8.20–8.00
    B. 8.5%
    C. 85.24–85.30
    D. 85 1/2

84. General obligation bonds are usually NOT sold short because

    A. they are backed by the full faith and credit of the issuing authority
    B. MSRB regulations prohibit short selling
    C. it is difficult to cover a short municipal position
    D. they trade over the counter

85. How long must a customer who sold a bond at a loss wait before he can buy back a substantially identical bond and not have the sale classified as a wash sale?

    A. 5 days
    B. 20 days
    C. 30 days
    D. There is no waiting period.

86. Which of the following includes the amount of anticipated competitive bid and negotiated sales in municipal bonds for the coming month?

    A. *Munifacts*
    B. *The Blue List*
    C. The visible supply
    D. Moody's Manual

87. Debbie Gold agrees to buy $10,000 of a new issue of municipal bonds that are being traded when-, as- and if-issued. Which of the following items would appear on her confirmation of this transaction?

    I. Amount of accrued interest
    II. Settlement date
    III. Description of the securities
    IV. Total cost of the transaction

    A. I, II and III only
    B. II only
    C. III only
    D. I, II, III and IV

88. A head and shoulders bottom formation is an indication of

    A. a bearish market
    B. a bullish market
    C. the reversal of an upward trend
    D. the reversal of a downward trend

89. The *dated date* on a municipal bond issue refers to the

    A. settlement date
    B. trade date
    C. date on which the bonds were originally issued
    D. date on which the bonds begin accruing interest

90. All of the following actions would increase a deficit in the U.S. balance of payments EXCEPT

    A. investments by U.S. firms abroad
    B. purchases by foreigners of U.S. securities
    C. U.S. foreign aid
    D. U.S. citizens buying Japanese cars

91. Doohickey Manufacturing, Inc. has a PE ratio of 8.0 and earnings per share of $1.30, and paid $.64 per share of common. What is the dividend payout ratio of Doohickey Manufacturing?

    A. 10%
    B. 12.50%
    C. 16.25%
    D. 49%

92. Moore Manufacturing declares bankruptcy and is to be liquidated. In what order of preference, starting with the first claims on the assets of Moore Manufacturing, will the following creditors be paid?

    I. Preferred stockholders
    II. Internal Revenue Service
    III. Bondholders of unsecured debentures
    IV. Common stockholders

    A. I, IV, III, II
    B. II, III, I, IV
    C. III, II, I, IV
    D. IV, I, III, II

93. Tech Data Company, with an EPS of $2.20, paid dividends of $.15 per quarter for the first three quarters of the year. Due to an excellent fourth quarter, the directors declared a $.30 dividend for the final quarter. What is the dividend payout ratio for Tech Data?

    A. 20%
    B. 29%
    C. 34%
    D. 49%

94. To tighten credit, the Fed begins selling securities in the open market. What is the first interest rate to feel this change in Fed policy?

    A. Money-market rates
    B. Prime rate
    C. Interest rates on long-term debentures
    D. Federal funds rate

95. Payment on Eurobonds is made in which of the following ways?

    A. Interest and principal in a foreign currency
    B. Interest and principal in U.S. dollars
    C. Interest in a foreign currency, principal in U.S. dollars
    D. Interest in U.S. dollars, principal in a foreign currency

96. The U.S. dollar has been appreciating against foreign currencies. All of the following statements are true EXCEPT that

    A. the U.S. dollar buys more of foreign currencies
    B. U.S. exports become more competitive
    C. U.S. goods become more expensive in foreign countries
    D. foreign goods become cheaper in the United States

97. Artco has 300,000 shares of common stock outstanding, no preferred stock and $500,000 in net earnings after taxes. Artco has a 1-for-3 reverse split. The new EPS will be

    A. $.55
    B. $1.66
    C. $5.00
    D. the same as the previous EPS

98. Which of the following statements concerning highly leveraged companies are true?

   I. Historically, utilities are highly leveraged.
   II. They are most likely to trade on equity.
   III. Their debt ratios are high.
   IV. If sales increase, EPS will increase dramatically.

   A. I and II only
   B. I and III only
   C. III and IV only
   D. I, II, III and IV

99. The economy has entered an uncertain period with interest rates fluctuating up and down. Which of the following statements are true?

   I. Short-term interest rates will fluctuate more sharply than long-term interest rates.
   II. Short-term bond prices will fluctuate more sharply than long-term bond prices.
   III. Prices of long-term bonds are most affected by changes in the yield.
   IV. The most volatile fluctuations are found in the federal funds rate.

   A. I, II and III only
   B. I, III and IV only
   C. II and IV only
   D. I, II, III and IV

100. When the Federal Reserve Board buys securities in the open market, which of the following will occur?

   I. The federal funds rate will tend to decrease.
   II. Treasury notes will tend to increase in price.
   III. Banks will have more money to lend.
   IV. The call loan rate will increase.

   A. I only
   B. I, II and III only
   C. III and IV only
   D. I, II, III and IV

101. Which of the following statements regarding the declaration of cash dividends is FALSE?

   A. Total liabilities increase.
   B. Total assets decrease.
   C. The market price of the stock may change.
   D. Growth companies are more likely to declare stock dividends than cash dividends.

Use the following information to answer questions 102 and 103.

Worthington Systems, Inc. is a start-up company formed by a group of investors to manufacture and market biomedical technology. At the time of its formation it had:

$1,000,000	7% $1,000 par debentures (convertible at $20)
1,000,000	10,000 shares of 5% preferred ($100 par)
2,000,000	200,000 shares of common ($10 par)
$4,000,000	Total capitalization

In its first year of operations, it had $1,000,000 of operating income.

102. What is the earnings per share of Worthington Systems, Inc. during its first year of operation?

   A. $1.89
   B. $2.65
   C. $2.82
   D. $3.05

103. What is the return on common equity during Worthington's first year of operation?

   A. 19%
   B. 25%
   C. 29%
   D. 50%

104. Stock is trading at $25 per share. If all the debenture holders converted, what would happen?

    A. EPS would decrease.
    B. EPS would increase.
    C. Neither the EPS nor the PE ratio would be affected.
    D. The PE ratio would be affected, but not the EPS.

105. Which of the following statements is NOT true of *inverted head and shoulders* formations?

    A. The price of the security is rising.
    B. It indicates a reversal of an upward trend.
    C. It is a clear indication of a bullish reversal.
    D. It signals a buy decision.

106. Middletown Power and Light has issued convertible bonds with a fixed rate of interest. Last year, Middletown increased its operating profit by 25%. The earnings per share for the company

    A. will increase
    B. will decrease
    C. will remain the same
    D. cannot be determined from the information given

107. After three consecutive quarters of decline, the Fed takes action to expand credit. Which of the following actions would have LEAST impact on the economy?

    A. Buying securities in the open market
    B. Lowering margin requirements
    C. Lowering reserve requirements
    D. Lowering the discount rate

108. Interest rates have been declining for the past three months. Which of the following statements are true?

    I. Long-term discount bonds benefit the most.
    II. Bond prices gain in proportion to the loss in yield.
    III. Bond prices of newly issued bonds remain the same.

    A. I and II only
    B. I and III only
    C. II and III only
    D. I, II and III

Use the following account information to answer questions 109 through 111.

    Buy 2 MCS Jun 40 calls at 2
    Sell 2 MCS Jun 30 calls at 4 1/4

109. What is this position called?

    A. Bearish spread
    B. Bullish spread
    C. Combination
    D. Variable hedge

110. What will be the investor's overall net profit or loss if both calls expire unexercised?

    A. $450 loss
    B. $450 profit
    C. $1,250 loss
    D. $1,250 profit

111. At what price in the stock will the investor break even?

    A. 30
    B. 32 1/4
    C. 40
    D. 44 1/4

112. The writer of a Twitco Jan 25 put would be considered fully covered if the writer also had which of the following positions?

    A. Long a Twitco Jan 20 put
    B. Short a Twitco Jan 25 call
    C. Long a Twitco Jan 25 call
    D. Long a Twitco Jan 30 put

113. Assume that ABC declares a 6% stock dividend. What will be the exercise price of the ABC Jan 50 call option after the ex-dividend date?

   A. 47
   B. 47 1/8
   C. 47 1/4
   D. 50

114. Using Table 21.2, how much money must the investor deposit to purchase 10 May 60 DWQ calls? (Reg T 50%)

   A. $2,250
   B. $5,950
   C. $6,000
   D. $8,250

115. Using Table 21.2, what price would DWQ need to reach in order for the investor who bought 10 May 60 DWQ calls to break even? (Disregard commissions.)

   A. 57 3/4
   B. 60
   C. 61 3/4
   D. 62 1/4

116. Using Table 21.2, when will the 10 May 60 DWQ calls expire?

   A. 11:59 pm EST Saturday, May 19th
   B. Noon EST Saturday, May 19th
   C. 4 pm EST Friday, May 18th
   D. 3 pm EST Friday, May 18th

117. Using Table 21.2, if the 10 May 60 DWQ calls expire unexercised, how much money will the investor lose?

   A. $2,250
   B. $5,950
   C. $6,000
   D. $8,250

Table 21.2

Option & NY Close	Strike Price	Calls—Last			Puts—Last		
		May	Jun	Jul	May	Jun	Jul
DWQ	60	2 1/4	r	r	1/16	7/8	1 3/8
58 1/4	65	1/4	r	r	7 1/2	8	8 5/8

118. A customer tells his registered representative to purchase $10,000 worth of shares in whatever pharmaceutical company the rep thinks looks good. In what type of account could the rep accept this type of order?

   A. Custodial account
   B. Discretionary
   C. Margin account
   D. Special cash account

Use the following information to answer questions 119 and 120.

On November 24, 1998, an investor buys 1 OEX Dec 575 call at 7 when the index was at 581.96. On December 1, 1998, the index closes at 584.50 and the investor would like to take some gain.

```
              Wednesday, December 1, 1998

                    OPTIONS
              CHICAGO BOARD
          S&P 100 INDEX - $100 times index
```

Strike Price	Calls - Last			Puts - Last		
	Nov	Dec	Jan	Nov	Dec	Jan
565	10 3/8	14	...	1 1/4	4 1/8	6 3/4
570	7 1/4	11 7/8	13	2 5/8	7 5/8	9 1/2
575	4 1/8	9 7/8	10 1/8	7 1/8	11 1/2	12 5/8
580	2 3/8	6 1/4	8 5/8	10 1/2	13	15 1/2
585	1 1/4	4 1/2	6 1/4	15	...	...
590	1/4	3 1/8	5	20	...	...
595	1/8	2 1/8	4 1/8	...	...	...

```
Total call volume 174,908   Total call open int.  1,282,742
Total put volume 164,129    Total put open int. 1,113,492
The index: High 585.78  Low 582.12  Close 584.50  +2.42
```

119. Which of the following courses of action would result in the largest gain?

   A. Sell the option at the close.
   B. Lock in a 2.54-point gain by exercising the option when the index is at 584.50.
   C. Exercise the option any time on December 1, 1998.
   D. Continue to hold the option and allow it to expire.

120. Which of the following OEX options were in-the-money at the close on December 1, 1998?

   I.   Jan 565 call
   II. Jan 570 put
   III. Dec 585 put
   IV. Jan 595 call

   A. I and III
   B. II, III and IV
   C. II and IV
   D. III

121. Individuals who have diversified stock holdings usually write covered calls so as to

   A. increase their rate of return on the stocks held in their portfolios
   B. increase the number of shares they own
   C. further diversify their portfolios
   D. lock in profits

122. An investor buys 1 ABC Apr 40 call and sells 1 ABC Jul 50 call. What is this position?

   A. Variable hedge
   B. Straddle
   C. Diagonal spread
   D. Vertical spread

123. Using Table 21.3, an investor purchased a deutsche mark Mar 64 call on the last sale of the day. How much did the investor pay for the option?

   A. $126.00
   B. $478.80
   C. $787.50
   D. $1,260.00

124. Using Table 21.3, the investor exercises the call with the deutsche mark at 65.50. What was the investor's net cost?

   A. 64.00 cents per mark
   B. 65.26 cents per mark
   C. 65.50 cents per mark
   D. 66.76 cents per mark

Table 21.3

Option & Underlying	Strike Price	Calls—Last			Puts—Last		
		Nov	Dec	Mar	Nov	Dec	Mar
62,500 German marks-cents per unit							
DMark	...63	0.21	0.42	r	0.23	0.89	s
67.60	...64	0.66	0.88	1.26	r	1.14	r
67.60	...65	r	r	0.74	r	r	r

125. An investor would like to profit from a market advance that she believes will occur in the near future, but she is uncertain which specific stocks will be affected. She also wishes to limit her risk to a specific amount. Which of the following actions would be most appropriate to take in attempting to meet this objective?

   A. Buy calls on a broad-based stock index.
   B. Sell puts on a narrow-based stock index.
   C. Buy calls on a narrow-based stock index.
   D. Purchase several blue chip stocks on margin.

◆ Answers & Rationale

1.   C.   This is a judgment question. The put is in-the-money by 15 points (the holder of the put could buy the stock at 45 and sell it at 60). Because the premium includes intrinsic value (amount in-the-money) and time value (intangible value), the premium must be greater than 15. Because there are only two weeks remaining before expiration, the time value will be very little; therefore, 15 1/4 is the best answer.   (Page 371)

2.   B.   The 5% markup policy applies to all types of secondary market transactions including riskless and simultaneous transactions.
                (Page 138)

3.   C.   A revenue bond is backed only by the revenue generated by the facility, whereas a GO bond is backed by the full faith, credit and taxing power of the issuer (and is therefore considered safer). A double-barreled bond is a revenue bond that is additionally backed by the full faith, credit and taxing power of the municipality.
                (Page 315)

4.   B.   Financial Guaranty Insurance Company (FGIC), Bond Investors Guaranty Insurance Co. (BIGI) and AMBAC Indemnity Corp. (AMBAC) all insure municipal bonds, as do MGIC and MBIA.   (Page 344)

5.   A.   Extra funds received normally are placed in the surplus fund or the general reserve. If at a later date the municipality decides to call the bonds, the funds will be transferred from the general reserve to the sinking fund (if there is one) and the bonds will be called.   (Page 317)

6.   A.   Municipal securities are quoted in yield to maturity, so that is the yield you must use. This is the formula for tax-equivalent yield.
                (Page 339)

7.   C.   One of the functions of the order book official (sometimes called the *board broker*) is to maintain a record of all limit orders. The OBO displays the inside market. The CBOE employs the OBO.   (Page 364)

8.   A.   The premium is the cost (or price) of the option. The profit on an option represents gain. The cost to exercise an option is the exercise or strike price. Premiums equal intrinsic value plus time value.   (Page 358)

9.   A.   The Options Clearing Corporation issues, guarantees and exercises options for the industry. The firm handles all of the clerical functions. The Options Clearing Corporation guarantees the performance of the option contract.
                (Page 365)

10.   A.   The manufacturing company wants to protect the value of the British pound payment. Just as in any hedge used to protect against a decrease in value, the hedger buys puts or sell calls.
                (Page 398)

11.   C.   If rates are rising, bond prices are falling. Buying puts or selling calls would be profitable.   (Page 394)

12.   B.   Systematic risk is also called *market risk*. Index options allow the investor to protect against any decrease in the value of stocks due to market factors. This is different from non-systematic or company-specific risk, which can be hedged with equity options. All stocks have both types of risks: the risk of what the market does and the risk of what happens to the individual company.
                (Page 392)

13.   D.   To determine which stocks are optionable, the CBOE considers the number of shares outstanding (minimum of 7,000,000), number of shareholders (minimum of 6,000), trading volume (minimum of 2,400,000 in the past 12 months on all exchanges) and market price (minimum of $10 for the past 3 months prior to listing).
                (Page 363)

14.   A.   Foreign currency options traded in the United States are always quoted in U.S. cents.
                (Page 398)

15. **A.** The corporate agreement (also known as the corporate resolution) which must be signed by the secretary of the corporation, identifies officers authorized to make transactions. In a margin account, a copy of the corporate charter and a hypothecation agreement would also be required.
(Page 154)

16. **C.** For tax purposes the LP will have a $50,000 loss. Loss is applicable to passive income.

$ 300,000	Revenue
– 200,000	Operating expenses
– 95,000	Interest
– 55,000	Depreciation
– $ 50,000	Loss

(Page 479)

17. **A.** When figuring profit or loss, subtract deductible expenses (these include expenses, mortgage interest and depreciation) from total income. For cash flow, subtract real-dollars-out from real-dollars-in (this would not include depreciation). Remember, the only way the $50,000 loss can be used is to offset a gain. Cash flow is taxable income with depreciation added back (–$50,000 + $55,000 depreciation = $5,000 cash flow).   (Page 479)

18. **C.** Depletion is a deduction taken for the removal and sale of a natural resource such as oil, gas, coal, peat, sulfur or timber. It does not apply to real estate.   (Page 466)

19. **B.** Because the participant's investment is $20,000, the deductions will be taken from that figure. A return of capital reduces the participant's risk and his basis; the allowable depletion also reduces the basis. Therefore, the participant has an adjusted cost basis of $2,000.   (Page 471)

20. **A.** SIPC insures the customer to a maximum of $500,000. The maximum amount of cash included in the $500,000 total is $100,000.
(Page 284)

21. **A.** To determine the deposit required when an investor writes an uncovered out-of-the-money call, take the premium for the option, add 20% of the current market value (CMV) of the underlying stock, subtract any amount the option is out-of-the-money (this gives you the total margin requirement), then subtract the premium; the result is the required deposit. The customer who wrote the ZZZ uncovered call would have a margin requirement of $250 plus $1,570 (which is the $7,850 CMV × 20%) minus $150 (the amount the option is out-of-the-money), for a total of $1,670. He would have to deposit $1,420, which is the margin requirement of $1,670 less the premium of $250 that he received for writing the call.   (Page 402)

22. **C.** Pension funds normally must follow very conservative investment strategies. Of the strategies listed, only answer C represents transactions that would be appropriate for this type of account. An investor who writes uncovered options or shorts securities is taking on very great risks for the returns that are possible.   (Page 394)

23. **D.** The requirement is that if a bond is callable, it must be quoted in yield to maturity or yield to call, whichever yield is lower. In relation to the coupon, the yield to call is farthest away, so if the bond is trading at a discount the yield to call will be the highest yield; if the bond is trading at a premium, the yield to call will be the lowest yield.   (Page 337)

24. **B.** Most states levy both income tax and general state sales taxes. They also charge licensing fees to private schools, hospitals, etc. Real estate taxes are normally charged by a county or city and are used for general expenses.
(Page 314)

25. **A.** Because this is a premium bond, the premium must be amortized over the life of the bond (this is true whether it was purchased in the primary or secondary market). The bond was purchased for a $100 premium and will mature in 10 years, so the bond will be amortized at $10 per year. After 5 years, the $50 ($10 × 5) amortized would have dropped the cost basis to $1,050 (or 105). Therefore, at the time of sale there is no loss or gain.
(Page 338)

26. **C.** If the interest rates change, geographic diversification will not help. A change in interest rates will affect all of the yields.   (Page 255)

27. **D.** Normally the concession is part of the takedown. However, in this example it has been separated. Because the total takedown includes the concession, it is 1 3/4% of $100,000, or $1,750. In this question, the total takedown is 1 3/4 points (takedown of 3/4 plus additional takedown of 1 point). A syndicate member that sells the bond will receive the whole takedown.   (Page 326)

28. **B.** Because this issue is a divided, or Western, syndicate, each member is responsible for a specified number of securities to be sold. If a member does not sell its share, it receives the bonds for its inventory. Answer A would be correct for an undivided, or Eastern, syndicate.   (Page 323)

29. **D.** IDRs are issued by municipalities to construct a facility that will be used by, or is being constructed for, the benefit of a corporation. When this is done, the corporation is required to sign a long-term lease. Although classified as a municipal security, IDRs are backed by the revenues of the corporation participating in the project.   (Page 316)

30. **D.** The bond counsel (bond attorney) is paid to do whatever research is necessary to render an opinion on the legality and the tax-exempt status of the issue, and may use any or all of the items listed when rendering a legal opinion.   (Page 314)

31. **A.** Answers B, C and D are revenue bond considerations.   (Page 341)

32. **D.** Because revenue bonds are backed solely by the user fees paid to the facility, it is important to know how these funds will flow (what is paid first, second, etc.). Because GO bonds have full faith and credit backing, flow of funds is not an issue.   (Page 316)

33. **B.** White's ratings are based on the marketability of an issue at a particular interest rate, rather than on the creditworthiness of the issuer.   (Page 344)

34. **A.** A general obligation bond may be backed by a specific tax, and that tax may be limited by a ceiling on either its rate or amount.   (Page 315)

35. **B.** An unqualified legal opinion is one that is issued by the bond counsel with no restrictions. It confirms that there is no problem or potential problem with either the tax-exempt status or the legality of the issue.   (Page 314)

36. **D.** The rate covenant will have within it the promise to charge enough for the use of the facility to cover expenses. It will also include a gross or net revenue pledge stating in what order the revenue received will be used.   (Page 313)

37. **A.** The manager of the syndicate buys the securities from the issuer and in turn sells them to the other members of the syndicate at a discount, known as the *takedown*.   (Page 326)

38. **A.** Municipal Bond Insurance Corporation (MBIA) and AMBAC Indemnity Corporation (AMBAC) both insure municipal bonds. Securities Investor Protection Corporation (SIPC) insures securities account holders from broker-dealer default; Federal Deposit Insurance Corporation (FDIC) insures bank account holders from bank default.   (Page 344)

39. **B.** In a gross revenue pledge, debt service comes first; in a net revenue pledge, operations and maintenance have first claim.   (Page 316)

40. **A.** When a customer makes a sale in a restricted account, 50% of the proceeds are released to SMA and can, therefore, be withdrawn by the customer. The customer sold $1,000 worth of securities, so $500 can be released.   (Page 188)

41. **D.** The customer owns stock that he purchased for $50 a share. To protect that price, he purchased (or paid for) a put that allows him to sell

the stock for $50 a share. The cost of the put was $500, or $5 a share. Therefore, he has invested a total of $55 for this position, which will be his breakeven. If the stock trades at 55 or above, he will be able to sell his stock for enough to cover the cost of the put he purchased, as protection against downside risk.   (Page 389)

42. **A.** The customer has sold short and purchased stock in a margin account. The requirement is 50% of the price for both. There will be no margin requirement for the options because the short sale covers the put and the purchase covers the short calls. Therefore, the total margin requirement is $12,000. The deposit will take into consideration any monies received as a result of the sale of the options for $400 for the put and $1,000 for the two calls; thus, the deposit requirement is reduced by $1,400. Therefore, the margin deposit will be $10,600.

$$
\begin{array}{ll}
\$\ 4,000 & \text{SMV} \\
\$ 20,000 & \text{LMV} \\
\hline
\$ 24,000 & \\
\times\ \ 50\% & \text{Reg T} \\
\hline
\$ 12,000 & \\
-\ 1,000 & \text{Proceeds of sale of ABC call} \\
\hline
\$ 11,000 & \\
-\ \ \ 400 & \text{Proceeds of sale of XYZ put} \\
\hline
\$ 10,600 &
\end{array}
$$

The written put is covered by the short sale of 100 XYZ, and the short call is covered by the long ABC stock.   (Page 402)

43. **A.** The client buys the stock for $4,000, with a margin requirement of $2,000. He sells a covered call against the stock, which requires no margin. The $400 he receives for writing the covered call offsets the margin required, so the net deposit required would be $1,600.   (Page 401)

44. **A.** This is a vertical debit spread. Whenever you have a debit spread, you know that the option you sold is covered by the one you bought; therefore, the margin requirement is based solely on the purchase. The customer purchased 10 con-

tracts for 1 1/8 (or $112.50 each × 10), which equals $1,125; and the customer received $500 ($50 × 10). Therefore, her margin call is $625.   (Page 401)

45. **C.** The dealer is buying for its inventory. This is called *position trading*.   (Page 134)

46. **C.** Tax preference items include certain income and gains associated with direct participation items, but are not applied to corporate inventories, other capital gains or corporate depreciation.   (Page 266)

47. **A.** Tax losses from passive investments can be deducted only against passive income.   (Page 466)

48. **D.** The trader may not be able to borrow the bonds to cover the short because many municipal issues have a thin float.   (Page 128)

49. **C.** By signing a letter of recourse, the limited partner accepts certain financial responsibilities in addition to the original investment.   (Page 480)

50. **D.** The MSRB has specified that all of the listed requirements be met by the broker-dealer.   (Page 331)

51. **D.** To exercise a put, an investor can either deliver the shares of the underlying stock or deposit the required amount of cash to sell short the stock.   (Page 374)

52. **A.** The largest portion of all broad-based indexes are industrial securities.   (Page 220)

53. **A.** Before a bid is placed, a preliminary price meeting of syndicate members is held. Each member enters onto *The Bond Buyer* worksheets proposed prices or yields for each maturity of the issue.   (Page 319)

54. **D.** A when-issued trade establishes the contract price but not the settlement date. Because the settlement date will not be established until the

securities become available, the amount of accrued interest and the total amount due cannot be calculated at the time of the trade. (Page 329)

55. **D.** The corporation receives interest free of federal tax while holding the bond. Appreciation or depreciation of the bond's value is treated as a capital gain or loss upon sale. The gain or loss is calculated using the purchase and sale prices, not the adjusted bond value. (Page 339)

56. **C.** Always assume a $1,000 bond face value unless otherwise stated. U.S. government notes and bonds are quoted as a percentage of par in 1/32nds. 97 16/32 (97.5% of par) is $975.00. 97 12/32 (97.375% of par) is $973.75. The spread is $1.25. (Page 63)

57. **D.** The number of contracts that a client owned (long) or owed (short) would not affect the option premiums. (Page 371)

58. **A.** The amount of the premium that would be amortized (and, therefore, affect the cost basis for determining capital gains or losses) is based on the price at which the bond is purchased, the date it was purchased, the length of time remaining until maturity, the sale date and the proceeds. (Page 339)

59. **B.** A dealer wishing to dispose of a block of bonds will seek a work-out quote or a workable indication from another dealer. The workable indication from another dealer is not a firm bid, but it is the price at which the other dealer is likely to buy. (Page 133)

60. **C.** $400 + $1,040 = $1,440. If this were an initial transaction in a new account, the margin requirement would be $2,000. (Page 403)

61. **D.** Part of the general partner's job is to actively manage himself, or to hire managers for, partnership properties. (Page 464)

62. **A.** The IRS makes the final determination of all tax matters. (Page 471)

63. **D.** *Munifacts* is a private wire system similar to the Dow Jones wire system. It continually prints general news affecting the municipal bond market, new information about issues and pricing information. (Page 321)

64. **C.** The MSRB has rules against manipulative practices such as this. (Page 354)

65. **C.** Because the client is investing $60,000, the breakpoint at $50,000 applies. Therefore, it is necessary to calculate the offering price at this breakpoint as follows. First take the net asset value and divide it by 100% less the sales charge percentage. $16.00 divided by 95% equals $16.84. $60,000 will purchase 3,562 shares at $16.84 per share. (Page 421)

66. **A.** In an undivided (or *Eastern*) syndicate, each member is responsible for its proportion of the offering, regardless of how many bonds it has already placed. If the member was committed to sell 10% of the original dollar value of the issue, it will be committed to sell 10% of any bonds remaining unsold. (Page 323)

67. **A.** Presale orders get filled first because they were placed even before the syndicate manager had purchased the securities from the issuer. Group net orders are filled next; although the buyer didn't indicate a desire to purchase the bonds until after the beginning of the sale period, the buyer has agreed to pay the public offering price and the entire group splits the takedown according to the percentage of their individual participation in the syndicate. Designated orders are the next orders filled; the buyer is still willing to pay the full public offering price, but would like to designate which syndicate members will receive the credit for the sale. The last orders filled are those of the members themselves, who will be allocated bonds minus whatever takedown or concession for which they are eligible. (Page 327)

68. **C.** There are no restrictions that specifically apply to the purchase of new issues in a custodial account, as long as the registered rep has discussed and reviewed the suitability of the investment. (Page 250)

69. **B.** The primary purposes of a legal opinion are twofold: the counsel attests to the fact that, to the best of its knowledge, the issuer has the legal right to issue the securities in question, and the interest that will be paid on the bonds by the issuer will be exempt from federal taxation.

(Page 314)

70. **C.** The term *standby* is usually used to indicate that a brokerage firm has agreed to purchase any part of an issue that has not been subscribed to through a rights offering.   (Page 104)

71. **C.** By interpolating, we know that the price of the 7.2% bond should be approximately 2/10ths (or 20%) of the way between the 102 price of the 7% bond and the 106 price of the 8% bond. Twenty percent of 4 points $(106 - 102 = 4)$ would be .8, so we add .8 to 102, which is 102.8.

(Page 33)

72. **D.** GO bonds are issued on a competitive basis. Revenue bond issues are typically negotiated.   (Page 319)

73. **C.** The official statement is used to disclose all material information that an investor would need to know about an issuer to make an intelligent and informed decision regarding the purchase of the issue.   (Page 313)

74. **C.** The bond counsel is not concerned with the amount of the underwriting spread.

(Page 314)

75. **A.** Because "How much money can we raise?" and "How much is it going to cost us?" are the only two things the issuer wants to know, they are the two things that a firm bidding on the issue would include in its bid. The investor would want to know the yield to maturity in order to determine whether the investment made sense for her. The members of the syndicate would want to know the underwriting spread so they could decide whether it would be profitable for them to take part.

(Page 319)

76. **B.** The municipal dealer does not have to disclose purchases of securities by individuals.

(Page 328)

77. **B.** The Trust Indenture Act of 1939 requires trust indentures to include clauses protecting the bondholders.   (Page 42)

78. **C.** A Ba rating is consistent with the client's willingness to accept moderate risk. The client's tax bracket might be too low to take full advantage of the bond's tax-exempt feature. The bonds would also not be very liquid because only 1,000 bonds were issued. If the client lost his job and needed cash, the bonds might be difficult to sell.   (Page 31)

79. **B.** Any bond subject to additional taxes, such as might occur with an investor subject to alternative minimum tax (AMT), would have a lower net yield than one that was not subject to additional taxes.   (Page 266)

80. **C.** The premium deducted yearly for the period held is deducted from the original cost to establish the new basis: $100 \div 8 = \$12.50$; $\$12.50 \times 6 = \$75$; $\$1,100 - \$75 = 102 \ 1/2$.   (Page 338)

81. **A.** The SEC regulates all securities, and was empowered to do so by the Securities Act of 1933. The IRS was not empowered to act directly in securities matters. The NASD and the NYSE are SROs empowered under the Securities Exchange Act of 1934 to regulate exchanges and broker-dealers, and are responsible to the SEC.

(Page 347)

82. **D.** Bond quotes are based upon a percentage of face amount. Bonds have a par value of $1,000. Therefore, a quote of 85 1/2 is 85 1/2% of $1,000, or $855.   (Page 43)

83. **B.** Municipal serial bonds are issued at one time with differing maturity dates. They are quoted on a yield basis such as 8.5%. Term bonds, in contrast, compose a large part or all of a particular issue and come due at the same time. These bonds (dollar bonds) are quoted in terms of dollar prices rather than yields.   (Page 22)

84.   **C.**   Because municipal trading is limited, municipal bonds are not *fungible* (that is, identical to the point of being interchangeable) securities. With fungible securities, such as listed equities, there are many equivalent securities trading at any time. It is easy to short 100 shares of GM (borrow the stock) because an equivalent 100 shares of GM can be purchased on the NYSE at any time. It is not easy to short 5M of 6% NYC GO bonds '05 because it would be very difficult to cover the short position with the same bonds.   (Page 128)

85.   **C.**   When a customer sells a security at a loss, he cannot buy back a substantially identical security between 30 days prior to and 30 days after the sale that established the loss.   (Page 263)

86.   **C.**   The 30-day visible supply is used by issuers and dealers to determine the amount of new issues expected in the market in the next 30 days. Published monthly, the visible supply is the par value of all competitive bids and negotiated sales that are scheduled to be reoffered by syndicates within the coming 30 days.   (Page 321)

87.   **C.**   When an order is taken for a bond *when-, as- and if-issued*, the bond is a new issue without a final settlement date. Because the settlement date is not set, the amount of accrued interest payable to the seller (the underwriter in this case) is not known. If the amount of accrued interest is not known, the total cost of the transaction cannot be determined.   (Page 337)

88.   **D.**   A head and shoulders bottom formation is also known as an inverted head and shoulders formation. It is that part of a graph where a down trend has reversed to become an up trend. It is not an indicator of the bullishness or bearishness of the market as a whole, however. It is only an indication of the direction of a trend, which may be either short or long in duration.   (Page 222)

89.   **D.**   The dated date is the date on which the bonds begin to accrue interest.   (Page 338)

90.   **B.**   There is a deficit in the balance of payments in the United States when the country has been paying out more money abroad than it has been taking in. This happens when the United States imports more than it exports, invests money abroad, or sends money to foreign countries in the form of foreign aid. However, when foreigners purchase U.S. securities, foreign currency flows into the country, not out. Answer B, therefore, will decrease the deficit in the balance of payments.   (Page 218)

91.   **D.**   The dividend payout ratio is 49%.

$$\frac{\text{Annual dividends per share of common}}{\text{Earnings per share}} =$$

$$\frac{\$.64}{\$1.30} = 49.23\%$$

In other words, Doohickey Manufacturing is paying out about half of its earnings in dividends.
            (Page 241)

92.   **B.**   In the event of a liquidation, the order of preference is:

1.   unpaid wages
2.   taxes (IRS)
3.   secured claims (e.g., mortgages)
4.   secured liabilities (bonds)
5.   unsecured liabilities (debentures)
6.   general creditors
7.   subordinated debt
8.   preferred stockholders
9.   common stockholders

            (Page 41)

93.   **C.**   Total dividends paid each quarter during the year are $.15 + $.15 + $.15 + $.30 = $.75. The dividend payout ratio is:

$$\frac{\text{Annual dividends per share of common}}{\text{Earnings per share}} =$$

$$\frac{\$.75}{\$2.20} = 34.09\%$$ (Page 241)

94.   **D.**   The Federal Reserve's actions to influence the money supply are first felt on the discount rate and the federal funds rates. These are the rates for loans of reserves.   (Page 215)

95. **B.** Eurobonds are denominated by either domestic or foreign corporations in a currency other than that of the country of issue. Typically they are denominated in U.S. dollars and payment of interest and principal is made in U.S. dollars.

(Page 84)

96. **B.** When the U.S. dollar strengthens, foreign goods become cheaper in the United States because the dollar buys more. At the same time, U.S. goods become more expensive in foreign countries because their currency would buy less of U.S. goods. Therefore, when the dollar appreciates relative to foreign currency, U.S. exports become less competitive and foreign imports become more competitive.

(Page 218

97. **C.** Earnings per share are earnings available for common divided by the outstanding shares. Because Artco has no preferred stock, all the earnings after taxes are earnings for common. The reverse split means that three outstanding shares will be traded in for one new share. Thus, after the split, the company will have 100,000 shares outstanding. The new EPS will be $5.00 per share ($500,000 ÷ 100,000 shares).   (Page 240)

98. **D.** Historically, utility stocks have a high percentage of debt in their capitalization. Thus, like all highly leveraged companies, their debt ratios are high. Because of this, they are most likely to trade on equity. Because they pay fixed debt interest fees, if sales increase there is no increase in debt cost. The earnings increase flows to the relatively small equity base and can increase earnings per share greatly. Because leverage magnifies earnings swings, it also magnifies EPS changes. EPS changes are direct influences on the stock's price.

(Page 237)

99. **B.** Short-term interest rates fluctuate more than long-term interest rates. Long-term bond prices fluctuate more than the price of short-term debt instruments (so choice II is false). Because long-term bonds must make up the difference in yield over the years, as yields change the prices on long-term bonds are affected the most. The federal funds rate is the rate at which banks loan money overnight to each other to maintain reserve requirements; due to its very short-term nature, it is the most volatile money-market rate.   (Page 217)

100. **B.** When the Fed buys securities in the open market, it is putting money into the banking system. This tends to ease the money supply and lower interest rates.   (Page 216)

101. **B.** Upon the declaration of a cash dividend, retained earnings are reduced because dividends are paid out of retained earnings. Until the dividends are paid, liabilities increase. Assets are not affected until the cash dividend is paid. A decision to pay a dividend impacts the market price of the stock. A corporation is not required to pay cash dividends to common stockholders; the decision is made at the discretion of the board of directors. Indeed, growth companies are less likely to pay cash dividends than stock dividends (which require no outlay of cash) because they want to retain most of their earnings for future growth.

(Page 235)

102. **C.** Calculate earnings per share as follows:

$1,000,000	Operating income
− 70,000	Interest on convertible debentures
$ 930,000	Income before taxes
− 316,200	Taxes at 34%
$ 613,800	Income after taxes
− 50,000	Preferred dividends
$ 563,800	Earnings for common

$$\frac{\text{Net income available for common}}{\text{No. shares of common outstanding}} = \frac{\$563,800}{200,000}$$

$$= \$2.82 \text{ EPS}$$
(Page 240)

103. **C.** The rate of return per share of common equals:

$$\frac{\$563,800 \text{ earnings for common}}{\$2,000,000 \text{ common equity}} = 28.19\%$$

(Page 239)

104. **A.** If all bondholders converted, no bond interest would be paid. Note the effect on the income statement:

$1,000,000	Operating income
– 0	Interest on convertible debentures
$1,000,000	Income before taxes
– 340,000	Taxes at 34%
$ 660,000	Income after taxes
– 50,000	Preferred dividends
$ 610,000	Earnings for common

These earnings are spread over 200,000 original common shares plus 50,000 converted shares. Because of this, earnings per share decreases:

$$\frac{\text{Net income available for common}}{\text{No. shares of common outstanding}} = \frac{\$610,000}{250,000}$$

$$= 2.44 \text{ EPS} \qquad \text{(Page 241)}$$

105. **B.** An inverted head and shoulders formation indicates that the price of the security has bottomed out and is now rising. It is a reverse downward trend and a clear indication of a bullish reversal. Thus, investors who follow technical indicators may want to buy this stock.

(Page 222)

106. **A.** Because a company's interest expense is fixed, if the sales and operating margin (operating profit) increases, the EPS (profit on equity) will increase. For example:

	Typical Year	Good Year
Sales	$1,000,000	$1,400,000
Expenses	– 500,000	– 775,000
Operating margin	$ 500,000	$ 625,000
Bond interest	– 100,000	– 100,000
Income before taxes	$ 400,000	$ 525,000
Income after taxes (34% rate)	$ 264,000	$ 346,500
EPS (200,000 common shares)	$1.32	$1.73

(Page 241)

107. **B.** Changing the margin requirement affects the credit extended only on securities transactions. The other actions listed will affect credit throughout the entire economy.   (Page 216)

108. **B.** When interest rates decline, long-term bonds benefit the most due to the compounding effect of the interest rate decline over the life of the bond. Because the bonds are still issued at or near par value, bond prices on newly issued bonds remain the same. However, as interest rates decline, the loss in yield will be accompanied by a gain in the price of bonds in the secondary market. This relationship between yield and price is not proportionate because of the different times to maturity. The price of a bond that will mature in one year will not move as much as the price of a bond that will mature in 30 years.   (Page 217)

109. **A.** The investor has a net credit, so he *sold* the call spread. When an investor sells a call spread by buying the call with the higher exercise price, the spread is considered *bearish*.   (Page 384)

110. **B.** If both calls expire, the investor will lose $400 on the calls that he bought and make a profit of $850 on the calls that he wrote, for a net profit of $450.   (Page 382)

111. **B.** The investor will break even if the MCS Jun 30 call is trading at 2 1/4. This price means that the stock was trading at 32 1/4.

(Page 384)

112. **D.** A short put is covered by a long put that has an equal or higher strike price with an expiration date that is the same or later than the short put.   (Page 402)

113. **B.** In the event of a stock dividend, the call contract would become a call on 106 shares. Divide 106 shares into the total contract price of $5,000 to determine the adjusted exercise price. After rounding off to the nearest 1/8th, the result is 47 1/8.   (Page 367)

114. **A.** Options are not marginable. Therefore, the investor must pay for these calls in full. Ten times $225 equals $2,250.   (Page 401)

115. **D.** Calculate the breakeven point of a purchased call by adding the cost of the call to the exercise price. In this case, 2 1/4 plus 60 equals 62 1/4. (Page 376)

116. **A.** Listed stock options expire at 11:59 pm EST on the Saturday immediately following the third Friday of the expiration month. (Page 368)

117. **A.** The investor will lose 100% of his investment if the calls expire unexercised, which means he will lose $2,250. (Page 377)

118. **B.** In a discretionary account a registered rep can make decisions with respect to the specific security and the quantity to purchase as well as to time and price. (Page 157)

119. **A.** If the investor sold the option at the close, the gain would have been 2 7/8 points, or $287.50 (9 7/8 closing sale price minus 7 opening purchase price). If the option had been exercised, the gain or loss would have been calculated based on the closing index value for that day. The gain would have been the difference between the closing index value (584.50) and the strike price (575) less the premium paid (7) for a net gain of 2.50, or $250. If the option expires, the investor has a loss equal to the premium. (Page 398)

120. **A.** A call is in-the-money if the index value is greater than the strike price, whereas a put is in-the-money if the index value is lower than the strike price. (Page 398)

121. **A.** Individuals with diversified stock holdings may write calls against their positions, thus deriving the premiums for these calls. Writing calls, therefore, increases the rate of return on the stocks that they hold. (Page 374)

122. **C.** Both the exercise price and the expiration date are different. This is a diagonal spread. (Page 379)

123. **C.** The premium of 1.26 represents 1.26 cents per unit times 62,500 units per contract, for a total premium of $787.50. (Page 399)

124. **B.** When the investor exercises the call, he must pay the strike price of 64 cents per mark, to which the premium of 1.26 cents per mark must be added, for a net cost of 65.26 cents per mark. (Page 399)

125. **A.** A broad-based stock index is designed to track the market as a whole rather than any particular market segment. If the market rises, both index call buyers and index put sellers will profit. (Page 392)

Notes

Notes

Notes